LABOR'S TIME

In the series *Labor in Crisis,* edited by Stanley Aronowitz

Philip Yale Nicholson, *Labor's Story in the United States*

Nelson Lichtenstein, *Labor's War at Home: The CIO in World War II*

Thaddeus Russell, *Out of the Jungle: Jimmy Hoffa and the Remaking of the American Working Class*

Steve Martinot, *The Rule of Racialization: Class, Identity, Governance*

Randy Martin, *Financialization of Daily Life*

Joe L. Kincheloe, *The Sign of the Burger: McDonald's and the Culture of Power*

Joshua B. Freeman, *In Transit: The Transport Workers Union in New York City, 1933-1966*

LABOR'S TIME

SHORTER HOURS, THE UAW,
AND
THE STRUGGLE FOR
AMERICAN UNIONISM

Jonathan Cutler

TEMPLE UNIVERSITY PRESS
Philadelphia

Temple University Press
1601 North Broad Street
Philadelphia PA 19122
www.temple.edu/tempress

Copyright © 2004 by Temple University
All rights reserved
Published 2004

Printed in the United States of America

The paper used in this publication meets the requirements of
the American National Standard for Information Sciences—
Permanence of Paper for Printed Library Materials,
ANSI Z39.48-1984

Library of Congress Cataloging-in-Publication Data

Cutler, Jonathan
    Labor's time : shorter hours, the UAW, and the struggle for American unionism /
Jonathan C. Cutler.
        p. cm. — (Labor in crisis)
    Includes bibliographical references and index.
    ISBN 1-59213-246-4 (cloth : alk. paper) – ISBN 1-59213-247-2 (pbk. : alk. paper)
        1. Hours of labor—United States. 2. Labor unions—United States. 3. Automobile
industry workers—Labor unions—United States. 4. Workweek—United States.
5. International Union, United Automobile, Aircraft, and Agricultural Implement Workers
of America. I. Title. II. Series.

HD5124.C88 2004
331.25'7–dc22

                                                                    2003067204

2 4 6 8 9 7 5 3 1

For Anne

CONTENTS

ACKNOWLEDGMENTS

Many people helped me conceptualize, craft, and complete this book. This project began the day I met Stanley Aronowitz—or, to be more precise, the night I first read his essay, "Why Work?" while sitting in my cloistered dorm room at Union Theological Seminary. That essay—and the many years of extraordinarily generous guidance, support, and friendship from Stanley and his partner Ellen Willis—initiated a series of intellectual and political transformations that continue to energize my work to this day. I was lucky to find members of the sociology faculty willing to facilitate my research and my writing, especially David Lavin, Bill Kornblum, and Patricia Clough, a brilliant teacher whose energy, speed, and dazzling originality helped me keep moving and thinking and whose friendship endures across time and space. Kristin Lawler, my CUNY reading partner and drinking buddy, has been an engaging critic, an enduring intellectual ally, and a fabulous friend through it all.

During my time in New York, I had the good fortune to work with many of the leading labor scholars of our time on a labor "teach-in" at Columbia University, and it was in that context that I became immersed in the study of organized labor. Early conversations with Tom Sugrue and Nelson Lichtenstein helped convince me that there was an important story to be told about the UAW and the fate of the shorter workweek. It was also during that time that I met Thaddeus Russell. I have benefited immensely from Thad's ferocious intellectual appetite, his inspiring acumen as a researcher and writer, and his indispensable friendship. He is a great interlocutor and collaborator. His extraordinary, path-breaking book *Out of the Jungle: Jimmy Hoffa and the Remaking of the American Working Class* (2003) is the opening salvo of a new generation of labor scholarship and represents one of the most original labor biographies ever crafted.

My colleagues at Wesleyan University have provided an invigorating space for research, writing, and teaching. In sociology, Algernon Austin, Mary Bosworth, Mary Ann Clawson, Alex Dupuy, Sue Fisher, Charles Lemert, Rob Rosenthal, Victoria Stahl, and Sharon Smith have helped make Wesleyan my home and provided thoughtful and judicious advice for navigating the academic universe. Thanks also to Henry Abelove and the Wesleyan University Center for the Humanities for a productive semester of dialogue and debate during the fall of 2000.

Thanks to Micah Kleit at Temple University Press for believing in this project from the start. Research for this book was made possible by the support of great librarians, especially William LeFevre at the Archives of Urban and Labor Affairs at Wayne State, and Kate Wolfe at Wesleyan University. Thanks also to the archivists at the Special Collections Division of the Michigan State University Library. Project grant funding from the Office of Academic Affairs at Wesleyan University also facilitated the research for this book.

My parents, Jerry and Nancy, gave me the latitude to explore and wander, and graciously stuck by me throughout extended years of schooling, even when they were not sure exactly where it was all heading. My father also generously agreed to read a final draft of the text and provided useful commentary. Kate and Peter Bergen generously welcomed me into their family and into their home; their kitchen table has been an unusually productive workspace for me, and I am grateful for their encouragement and support. Kenny Fass has been a friend and a muse since I met him in third grade and I cannot imagine the life of the mind without him. Joseph and

Nathaniel, the best little boys a dad could wish for, have patiently waited for this project to be completed so they could teach me about the really important things, like baseball. And then there is Anne. As with the essay that first inspired this book, I first encountered Anne Bergen within the cloistered walls of Union Theological Seminary and life has never been the same since. Anne helped me remember what it meant to embrace life—a lesson that informs the political unconscious of this book as much as anything else. Anne has endured all of my anxieties and fears; she has embraced and encouraged my hopes and desires. She makes everything possible. She is my best friend, pure and simple.

LABOR'S TIME

INTRODUCTION

On Wednesday, January 8, 1964, only seven weeks after the assassination of John F. Kennedy, Lyndon Johnson stood before a joint session of Congress to deliver his first State of the Union Message since being installed as president. The next morning, a *New York Times* headline dutifully publicized the now-famous White House call for an "unconditional war on poverty in America." Little noticed by the *Times*, but prominently featured in a *Wall Street Journal* headline, was a second announcement: "Johnson . . . Spurns a 35-Hour Work-Week." "I believe the enactment of a 35-hour week," said the President, "would sharply increase costs, would invite inflation, would impair our ability to compete, and merely share instead of creating employment."[1]

The president's opposition to the shorter workweek did not come entirely as a surprise. Both the idea of a War on Poverty and the opposition to the shorter workweek were inherited from the Kennedy administration. Indeed, Kennedy, in his 1963 State of the Union address, had declared his opposition to the movement for a shorter workweek. Kennedy stated that he looked forward to "an end to the growing pressures for such restrictive measures as the 35-hour week, which alone could increase hourly labor costs by as much as 14 percent, start a new wage-price spiral of inflation, and undercut our efforts to compete with other nations."[2]

Today, there is almost no memory of shorter hours as a road not taken on the way to Johnson's Great Society. What ever happened to the idea of a shorter workweek? What ever happened to the future in which progress was to be marked by growing abundance and diminished work? What ever happened to organized labor's perennial demand for shorter hours and higher wages?

The juxtaposition of Kennedy and Johnson's repudiation of shorter hours and the simultaneous initiation of a War on Poverty illuminates some of the ways in which social policy discourses in the United States were transformed during these years. Nobody today remembers what the War on Poverty *was not*; but in the early 1960s Kennedy and Johnson were crystal clear that it was not a shorter workweek. At the start of the Great Society debates, the War on Poverty was a state-sponsored alternative to a labor-led shorter hours initiative. Four decades later, the War on Poverty has many critics and defenders, but no major competitors—least of all the forgotten shorter hours movement. Scholars have argued for forty years about the benefits and liabilities of particular Kennedy and Johnson administration social policy initiatives, but the most enduring influence of the War on Poverty may well be the framing of political discourse itself, including the almost complete displacement of the idea of a shorter workweek as a mechanism for mitigating unemployment and increasing wages.

Comparison of the forgotten discourse of shorter hours with the inherited politics of the War on Poverty also illuminates a surprising and relatively unexplored dimension in the interaction of race and labor in the postwar era. It is commonly asserted that the liberal leadership of the industrial union movement supported civil rights and the War on Poverty, even as these progressive efforts often were undermined by the racial bigotry of the old skilled trade unions. As Jill Quadagno has explained, "the War on Poverty—especially Federal initiatives to pressure craft unions to open apprenticeship programs to minorities—inflamed a long-running conflict between these two Democratic party constituents—trade unionists and African Americans—triggered a backlash among resentful skilled tradesmen . . . and [created] a constituency of Reagan Democrats in the 1980s."[3] According to this scenario, the backlash was represented by the leader of the skilled trades unionists, George Meany, "a former plumber who envisioned a narrow role for trade unionism and who ruled the AFL-CIO with an iron fist." By contrast, United Automobile Workers (UAW) president, Walter Reuther, was represented as the progressive alternative to Meany, an advocate for a more expansive vision of organized labor, a union official who ruled his organization with a velvet glove, and "a man deeply committed to civil rights and to organizing the unorganized."[4]

But this common refrain about Reuther and Meany, and about the politics of labor and race, is rendered suspect by the lost history of the shorter hours struggles of the 1950s and 1960s. One unalterable fact at the core of this book must be made explicit from the start: Walter Reuther *opposed* the movement for a shorter workweek. He did not simply neglect the movement. As president of the UAW, Reuther used every weapon at his disposal to subvert the movement for a shorter workweek throughout the 1950s and early 1960s.[5] When Kennedy and Johnson were compelled to address "growing pressures" for shorter hours during the early 1960s, the source of that pressure came, not from Walter Reuther, but from George Meany and the skilled trades unions of the old American Federation of Labor. It was Meany, with his narrow vision of trade unionism, not Reuther and his allegedly expansive commitments to the unorganized and the unemployed, who led the agitation for a 30-hour workweek in response to the unemployment of the early

1960s.[6] The Kennedy administration—including the president himself—was repeatedly forced to reiterate his opposition to shorter hours in response to Meany's public agitation.[7]

Meany was neither a labor militant nor a vanguard force for interracial solidarity and Quadagno is probably right to assume that Meany's own inclinations were probably hostile toward the demands of black and Hispanic workers. But Meany was not immune to grassroots pressure politics from an emboldened civil rights movement. In the late 1950s and early 1960s, civil rights activists inside and outside the labor movement began to press Meany regarding the growing crisis of black and Hispanic unemployment.[8]

The effectiveness of minority grassroots pressure on Meany was enhanced by conflict among a divided union leadership.[9] Meany would have been largely insulated from grassroots pressures inside and outside the labor federation if not for the fact of an ongoing leadership feud between Meany and Walter Reuther. Meany's position as AFL-CIO president was not secure so long as Walter Reuther repeatedly flirted with the idea of challenging Meany's leadership of the merged labor federations. Furthermore, analysts predicted that any contest could be close, with both sides potentially dependent on the support of African-American trade unionists in a battle for dominance.[10] Meany's shorter hours agitation was completely opportunistic and was carefully aimed to exploit Reuther's major vulnerability as a labor leader: his repudiation of the classic demand for shorter hours. Not surprisingly, Meany's own shorter-hours activism seemed almost perfectly timed, not only to the ebb and flow of the labor market, but also to the periodic flare-ups in his ongoing battle with Reuther.[11]

Within organized labor, the discourse of shorter hours was traditionally used to defuse the social panic that accompanied frantic competition for work during periods of rising unemployment. It was a market strategy that aimed to meet diminished demand for labor with diminished supply. Most other populist gestures toward labor solidarity aimed to mitigate job competition by conjuring imagined communities (of men, of whites, of Americans) for the protection of privileged labor market positions, chiefly through immigration restrictions and race and gender-based limitations on access to skilled trade apprenticeships.[12] But the core logic of these labor supply strategies necessarily generated ferocious market exclusions (of women, of people of color, of "foreigners").[13] By contrast, the logic of shorter hours was unique in its capacity to articulate a vision of diminished job competition on the basis of less work for all rather than protected work for the anointed.[14]

Historically, the movement for shorter hours within the old AFL was by no means sufficient for transcending racist restrictions on union eligibility. Indeed, the historic campaigns for a 10-hour day and an 8-hour day were largely undertaken in order to maintain intra-union solidarity *within* a context of racist exclusion, rather than as part of an effort toward interracial solidarity within the working class.[15] However, when emboldened civil rights activists rebelled against these racial restrictions in the 1960s, vulnerable trade union leaders like Meany embraced the shorter hours demand as a plausible way to respond to the rising call for racial justice within and beyond the house of labor.

Meany was not the only skilled trade unionist to respond to the demands of civil rights groups with appeals to the unifying power of the shorter hours movement. Indeed, beginning in the late 1950s, Harry Van Arsdale, president of Local 3 of the International Brotherhood of Electrical Workers in New York City and head of the Central Trades and Labor Council in the City, responded to pressure from local civil rights activists by arguing for a shorter workweek "as the answer to growing unemployment in the city . . . particularly among Negroes and Puerto Ricans."[16] In 1962, Local 3 made national headlines when it initiated an unprecedented and ultimately successful strike for a 25-hour workweek. Prodded by civil rights groups and local politicians, the Local agreed to include "a substantial number of Negroes and Puerto Ricans among its apprentices. In the end, more than 200 were admitted."[17] President Kennedy responded to the national headlines by announcing that he was opposed to Local 3's drive for shorter hours.[18]

There was also a popular movement for 30 hours' work at 40 hours' pay in Walter Reuther's UAW during the 1950s and early 1960s. It was based in the largest UAW local, the massive Ford Local 600, with over 15,000 African-American members of a total 1950s membership of approximately 60,000. The 30-40 movement at Local 600 attracted a broad-based movement of African-American militants, along with Irish, Italian, and Polish skilled tradesmen, and a broad array of semi-skilled mass-production workers, all of whom supported the demand as a progressive response to the challenge of automation and the threat of technological unemployment. This book is a study of that movement. The fight for shorter hours within the UAW, however, faced the determined opposition not only of the White House and the automobile industry, but also the leadership of the union itself.

It was Reuther, as much as Meany, who insisted on a narrow, even fatalistic conception of the role of collective bargaining, especially in the battle against unemployment. As Nelson Lichtenstein has suggested, Reuther "lectured" his rebellious membership about the limits of collective bargaining. "You can't solve the problems of unemployment at the bargaining table," he said.[19] And it was Reuther, as much as Meany, who sought to rule with an iron fist, even if it meant using repressive tactics to undermine an interracial movement of local union dissidents who championed a shorter workweek throughout the 1950s and early 1960s.[20]

Reuther's suppression of the shorter hours demand during the 1950s and early 1960s had significant consequences for the political discourses of race and labor in the postwar era.. As David Roediger has suggested, "Reduction of working hours [can become] ... an explosive demand because of its unique capacity to unify workers across the lines of craft, race, sex, skill, age, and ethnicity."[21] Roediger has also suggested that any framework for understanding the intersection of race and labor must move "beyond explanations based on the labor market" toward investigations of the interactions between cultural discourse and possessive investments in whiteness.[22]

To be sure, the historic shorter hours discourse demonstrated only a limited capacity to alter the investment climate for identity formation and its influence left untouched deep investments in whiteness, masculinity, and heterosexuality. Within the workplace, the movement for shorter hours has never substituted for militant mobilization against racist and sexist divisions of labor.

Nevertheless, there are important ways in which a comparative analysis of the contrast between the discourse of shorter hours and the War on Poverty can contribute to Roediger's demand for explanations that move beyond a simple labor market analysis to an examination of work, desire, and race.

The ultimate aim of the shorter hours movement, as John R. Commons suggested at the start of the twentieth century, was to disarm the "whip of unemployment," and in this regard its aims seemed to accord with the subsequently articulated goals of the War on Poverty. But unlike contemporary anti-poverty crusades, the strategic basis of the shorter hours movement rested on notions of "joint aggrandizement," rather than paternalistic discourses of moral obligation and pity.[23]

Michael Harrington's book *The Other America*, a central text in the construction of the anti-poverty discourse of the 1960s, took no notice of the shorter hours movement.[24] For Harrington, the Other America "cannot really speak for itself."[25] In place of joint aggrandizement, and what George Rawick called "working class self-activity," Harrington's discourse appealed directly to the paternalistic inclinations of his audience. "How long shall we ignore this underdeveloped nation in our midst? How long shall we look the other way while our fellow human beings suffer? How long?"[26]

Harrington's anti-poverty discourse depends, ultimately, on an exaggerated distinction between the obligated subject and its passive object. "The poor," Harrington concluded, "are not like everyone else."[27]

One might suggest that Harrington's harangue was an assault on privilege, especially the privileges of whiteness. And, indeed, those who felt most threatened by such an assault took refuge in an illiberal backlash against racial change. As George Lipsitz suggests, this ongoing backlash is championed by "demagogic politicians [who] try to reassure white people that whatever else they lose, they will retain the possessive investment in whiteness."[28]

Harrington's discourse not only reinforced investments in whiteness among the illiberal opponents of his anti-poverty crusade, but also reinforced the possessive investment of whiteness among his most conscientious liberal supporters. As Rawick argued in reference to slavery, "The entire view of ... Victim and Object is related to the matter of guilt. Only those who feel themselves innately superior can feel such guilt about the conditions of others."[29] Harrington explicitly embraced the necessity of promoting a discourse of "shame" and insisted that "the fate of the poor hangs upon the decision of the better-off."[30] Lipsitz is correct when he concludes—against the grain of discourses like that of Harrington—that "liberal social welfare policies" cannot "solve the 'white problem' in the United States" insofar as they "reinforce the possessive investment in whiteness."[31]

Nowhere is this phenomenon more transparent than in the racial politics of work. At the heart of the shorter hours movement, asserted John Commons in 1906, is the allure of "more wages and less work."[32] Half a century later in 1962, the editorial page of the *Wall Street Journal* reached the same conclusion. "The drive for a shorter workweek may have the appearance of a 'more jobs' campaign, but what it comes down to is a plan to get more pay for less work."[33]

But what happens when the desire for less work is obstructed and repressed? Writing about the nineteenth century, Roediger called attention to the ways in which "whites could . . . use Blacks as a counterpoint to come to terms with their own acceptance of steady and even regimented labor."[34] As white workers repressed the desire for less work and more wages, compensation could be found in the category of whiteness wherein the desire for less work was first disavowed, then pathologized, and finally projected onto Others. As Rawick explained, "The Englishman met the West African as a reformed sinner meets a comrade of his former debaucheries . . . He must suppress even his knowledge that he had acted that way or even that he wanted to act that way. Prompted by his uneasiness at this great act of repression he cannot leave alone those who live as he once did or as he still unconsciously desires to live. He must devote himself to their conversion or repression."[35]

In the twentieth century, the War on Poverty reinforced the inclination to conversion among its liberal supporters and repression among its illiberal opponents, but in both cases, it drew upon and reinforced the nineteenth century valorization of whiteness and work, disavowing pleasure and play among whites; pathologizing it among blacks. The illiberal opponents of the welfare state lashed out at signs of laziness and pleasure. But the liberal defenders did not differ from the illiberal opponents in their disdain for laziness and pleasure. Instead, liberals went to great lengths either to deny that the Victims preferred pleasure to sacrifice and work (as when Harrington confided that "on the surface of Harlem life . . . [you] will find faces that are often happy, but always, even at the moment of bursting joy, haunted"[36]) or to insist that those who do parade such preferences were ripe for conversion (as when Harrington lamented that the Other Americans "do not postpone satisfactions . . . When pleasure is available, they tend to take it immediately," but conversion remained possible insofar as "their sickness is often a means of relating to a diseased environment"[37]).

Scholars seeking to explain the backlash against the War on Poverty often assume that a coalition of racially sensitive labor elites, liberal politicians, and African-American civil rights activists was undermined by the intractable racism of the entire skilled trade union movement and the white rank and file of the industrial union movement. Kennedy, Johnson, and Walter Reuther come up smelling like roses, while the remainder of the labor movement is dismissed as having been always already destined for Reagan country.

Tom Sugrue argues that the "UAW's record on race relations was mixed ... On the national level, the UAW was on the cutting edge of civil rights activism throughout the 1940s, 1950s, and early 1960s ... On the other hand ... white rank-and-file union members, often abetted by local leaders, worked to protect the color line in many plants. [Because of the] organizational structure of the UAW—especially its localism ... UAW International officials were reluctant to interfere with the internal affairs of union locals."[38] Reuther, according to this view, was a great progressive whose one flaw was that he was either unable or unwilling to impose his progressive will on autonomous union locals.

If Sugrue emphasizes the illiberal culture of racism among white rank-and-file workers, scholars like Judith Stein blame the decline of liberalism on the "narcissism"of civil rights activists who diverted attention from the underlying class interests of all workers.[39] Sugrue has rightly accused Stein of minimizing the grievances of African Americans in an effort to subordinate race politics to an abstract politics of class. Yet, for all the important differences between Sugrue's culturally sensitive assessment of the racism of Detroit's white rank and file and Stein's scandalous attempt to minimize the grievances of African-American workers, Stein and Sugrue—like Quadagno—exonerate Reuther. Stein makes the exoneration explicit, concluding that it was "not Reuther's policies, that doomed labor and liberalism."[40]

Sugrue and Quadagno blame the breakup of progressive politics on the racism of the white rank and file, and Stein pins the blame on the narcissism of civil rights activists, but all three pin their hopes on Walter Reuther. These hopes, however, are entirely misplaced. Although it would certainly be a mistake to underestimate the racism of the white rank and file, Reuther's contribution to the politics of postwar labor and race relations can only be celebrated if one is either unaware of his opposition to the movement for a shorter workweek, or unmoved by the eclipse of a progressive alternative to the path of intense racial polarization that ultimately undermined both the labor and civil rights movements.

Reuther's opposition to the shorter workweek, although perhaps surprising to some, was part of the public record during his tenure as president of the UAW and the CIO, and his repudiation of the demand has been noted, if only in passing, by several scholars, including Reuther's recent biographer, Nelson Lichtenstein.[41] Furthermore, rejection of the shorter hours movement was far from incidental or arbitrary. Rather, it marked a key point of departure for Reuther's more general break with the syndicalist tradition in the American labor movement and the development of his own brand of union corporatism.

According to the syndicalist theories of figures like John Commons, "A trade union is simply a combination to get a larger return."[42] This "pure and simple" notion of a labor union maintained that any authentic labor movement must abandon "the field of production" and focused exclusively on the terms and conditions of the sale of labor-power to employers. By contrast, corporatist unionists seek a far more expansive role for labor, including direct participation in the management of production.

In the classic terms of organized labor, a syndic—a delegate or agent in a business exchange—represents organized combinations of workers in the sale of labor-power. As George McNeill explained in 1887, the shorter hours movement constituted a centerpiece of syndicalist labor philosophy. According to McNeill, workers "desire to sell the smallest portion of their time for the largest possible price. They are merchants of their time. They feel that, if they flood the market—that is, sell more hours of labor than the market requires—stagnation will follow."[43] The entire bargaining process was to be mediated through market exchange and shop-floor bargaining with the simple aim of winning more wages, less work, and better working conditions.[44]

The leading figures of American corporatism explicitly repudiated the syndicalist worldview, especially the idea that labor should abandon the field of production.[45] Jacob Benjamin Salutsky (J.B.S.) Hardman, the most articulate defender of American corporatism and a great admirer of Walter Reuther, never missed an opportunity to heap scorn on the syndicalist traditions of the American labor movement. In 1928, Hardman protested against the triumph of syndicalism.

> The chieftains of labor were bargainers, shrewd politicians, and, save for rare exceptions, they were totally unrelated to the fundamental processes and problems of industry. The opportunity . . . lay in a direction more significant than collective bargaining. Labor could, if it would, assume responsibilities for production and ascend to active participation in the control of industry. But leaders of labor stuck to what they thought was their God-ordained job: they would sell labor for as good a price as they could command, but exercise control of industry they would not. They brushed aside the power that lay in their reach. They lacked the will to power.[46]

Commons was, in turn, as critical of Hardman's perspective as Hardman was of Commons. Commons complained that if a union underwent "the changes necessary in the character" required for it to "direct its energies to the production of wealth," it would "cease to be a trade union."[47] Commons was not simply fearful that corporatist experiments might not work. In fact, he was more concerned with the consequences for workers, if corporatist labor leaders *succeeded* in establishing their agenda within organized labor. Any union that concerned itself with "the risks and responsibilities of production . . .

raises up [a leadership] element interested in profits rather than wages . . . and, sooner or later, [it] goes over to the . . . employers."[48]

Although the anti-corporatist discourse of syndicalism has often been understood to imply business-friendly labor relations, while the audacious and even revolutionary rhetoric of corporatist discourse seems to point in the direction of labor militancy, these caricatures tend to obscure some of the underlying tendencies of the two labor philosophies. The syndicalists, in fact, were convinced that there was a constitutive antagonism at the core of the relations between the buyers and sellers of labor-power. Commons, for example, spoke of "the irrepressible conflict of capital and labor . . . The methods of unions cannot be understood except in terms of conflict."[49]

The defenders of corporatism were also keenly aware of these conflicts between labor and capital, but they argued that such employment relations were *needlessly* antagonistic. Clinton Golden and Harold Ruttenberg, two great defenders of corporatist labor relations, described the "almost universal desire of workers to tell the boss 'to go to hell,'" a desire accompanied in practice by workers who possess "the freedom to quit when the boss insulted or humiliated them, or when the work was not to their liking." But Golden and Ruttenberg interpreted this proto-syndicalist rebellion not as "a revolt against the authority of management as such, but against its arbitrary use and abuses."[50] On the other hand, when management had "the vision and courage to share . . . responsibility with its workers through their unions, then, and only then, will full production be achieved."[51]

For corporatists, the syndicalist retreat from responsibility for production was an understandable but avoidable response to the arbitrary and capricious misuse and abuse of managerial authority. Enlightened or sophisticated management should meet little or no resistance from labor once responsibility is shared on a cooperative basis. Corporatists embraced "a prophetic vision" of industrial relations founded upon "workers' participation in responsibility for the conduct of business."[52]

As C. Wright Mills explained, "Ideally, if all management personnel did not show up for work, the plant could be effectively operated by the workers and their unions."[53]

In many respects the corporatist vision of full production on the basis of shared responsibility and industrial democracy is consistent with both middle-class discourses of anti-market republicanism and socialist visions of worker control. Like the independent, self-employed, yeoman farmer, the industrial worker is called upon to stand apart from the haggling of the market and participate fully in the self-management of society. As Mills suggested, "Classic socialism shares its master purpose with classic democracy. The difference between Thomas Jefferson and Karl Marx is a half century of technological change."[54]

The syndicalist discourses of George McNeill and John R. Commons, however, stand in stark contrast to these corporatist schemes that aim to transcend the market in the name of an expansive industrial democracy. McNeill's merchants of time aimed to find leverage within the market; Hardman and the corporatists envisioned an industrial democracy able to transcend the market. The shorter hours movement, as both sides understood, was firmly rooted in the syndicalist tradition of the American labor movement.[55]

Corporatist ideology tends to assume an underlying social harmony, but should such harmony fail to appear on cue, the establishment of corporatist labor relations is secured by structural transformations that establish new mechanisms of authority in the relations between unions and members.[56] As Golden and Ruttenberg explain, "Police powers or disciplinary powers are vested in the union in direct proportion with the amount of responsibilities it assumes . . . To fulfill these responsibilities the union must have sufficient authority to discipline those workers who, for example, may stop work in violation of the contract."[57] Similarly, corporatist labor relations also rely on a transformed business and legal environment in which labor unions are provided with the institutional security that makes union-employer collaboration possible.[58]

The eclipse of the shorter hours movement within the American labor movement was one of the central manifestations of the triumph of corporatist labor relations in the United States. Within the UAW, in particular, the victory of the Reuther administration over the syndicalist movement for a shorter workweek was achieved primarily through the increasingly pronounced disciplinary powers that were vested in the union as a result of the historic, structural transformation of organized labor.

For more than two decades, UAW president Walter Reuther managed to resist popular pressure to put the syndicalist demand for a shorter workweek at the top of the postwar union bargaining agenda. A biographer might hope to gain some sympathetic insight into the psychic life of Walter Reuther in order to explain the pattern of his leadership activity, but for a sociohistorical analysis of the UAW and the shorter hours movement, the question of Reuther's motivation recedes in importance relative to the *structural* and *historical* factors that allowed Reuther to take the positions that he did without losing his leadership position within his own union.[59] As David Brody once suggested, it is not enough for labor history to simply publicize or criticize the intentions of corporatist labor leaders like Reuther. "Who would deny what [the leadership of the CIO] made abundantly clear in the public record? But why did they succeed?"[60]

Within the UAW, the fate of the shorter hours movement functions as a kind of proxy for the corporatist transformation of the union: the more vulnerable the leadership, the more voluble the syndicalist discourse of shorter hours; the more secure the leadership, the less effective the shorter hours agitation. How did Walter Reuther accumulate sufficient institutional power to make *his* corporatist ideology count despite the enthusiastic syndicalism of the union rank and file?

Nothing illustrates the urgency of a structural, rather than a motivational, analysis of Reuther's postwar opposition to the shorter hours movement than the fact that he had once been a leading promoter of the shorter hours demand. In 1938, when Reuther was himself an opponent of the incumbent UAW administration, he served as the chief spokesperson for a dissident insurgent caucus in the UAW and led a campaign for a 32-hour workweek in the automobile industry.[61] One might conclude, from this fact, that the young and militant Reuther understood the importance of the syndicalist shorter hours demand, but that he subsequently lost his nerve and knowingly betrayed the movement. One might just as easily conclude, however, that as a young Socialist, Reuther was deeply committed to corporatist visions of work and self-discipline and that even in the early years, he never actually believed in shorter hours or shared the syndicalism of the rank and file. But as an anti-incumbent insurgent in the UAW of the 1930s, even a would-be corporatist like Reuther was compelled to give lip service to syndicalist schemes in order to win the support of the membership. Only later, when Reuther was the leader of the incumbent administration and had established his authority within the union, could he successfully impose his own corporatist vision on the life of the union. How, then, did he succeed? What changed, structurally and historically, between 1938 and 1958 that allowed Reuther to reverse his public position on the question of shorter hours? In what sense might Reuther have been more insulated from rank-and-file pressures in the late 1950s and early 1960s than he had been in the 1930s?

In some cases, the union bureaucracy became insulated from the rank and file through changes to its own organizational structure. In one such instance, a change in membership rights helped to relieve pressure for a shorter workweek within the UAW. In October 1938, when Walter Reuther proposed that the International Executive Board of the UAW seek a 32-hour workweek throughout the automobile industry, a *Wall Street Journal* article announced, "32-Hour Week Idea May Become Troublesome Issue."[62] In seeking to understand the base of support for the shorter hours movement, the *Journal* pointed to the question of union membership rights and the pressure to reconcile the demands of the employed and the unemployed members. "The actual voting membership of many locals (those members who regularly attend meetings) are in the majority still unemployed. It is the pressure of these," the *Journal* explained, "which is causing presidents of locals to back the 'spread-the-work' plan. At the same time . . . local leaders are now trying to convince the working membership that 40 hours pay for 32 hours of work will be obtained for them if they agree to the plan."[63] *Ward's Automotive Reports*, an industry newsletter, suggested that "the persistent 32-hour week agitation for a six-hour, five-day week . . . would undoubtedly be accompanied by a demand for wage raises proportionate to the decreases in working hours."[64]

As a union that was, for the most part, established and led by skilled trade unionists, the UAW allowed members to retain membership rights during periods of unemployment.[65] As one early student of the UAW noted, "The strength of the unemployed in controlling union decisions may be important in the determination of policy . . . [In] the UAW-CIO [a person who has lost a job] can continue indefinitely as a member in good standing . . . As a result of this general situation, policies of the UAW-CIO with reference to such questions as seniority and work-sharing will, as time goes on, be influenced more and more by the unemployed members, unless the constitution is changed."[66]

Reuther was already thinking along these same lines. He suggested that, in light of the massive number of unemployed in the auto industry, the union "should be careful not to bring in a large section of these people into the union. If they do, they will be creating a very difficult position for the union because . . . we can't make more jobs and we should be careful not to organize all of these people in the hope of getting them back in the plant."[67] With little fanfare, the convention adopted a constitutional provision that a union member "must, at the time of application, be an actual worker in and around the plant."[68]

The structure of union membership also influenced the fate of the shorter hours movement in more immediate ways at Ford Local 600, which provided the primary institutional base for shorter hours agitation throughout the 1950s. During the height of World War II, the Ford Local 600 membership swelled to include more than 80,000 Ford employees. After the war, Ford embarked on a massive initiative to reduce its dependence on the militant and centralized workforce at the Rouge through a combination of automation (Ford engineers coined the phrase in the early 1950s) and plant relocation (called "decentralization" at the time). By the end of the 1950s, Local 600 was a mere shadow of its former self. Those older members who managed to hang on to their jobs were either retired or near retirement and they ultimately outnumbered the actively employed element of the membership. Among retirees, the attention shifted from shorter hours to early retirement. Local union officers discovered that they could ignore the shorter hour demands of actively employed workers with impunity so long as they carried the vote of the retirees.

Some of the most consequential changes during these years related to larger transformations within organized labor and within the basic framework of industrial relations in the United States. For example, Reuther's rise to power within the UAW was accompanied by the establishment of the UAW as the legally recognized, sole representative of the autoworkers. In the context of the rivalry between the AFL and the CIO in the late 1930s and early 1940s, however, the authority of the UAW-CIO was directly challenged by the UAW-AFL, a breakaway, rival auto union. It was in the context of this battle that Reuther and his allies had initiated the drive for a shorter workweek.

In January 1940, amidst the union rivalry, *Ward's Automotive Reports* announced with considerable alarm that the industry's worst fears had recently been confirmed "in the announcements from the two UAW camps" regarding "demands for contract revision" in the spring of 1940. "Outstanding in the platforms are 30-hour work-weeks at present 40-hour pay, paid vacations, higher pay levels and others." *Ward's* was quite explicit about the connection between the rival unionism and the demands for less work and more pay. Union competition for the loyalty of the workers "resembles any other election, in which the candidates promise whatever they believe will bring votes their way . . . The difficulty in this development is that . . . the men may seek delivery on the promises made them. Should this ensue, trouble will again be visited on the labor front."[69] Any prolonged rivalry might force union leaders to be as militant in delivering on contract demands as they had been in formulating those demands. *Ward's* reported, "The general hope is that one side or the other acquires complete dominance and thereby is enabled to exercise control over the men."[70]

If the UAW-CIO ultimately managed to acquire such dominance—and exercise control over the membership—it did so in the context of a changing legal environment for labor relations. In 1940, the "exclusive representation" provision of the National Labor Relations Act of 1935 was used by the UAW-CIO and the automobile industry to terminate the rivalry between the UAW-AFL and the UAW-CIO.[71] *Ward's* reported that National Labor Relations Board (NLRB) elections might contain a "seed of tranquility in them. . . insofar as they may go to end the interunion factionalism."[72] Immediately after the UAW-CIO was certified as the exclusive representative at General Motors (GM), *Ward's* confidently predicted, "At this writing it does not appear that disagreements which will develop in the new contract over such issues as larger pay, shorter hours, etc. will eventuate in strike action . . . the best opinion in both labor and management circles is that a strike, at least one of large dimensions, is improbable now."[73]

On May Day, a holiday historically associated with labor's fight for shorter hours, *Automotive Industries* reported "the union's decisive victory" in the NLRB election, along with a statement by Walter Reuther, then director of the GM department of the UAW-CIO, that the demand for "a 30-hour week with 40-hour pay" would not be pursued in the short term, although it remained a "long range goal of the union." It was the explicit aim of the newly certified CIO union, announced Reuther, to negotiate "in an orderly and constructive spirit."[74] Reuther, already in retreat, was ready to test the limits of his newfound insulation from the challenges of rivals.

The UAW-CIO was, for the most part, unchallenged in its dominance of auto industry unionism after its decisive triumph over the UAW-AFL. The 1950s witnessed a considerable reduction in amount of union rivalry and raiding, aided not only by the altered legal environment, but also by the 1953 no-raiding pact between the AFL and the CIO, and the 1955 merger of the two federations. The *Wall Street Journal* took note of the merger process and affirmed, in a sub-headline, that the truce "Could Help Businessmen, Too."[75]

The National Labor Relations Board continued to protect the peace pact between the auto industry and the UAW-CIO from those rival union challenges that did arise. The NLRB adopted a so-called contract-bar rule that barred, during the life of a contract, petitions for elections that challenged incumbent unions. During the early 1950s, GM joined with the UAW-CIO to fight off one of the most significant remaining rival challenges to the union. The company and the union contended that their pioneering five-year contract—the famous 1950 "Treaty of Detroit"—should serve as "a bar to the requested election" of a rival union.[76] Mindful of the "salutary and stabilizing effect" of the relationship between GM and the UAW-CIO, the NLRB decided that "the time has arrived when stability of labor relations can better be served . . . by holding as a bar collective-bargaining agreements even for 5 years' duration" and dismissed the petition for a challenge election.[77] As Christopher

Tomlins has argued, the "Board … succeeded in turning contract-bar into a major tool for securing incumbent unions."[78]

Although the institutional security of incumbent unions was certainly enhanced as a result of NLRB limitations on challenges from rival unions, these measures did not completely extinguish all rank-and-file leverage *within* unions. In some cases, however, the incumbent union bureaucrats could depend on employers for institutional security. Confronted with various forms of "dues" protests and individualized defections, for example, union leaders and employers often united in support of responsible unionism. As Reuther insisted, "if General Motors wants stable labor relations, if they want us to live up to all these responsibilities that they talk about, I think General Motors had better make up its mind that they can get this type of labor relations only by giving our Union … the type of recognition that makes it possible to carry out that responsibility. We cannot accept responsibility without authority, and you cannot have authority unless you have these other things."[79] GM did make up its mind and provided Reuther with the tools he would need to reinforce his authority.

Even with his authority largely secured through corporate and governmental mechanisms, Reuther remained vulnerable to one major challenge: *internal* union factionalism. Ensnared within the confines of exclusive representation, the contract-bar rule, and the union shop, all opposition was compelled to forgo exit strategies and to operate, instead, within the circumscribed boundaries of loyalty and voice. Internal union battles, especially in the context of union election campaigns, provided the membership with a limited opportunity to exert leverage on otherwise insulated incumbents. As with union rivalry, the factional competition helped to keep elites on their toes.[80]

It was against this backdrop that the movement for a shorter workweek struggled to be heard within the UAW and within the massive Ford Local 600 that served as its most active wellspring of agitation. In 1941, when Ford recognized the UAW local as the collective bargaining unit for employees at the gigantic River Rouge plant, Ford had approximately 85,000 autoworkers on the payroll. The Local was itself the size of many International unions in other industries, and in terms of internal political structure, the Local was divided into approximately eighteen different buildings or units that were themselves the size of *very large* local unions. Local 600 was not a rival union, but it was the size of one and in some respects it came to function as one.

Factionalism in the UAW was almost always a consequence of Cold War polarization. The enormous Ford Local captured the imagination of all the key players in the drama of Communism and anti-Communism in the American labor movement. From the inception of production at the Ford's River Rouge plant, those who dreamed of capturing the flagship of American industrial labor dreamed of capturing the Rouge. As a result, the factional history of UAW Local 600 at Ford's complex cannot be told without reference to the Cold War groupings that battled for hegemony within the union. The Communist Party (CP) targeted the Rouge almost immediately and established a strong following by the start of the 1930s.[81] At the same time, and largely in reaction to the successful Communist infiltration of the American labor movement, the Association of Catholic Trade Unionists (ACTU) was established as an enduring and potent anti-Communist force within organized labor in the United States. By the end of the 1930s, ACTU had committed itself to the battle for the Rouge.[82] Finally, local activists with links to several smaller independent socialist groups also joined the factional battles at the Rouge, although in the context of Cold War polarization these anti-Stalinist leftists were reluctantly but almost inevitably defined by their position in the larger battle between Communists and anti-Communists. The smaller groups included the Trotskyist Socialist Workers Party (SWP)[83], and two of its offshoots, the Workers Party (WP, subsequently known as the

Independent Socialist League, or ISL[84] and the Socialist Union, led by Harry Braverman and Bert Cochran, who broke away from the SWP in 1953.[85]

Apart from any role that these groups may have played in the factional battles at Local 600, their enduring interest in the Rouge guaranteed that they provided very detailed reporting about union politics at Local 600. The Communist Party newspaper, the *Daily Worker* provided considerable coverage of Local 600 and, after 1948, supplemented this reporting with a special, weekly *Michigan Edition* of the Sunday *Worker* newspaper. The Association of Catholic Trade Unionists published a bi-weekly newspaper, the *Wage Earner*, which became a monthly newspaper in 1949. These papers existed alongside two other weekly papers: the Workers Party newspaper, *Labor Action*, and the Socialist Workers Party newspaper, the *Militant*. In addition to these four newspapers, a monthly journal called the *American Socialist*, published by Braverman & Cochran's Socialist Union, devoted considerable attention to affairs at Local 600.

Like these political periodicals, the business press—especially *Business Week* and the *Wall Street Journal*—provided detailed coverage of the factional battles at Local 600 and the movement to put the demand for a shorter workweek at the center of the UAW bargaining agenda. Neither the political periodicals nor the business press were disinterested observers of the events they described, but all remain essential sources for reconstructing the factional politics of the Rouge. Biased newspaper coverage can be quite useful so long as one reads against the grain of bias.[86]

The first chapter of this book examines the political context in which the shorter hours movement emerged within Local 600 during the 1940s. The second chapter chronicles the attempts by Walter Reuther to suppress the demand for 30 hours' work and 40 hours' pay within the UAW. The third chapter considers the changing role of the CP in relation to Walter Reuther and the shorter hours movement. The fourth and fifth chapters document the ways in which the UAW was forced to respond to rank-and-file pressure for a shorter hours movement, and also the ways in which changes within the union set the stage for the demise of the dissident movement for a shorter workweek. The sixth chapter describes the specific organizational dynamics at Local 600 that ultimately enabled Walter Reuther's administration to gain control of the local and silence the movement for a shorter workweek.

1.

THIRTY HOURS'
WORK FOR FORTY
HOURS' PAY

In the earliest years of CIO activity at Ford's River Rouge factory, the two most powerful political factions within the Rouge, the Association of Catholic Trade Unionists (ACTU) and the Communist Party (CP), competed with each other for the support of the tens of thousands of workers at the giant manufacturing facility.[1] At the Rouge, the anti-Communist ACTU factionalists—commonly called "ACTists"—were clearly on the defensive until the summer of 1941. Percy Llewellyn, an ally of the CP, was president of the local and controlled thirteen of the executive board seats, compared with six seats for Paul Ste. Marie, ACTist leader at the Rouge and a founder of ACTU in Detroit. Paul Weber, president of ACTU-Detroit, wrote asking CIO president Philip Murray to support ACTU's failing opposition to the CP machine at Local 600. Driving home the need for support, Weber told Murray, "This opposition is likely to be liquidated soon unless some aid is forthcoming."[2]

Weber could not have hoped for more support than he would receive; however, it came, not from Philip Murray, but from Adolph Hitler. On June 22, 1941, the German army crossed the border into the Soviet Union, and adopted the slogan, "Everything for Victory." The CP joined the war effort to the *right* of almost every other political elite inside the trade union movement, enthusiastically and infamously supporting the no-strike pledge and incentive pay.[3] Communist Party leader William Z. Foster insisted that working hours "should be the maximum possible" and that "in the matter of working conditions, the trade unions need to show real flexibility."[4]

This line did not find favor with the rank-and-file workers in Local 600, and the CP paid dearly for its abandonment of the membership. Early in the war, considerable support within the Local shifted to Paul Ste. Marie and the ACTists.

At Local 600, the ACTists seized the opportunity and presented a program that was considerably more militant than the CP program. Fear of postwar unemployment was common and ACTists responded by endorsing the shorter workweek. In 1945, ACTist Joseph McCusker ran for Local 600 president, with Rouge ACTU leader Joseph Fitzpatrick as his campaign manager, and won on a program that led with the demand for a shorter workweek. An ACTU election leaflet boldly announced the top item of the campaign program.

> Change Standard Work-Week: This program advocates and will work to change the present standard 40-hour week to a standard week of four 8-hour days, with overtime beginning after the 32nd hour. The enormous advance in labor-saving devices, developed during the war, makes this an absolute imperative if the United States is to provide employment for all of its citizens who are willing and able to work and who need a job.[5]

The ACTists clearly positioned themselves to the left of the Stalinists during the war. That was not difficult, considering the CP wartime position. The real challenge that kept the ACTists on their toes, however, came from Max Shachtman's small Workers

Party (WP), an offshoot of the Trotskyist movement in the United States.

In the late 1930s, James Cannon and Max Shachtman—the two leading American followers of Leon Trotsky—formed the Socialist Workers Party (SWP). In line with Trotsky, the SWP was deeply opposed to Stalin, but still offered critical support for the Soviet Union. In a prewar break with Cannon and the Trotskyists, however, Max Shachtman split from the SWP and formed the WP as an alternative to the CP and the SWP. Shachtman concluded that there was no basis for the ongoing defense of the Soviet Union.

The implications during World War II were quite dramatic. Shachtman and the labor activists who broke from the SWP found no reason for caution in competing for the support of wartime workers. The SWP, however, was left with a somewhat contradictory labor policy. Although less audacious in their pro-war fervor than the CP, the SWP was nevertheless committed to the defense of the Soviet Union, and thus to wartime production requirements. The result was a policy of relative caution during the war years.[6] As a result, the SWP did not compete in articulating the most militant demands of workers during the war.

During the war, the WP helped initiate a "Rank and File Caucus" that championed a war-time call to "fight general unemployment by instituting a thirty-hour week at a livable wage."[7] The Caucus intended to function as "a major contender for power in the UAW."[8] The militant leadership of the Rank-and-File Caucus forced the ACTists and their Socialist ally Walter Reuther to move left in order to maintain rank-and-file support during the war. In 1944, Reuther supported a shorter workweek for the postwar era. Reuther, then a UAW vice-president, rallied his troops to the program, arguing, "I think it is better to have a 30-hour week and have all the people employed, all the people participating, than to have some people working 40 and 50 hours a week with great masses of unemployed."[9] Reuther clearly understood not only the appeal of the program and its popularity within the UAW membership, but also the logic of the program. In a 1944 debate with the president of the Chamber of Commerce, Reuther made this precise point. "We can in America," he argued, "on the basis of a 30-hour week create all of the wealth that we could create before the war on the basis of a 40-hour week. We have made that much technical progress during the war."[10]

During this same period, Earl Browder, leader of the CP in the United States, proclaimed that a new era of class cooperation had been born in the war alliance among the Soviet Union, Britain, and the United States. Browder embraced the idea that "capitalism and socialism have begun to find the way to peaceful coexistence and collaboration in the same world" and announced that "class divisions or political groupings" would "have no significance now" and revolutionary socialism would no longer be a public aim of the Communists. "Management and labor working with government, have demonstrated that they have the ability to solve any and all technical problems."[11] This analysis, combined with continued enthusiasm for war mobilization, led the CP to support Roosevelt's 1944 proposal that wildcat strikers should meet with harsh punishment for their treason. Communists even supported the idea of extending the no-strike pledge after the war.[12]

However, in 1945 the Communists abruptly reversed course, with important consequences for the postwar configuration of factional politics within the UAW. The postwar reversal resulted in a series of prolonged intellectual attacks upon Browder and "Browderism." The era of U.S.-Soviet alliance was over and the Cold War had begun. Although the alternative to "Browderism" within American Communism was not always clear, there could be no doubt that the renewed strength of William Z. Foster's leadership during this period implied some kind of alternative to Browder's corporatism.[13] The new Foster line did embrace a mild shift toward militancy within the labor movement, especially within CIO unions that the CP did not control.[14] Within the International Union of the UAW this meant a policy of advocating for a program somewhat more militant than anti-Communist factional opponents.

During the war, Browder had not only dissolved the CP as a political party, renaming it the "Communist Political Association," but he had dissolved the factional groups and "plant clubs" within the trade unions, including the Rouge clubs, which had been in existence for eighteen years.[15] In the fall of 1945, this period of liquidation ended and the militants reconstituted themselves in order to compete, once again, for support among the Rouge workers. After three years away in the Pacific, William Allan, Michigan labor correspondent for the *Daily Worker*, began working with Paul Boatin, the leading CP activist working in the Rouge, to develop a new militant line that would be attractive to Ford workers.[16] The *Wage Earner* kept a careful eye on these events, reporting that

> William Allan, Daily Worker correspondent ... was commissioned a month ago to reorganize Communist Forces at the River Rouge plant and to martial the 'fractions' for the all-out fight against the regime of President Joseph McCusker.[17]

Having campaigned and won office on a militant line of shorter hours at standard pay, McCusker governed on a very different basis. In contract negotiations, Ford demanded and received McCusker's approval for the introduction of a so-called "company security" clause that gave union support for company-imposed penalties against workers involved with or supportive of wildcat strikes. This was a major concession that opened McCusker to attack from the reconstituted Communists. The CP led a prolonged campaign against the clause at Local 600 and McCusker paid dearly for his support of the measure.[18]

During the war, McCusker had been compelled to adopt a more militant posture because of pressure from Shachtman's WP. After the war, however, the Shachtmanites faced a new set of alternatives within the UAW. Indeed, the WP was noticeably self-conscious about the changed political landscape. First, it understood that the near-monopoly on militant leadership that they had enjoyed during the war was now slipping away. Not only had Reuther "bowed to the pressure of the rank and file" during the latter days of the war, but now, as one Shachtmanite put it, the Stalinists, "reacting to the needs of the rulers of Russia in its conflict with the United States and Great Britain ... appeared to become 'radical' once again." Thus, it was "not surprising" that rank-and-file support was "temporarily flowing back into the channels of the two big ... factions." The political landscape had become "blurred over and unclear to the rank and file." More to the point, the direction and mission of the WP had become blurred and unclear.[19]

Was it more important for the Shachtmanites to support militant rank-and-file movements within unions like the UAW or to support the battle against the Stalinists? The Shachtmanites feared that it would be difficult to compete with the CP for the defense of rank-and-file demands without simultaneously lending aid and comfort to CP-led initiatives. Beyond the problem of competing with the CP was the WP desire to *crush* the Stalinist menace. The WP understood its own predicament quite clearly. In places like Local 600, it had to choose between, on the one hand, "a weak Stalinist regime, which in order to maintain its power has been forced to conduct a militant policy and operate in a relatively democratic manner," and on the other hand, "a powerful, reactionary and totalitarian labor bureaucracy."[20]

In the UAW, the Shachtmanites acted decisively, throwing themselves into the Reuther administration caucus, along with Reuther's old Socialist Party and ACTist alllies. The question of the rank and file disappeared as the Shachtmanites joined the administration. "Our party and *Labor Action* have consistently taken the position that the militants in the UAW should support (or continue to support) the Reuther group." Shachtman considered the Reuther camp, rather than the Stalinist faction, to be "unmistakably the *left wing* of the UAW ... Our party decided, years ago, to support unhesitatingly the authentically reformist and even conservative labor leadership for control of the labor organizations as against the Stalinist leadership."[21] The Shachtmanites, including New York-based Irving Howe and Detroit-based B. J. Widick, published glowing treatments of Reuther's leadership, including the 1949 book, *The UAW and Walter Reuther*.[22] Shachtmanites had, in effect, decided that any notion of rank-and-file militancy was now foreclosed. The Shachtmanites declined to compete in articulating the desires of the rank and file. Shachtman simply remarked, "By 'the labor movement,' we must perforce refer today [to] the politically active officialdom."[23]

A small Detroit group of Shachtmanties, known within the WP as the Johnson-Forest tendency, chose a different road. Always more closely linked with the rank and file, and animated by a powerful critique of labor bureaucracy arising from the experience of internal union repression during wartime, the Johnsonites kept a keen eye on shop-floor grievances and popular culture. Facing the scorn of Irving Howe and others, this group broke from the WP and briefly merged with the SWP.[24]

The SWP, which had adopted a less militant stand than the WP during the war, faced similar dilemmas in the postwar era. The leadership most closely associated with James Cannon joined the Reuther parade and derided the rank-and-file campaigns of Local 600, mocking SWP members who were sympathetic to these struggles.[25] But Cannon's party, like Shachtman's, was torn apart by the dilemmas of the postwar political landscape.[26] Bert Cochran, the leading wartime trade union strategist within the SWP, ultimately opposed an alliance with Reuther and split with the party in 1953 along with George Clarke and Harry Braverman to form the Socialist Union.[27] Similarly, some SWP activists, including labor writer Art Preis, were supportive of Local 600's militancy, despite its association with the leadership of the CP.[28]

And yet, the remarkable fact of the postwar era was that so many factional elites abandoned the rank and file and embraced the bureaucratic anti-Communism of the emergent Reuther administration. They walked away, not because they failed to attract rank-and-file support for militant positions, but because they lost interest in the battle for rank-and-file demands once anti-Communism became the central aim of the bureaucracy.

In 1946, Walter Reuther had not yet secured his leadership of the UAW. During that year, he campaigned against R. J. Thomas, an incumbent president hobbled by his own wartime record and his sympathy for Stalinist-supported productivity drives. Reuther won the presidency by an extremely narrow margin based upon perceptions that his leadership of GM workers in a major strike had been militant and successful.[29] Reuther's base of support, however, was not yet broad enough to secure control of the International Executive Board (IEB). As a result, Reuther was forced to retain, if only temporarily, his militant posture.

On October 12, 1947, Charles Erwin Wilson, president of GM, proposed that expanded production targets could best be met if the legal workweek were extended from 40 to 45 hours.[30] On November 9, 1947, as Reuther prepared for his UAW convention election, he presented his opening remarks to the convention delegates, lashing out at Wilson and adopting a militant position.

They want to take away overtime up to 45 hours a week. They cannot give us 40 hours, let alone 45 hours. I want to say to Mr. Wilson and N.A.M. [National Association of Manufacturers] we are not going back, the Auto Workers don't believe our future and the future of America lies in going back. With the advanced technology we have— we are on the threshold of the atomic age; let us mobilize that power, let us mobilize that technology, let's not go back to the 45-hour week— we are planning on a 30-hour week, with higher pay and higher living standards than we ever had, and we can do it.[31]

At the 1947 convention, Reuther championed the fight for the "30-hour week, with higher pay," and was swept to re-election. Significantly, the 1947 convention delegates also rewarded Reuther with control of the IEB for the first time. Almost immediately after the convention, however, Reuther changed his tune. Although remaining critical of Wilson's campaign for legislation to establish a 45-hour week at straight time, Reuther quickly abandoned the program for a 30-hour week with higher pay and higher living standards. In response to Wilson's offensive, Reuther retreated. Reuther backed away from a militant program of struggle and instead sought to establish his credentials as a labor statesman willing to impose discipline in the face of rank-and-file militancy. He moved swiftly into a corporatist mode, arguing for a harmony of interest between auto manufacturers and the union leadership.

Business Week predicted that Reuther's triumph would mean the "Hillmanization" of the UAW with Hillman representing "the prototype of the radical tamed by the responsibilities of running a large union . . . In the end, the Hillmans and the Reuthers manage to split their personalities. As trade union operators, they look a lot like their more conservative brethren. But on the slogan front, they are as radical as ever."[32]

On January 17, 1948, Paul Boatin, a Communist and building unit committeeman at the Rouge, took up Reuther's now-abandoned militant convention challenge to GM's Wilson. In an article in *Ford Facts*, Boatin launched a new campaign for the Rouge "Progressive Caucus." As the top demand of a new program, Boatin wrote, "To all the Big Shots we say: 1. We won't let you abolish overtime! We say: place the benefits of science and new invention at the service of the people. Let's have the 6-hour day—and get paid for 8."[33] Reuther had created an opening for militancy on his left wing and Boatin stepped right up. Reuther's reversal was soon to become even more public, and Boatin's appropriation of the shorter hours line would be rewarded at the Rouge.

On February 4, GM's Wilson repeated his proposal at a news conference announcing the opening of a new assembly plant in Wilmington, Delaware. The next day, Reuther was scheduled to be a witness before the concluding day of Senate Foreign Relations committee meetings on the proposed European recovery program. The *New York Times* reported that as he testified, Reuther spoke extemporaneously, "disregarding a long, prepared statement of his organization's views on the Marshall Plan."[34]

Reuther spoke about the Cold War implications of the program, advocating support for the Marshall Plan as a tool for combating the strength of the CP in Europe, especially in France and Italy. He argued that "the men in the Kremlin ... know that they can't beat us, but they hope to take over all Europe by default."[35]

In a complete reversal of his convention commitment to fight for the 30-hour workweek at 40 hours' pay, Reuther announced that autoworkers would be "ready to work longer work weeks whenever management ... can supply the materials and the work" because "there is no present limitation on the work week." Furthermore, Reuther calculated that under a 44-hour week, the extra four hours "will cost the employer only 4.4 percent more in hourly wages while he gets 10 percent more production."[36]

Reuther's new position on the hours of labor clearly pointed to a potential weakness in Reuther's reputation as a militant leader. Boatin had responded to this opportunity. But the coincidence of Reuther's flagging commitment to shorter hours and his increasing commitment to the Marshall Plan gave the CP leadership—first in Michigan and ultimately in New York—exactly the kind of program issue for which they had been searching. When Reuther abandoned the fight for shorter hours and linked his longer hours plan to anti-Communism, Nat Ganley and other Detroit-based CP leaders began to make the issue their own.

Thus, the early days of 1948 marked, not the death of the CP in the UAW, but a moment of new promise and opportunity.[37]

Everything fell into place. The CP was totally opposed to the anti-Communist political intent of the Marshall Plan. Reuther supported it. When Reuther linked his support for the Marshall Plan to his support for longer hours, William Allan and Nat Ganley used the opportunity to promote CP foreign policy couched in terms of militant trade unionism. Allan published a "first draft" of the CP response to Reuther's longer hours program. Noting the coincidence of recent Detroit layoffs and Reuther's hours testimony, Allan sought to emphasize a guarantee of work in the face of layoffs. In response to Reuther's claim that "there's no present limitation on the work week," Allan stated, "the auto workers here are talking in different terms. They want a full work week and a guaranteed 40 hours pay."[38] But when Ganley rewrote the article for use in the Michigan Edition of the *Worker*, he recalled for his readers how, in his Senate testimony, "[Reuther] explained to the Senators how a 44-hour work week is very beneficial to management and the Marshall Plan . . . But the auto workers are talking in a different language. At present they demand the guaranteed 40 hours pay and in the days and months to come they will think more in terms of a basic 30 hour work week, without reduction in weekly earnings, and with double time for all overtime."[39] The 30-40 campaign had begun, as the CP slowly and tentatively embraced the shorter hours movement emerging from the Rouge.[40]

The CP embrace of the shorter hours initiative began tentatively. Ganley made the link to 30-40, but his language is filled with hesitancy. The guaranteed pay proposal was borrowed from Reuther and the 30-40 demand was directed toward the days and months to come, rather than the present. Only in the future, Ganley had suggested, would workers think more in terms of 30-40. Ganley seemed more pleased to catch Reuther in the act of reversing himself than he seemed intent on launching a bold, new program.

At Ford, the start of 1949 was greeted with a wave of layoffs and the CP took note of a company newsletter proudly announcing

Ford's ability to produce more cars with fewer workers.[41] On January 23, 1949, the first major announcement of the "new" CP program came in the form of a large, front-page *Worker* cartoon that showed a worker holding a placard calling for a 30-cent raise and a 30-hour week without pay cuts in '49. The accompanying article noted a rise in unemployment, warning,

> These layoffs may not be temporary. Even if for a time production increases ... the rising speed-up means that Ford will try to get fewer workers to the job ... The threatened workers, confronting a contracting job market, are looking for help from their union. That is why, in the UAW, the demand is rising for a real determined fight for a 30-cent wage increase and for a guaranteed 30 hours work at 40 hours pay.[42]

The same placard appeared on the front page of the next edition of the *Worker*, and in his column, Ganley made much of the new demand for "30-30 in '49" (a 30-cent raise and a 30-hour week without pay cuts). This sudden devotion to the 30-hour week was well timed to prepare for a February 19, 1949 UAW "National Conference on Economic Objectives" for the next round of contract negotiations. Reuther had announced that the purpose of the meeting was to discuss the demands "as formulated by the International Executive Board."[43] The IEB had argued that negotiations should focus on the creation of a pension plan for retiring workers. The CP could not beat Reuther on this demand. Rather, they were forced to "agree" that pensions were important.[44] The administration at first ignored the CP-led campaign. Ganley shot back stating that autoworkers "can't understand why their top UAW leaders should use pensions to knife the demands for a 30-cent raise, for a 30-hour week with 40 hours pay and for curbing speedup and layoffs."[45]

By the time the February conference was called to order, Reuther was forced to confront the popularity of the 30-hour week demand. Reuther's report began with a demand for economic planning and union support for auto industry attempts to get more steel at lower prices. Then, Reuther presented the IEB proposal for company health insurance and a $100 minimum monthly pension for those over age sixty with twenty-five years of service.[46] Having put forward his own positive program, Reuther turned next to confront the programmatic challenge led by the Communists. Reuther lifted up a copy of the Michigan Edition of the *Worker*, noted the "30-30" demand, and suggested that the CP was trying to "sabotage" IEB demands.[47] Reuther knew that the CP had tapped a rank-and-file desire. He had tapped it himself, most recently at the November 1947 convention. "That's not bad—if you can get it. The 30-hour week demand is a popular demand," he acknowledged. But Reuther was opposed to the demand. "If you have a 30-hour week . . . you get a reduction in over-all production of 25 per cent . . . so you have a 25 percent decrease in production energy and activity . . . Now does anybody think there is a Santa Claus comes down from the North Pole with all these things in a big red bag and dumps them in the distribution channels? . . . Our basic fight is to get the purchasing power to buy the things we make. Not to make less things, but to make more things and to get more money to buy the more things we make . . . We don't want more leisure. We want more goods, and when we have enough goods, then we will fight for more leisure." Reuther then underscored the fact that the shorter hours demand was wrapped up with the Cold War interests of the CP. "But you see," he argued, "this is a political demand. If you can sabotage the American economy, reduce its production output, you weaken the position of America in the total world picture at a time when that happens to be the most important objective."[48]

Reuther's red-baiting attack on the 30-40 demand was an early taste of things to come. At Local 600, however, the true battle of 1949 was a strike against the "speed-up" of the pace of work provided additional opportunities for mobilization. A CP-crafted pamphlet scrutinized the shortcomings of the Ford-Reuther settlement.[49]

Moreover, the CP explicitly and articulately connected the speed-up strike to the historic fight for shorter hours and higher wages, arguing, "A halt to speed-up will help stem the growing army of the unemployed and protect the health and safety of the workers." In the accompanying "Program to Put the Guts Back in UAW-CIO," the 30-40 was once again featured prominently, and the pamphlet argued that the "fight against speed up is on par with the historic fight of laboring men and women to win the 6-hour day."[50]

In the month prior to the July 1949 UAW convention in Milwaukee, the CP continued to push the 30-40 demand. Ganley used his June 19 column to advocate for shorter hours in the face of recession layoffs, and the *Worker* ran a pre-convention front-page article that asked, "Will the convention tackle the question of looming layoffs in auto? Will it press for a shorter workweek at 40-hours' pay?"[51]

In November, as Ford workers faced layoffs, the CP recalled how they had "warned" of layoffs months ago and how they had "raised the issue then of a 30-hour work week with 40 hours pay. Reuther sneeringly termed it 'idealism.'"[52]

At the Rouge, however, the political configuration of the 1950 local union elections led the CP into an awkward retreat from its militancy. Rank-and-file anger with the terms of the speed-up strike were not only directed at Reuther, but also at the incumbent Local 600 president, Tommy Thompson, a one-time ally of the CP who had become a self-proclaimed "middle-road" figure. Thomson struggled to stay in the good graces of the Local 600 rank and file without forcing a showdown with the Reuther administration—not any easy task.

Nevertheless, because Thompson had once been aligned with the CP, anti-incumbent sentiment could just as easily shift to the right as it could to the left. Early in the election cycle, most observers noted that, for all his efforts to accommodate the Reuther administration, Reuther would not support Tommy Thompson in the 1950 elections. Thompson had flip-flopped too many times in the past. Moreover, Joe

McCusker and the ACTists, still stung by Thompson's CP-aligned victory over their administration in 1946, had never warmed to Thompson. ACTU's *Wage Earner* reported that it was "no secret that Thompson and McCusker were violently opposed to one another" because of the 1946 election and Thompson's historical tendency to "make political deals" with the Communists.[53] Now, implicitly recognizing Thompson's post-strike settlement vulnerability, even the ACTists who helped craft the terms of the settlement tasted blood. The CP reported, as "Joke of the Week" at Local 600, that "Joe McCusker ... together with John Fitzpatrick ... [will soon] ask the left wing for a united front with the right wing to 'beat Thompson.'"[54]

Late in 1949, however, the CP decided to try to undermine Reuther and the ACTists by embracing Thompson, constructing a "unity" coalition, not with the ACTists, but instead with members of Thompson's administration. The first "deal" with a member of Thompson's administration was made with Bill Hood, a leading African-American trade unionist and the incumbent recording secretary of Local 600. Hood had originally aligned himself with the Communists but broke with the CP in 1948 when Thompson abandoned his strategic alliance with the Communists. In 1948, the CP had denounced Hood as a "renegade" who had become a tool of Thompson's "do-nothing administration."[55] Less than a year later, Hood was featured in a flattering *Worker* piece for his support for Reverend Charles Hill—a black, Detroit community leader and long-time defender of the progressives at the Rouge—in Hill's run for the Detroit Common Council.[56] Next, after nearly two years of relentless critique of Tommy Thompson's "sell-out" Local policies, the Worker quite suddenly and dramatically warmed up to Thompson, as he desperately sought to renew his link with the militants. For good measure, the CP published a report implying that Thompson would "seriously think of doing something on a program of the 30-hour week with 40-hour pay as one of the ways to ease developing unemployment."[57]

Reuther must have enjoyed watching the CP embrace Thompson and shift uncritically to the right. Far from seeing in this an impassable "united front" against his administration, Reuther correctly saw a potential opportunity to shift left in order to win control of Local 600. Of course, Reuther himself could not actually shift left at this point, nor could well-known Reuther loyalists Joe McCusker, John Fitzpatrick, or Gene Prato. But a relatively unknown staff member in McCusker's regional office was selected for the job of capturing the Rouge for Reuther by running as a militant.

Carl Stellato never received a formal education beyond the eighth grade, but he was nobody's fool. In the eight years that he spent working at Ford's River Rouge—from age eighteen to age twenty-six—Stellato was employed as a machine-setter and devoted his energy to building a union at the Rouge. After the recognition victory, he became the first Chief Steward in the Motor Building. He worked his way out of the plant, riding on the political coattails of a CP-aligned regional coordinator at the 1943 UAW convention. When Stellato had last been seen on the shop-floor of the Rouge, he was aligned with the CP, albeit during the period of Communist wartime productivity drives. When the CP lost control of the regional director position, Stellato managed to keep his office job and work for McCusker.[58]

The rumor at the Rouge was that McCusker actually had to threaten to return Stellato to the shop before the latter agreed to leave his staff post and make a run for the presidency of Local 600.[59] Not only did Stellato agree to run, but he also convinced Pat Rice to join his slate. Rice had been associated with the progressives for many years. The Reutherites had not asked the left wing for a united front with the right wing to beat Thompson, but they had constructed the semblance of a united front, without the CP.

Stellato's ticket campaigned against four years of "Thompsonism" and asked workers to join a campaign "to end company-unionism, to end speed-up, to end job movement, to restore militant union leadership in Local 600."[60] Perhaps most significant was the fact that Stellato refused to engage in red-baiting.[61] He went one step further, joining the progressives—and Tommy Thompson—in signing a leaflet demanding the reinstatement of Art McPhaul, an African-American militant who had been fired for speaking out in the lunchroom of the building, arguing for a fighting campaign against the speed-up.[62]

Going into the election, the CP did not actually endorse Thompson. While the *Worker* had transformed him miraculously into a militant fighter, the Party had obligations to fulfill at Local 600. Percy Llewellyn, Stellato's old mentor, had not met with much political success since he lost his Regional Coordinator post in 1947. The CP tried to get him elected to that post again in 1949, but in the face of likely defeat, Llewellyn withdrew his candidacy prior to the 1949 convention.[63] Llewellyn was put on the CP-sponsored slate for president of Local 600 in 1950. Going into the elections, the CP "developed a bold, new approach by entering into the race a list of the best fighters, regardless of caucus affiliation."[64] What this actually meant was that the CP endorsed Llewellyn from its own caucus, Hood from the Thompson slate, and Pat Rice from the Stellato slate.[65]

Nevertheless, it was widely understood that the CP would back Thompson in the event of a run-off election between Stellato and Thompson. The CP reversal on Thompson was so unpopular with the rank and file that the progressives at Local 600 split. A group of independent local militants broke with the CP leadership and formed a group that the *Worker* referred to as the "Broom Slate," presumably so-named for its intent to sweep Thompson from office, or for its intent to make a clean sweep with a new progressive caucus.[66]

The CP made desperate attempts to expose Stellato and to heal the split on the left. Johnny Gallo, a long-time Communist activist at Local 600, issued a leaflet that declared,

I charge that the Reuther-McCusker Right Wing Ticket is trying to present itself to the militant Ford workers as a 'Progressive' ticket. For example, they are running Pat Rice for vice-president, who has long been associated with Progressive policies in Local 600.[67]

Similarly, Ganley argued,

Reuther knew his name was 'mud' among the Rouge workers because of his betrayal of the anti-speedup strike last year and his 2 1/2 year company security freeze this year for Ford workers. Hence he had to sneak into the elections, backing a ticket headed by a renegade left-winger.[68]

The split among the historically united bloc of progressives only increased CP fears that Stellato would win support from some anti-Thompson militants. One *Worker* article sent out an order to CP troops, "Fight Ford—Not Each Other," and called on the "Broom Slate" and the "Progressive Slate" to unite in a fusion slate. No fusion slate for local-wide offices developed, although independent progressives and CP activists were united in many of the building unit races.

When the elections were held, between March 21 and March 23, 1950, the building elections were an extraordinary triumph for the progressives. Many independent progressives and CP activists were elected without the need for a run-off.[69] But all of the top four local-wide offices required run-off elections. The primary left Thompson and Stellato headed for a run-off, with 12,516 votes to 11,883 votes, respectively.[70]

As anticipated, the CP endorsed Thompson in the run-off election.[71] The legendary Rouge CP leader Bill McKie issued a leaflet that warned the membership about Stellato's connection to Joe McCusker and simultaneously endorsed Thompson.[72] The Communists likened the run-off campaign to the anti-fascist war years.

Communists and progressives advanced a minimum unity program as the basis for alliances with former political opponents, including candidates running on Right-wing and Center slates . . . It was not the full, advanced program usually put forth by the progressive coalition at Ford's.

Many progressive caucus leaders opposed any electoral united front. They charged Communists with "unprincipled deals" . . . While rejecting a united front on a minimum program to stop the Reuther-ACTU bid for complete control, some progressives were in favor of an electoral alliance with these forces, to "get Tommy Thompson."

Such attitudes were exploited by Trotskyites, who sought to drive a wedge between the Communists and their progressive allies.[73]

The CP conceded "progressive forces were split in their estimate of Stellato. In the run-off, some supported him. His militant promises, convincing personal manner, and his plea for a chance to prove that 'I really am an independent' was effective. Many progressives and some Communists were confused and uncertain."[74]

Stellato beat the incumbent president Thompson 15,317 to 14,758 votes in the run-off. Rice also beat the incumbent vice-president, Lee Romano 15,902 to 12,249 votes. Bill Hood, who received more votes than any other local-wide candidate in the primary election, kept his job by out-polling Stellato's right-wing candidate. In the units where run-off elections were necessary, progressives Paul Boatin and Bill Johnson were elected. Both beat Reuther-backed, right-wing candidates.[75]

The *Wage Earner* exclaimed, "A right wing president with a left-wing executive board! . . . What will happen at 600 with the changes in office?"[76] The CP made a bid for peace and preached reconciliation to the ranks. In the aftermath of the election, the Communists warned the independent militants and any "confused" Party members that

any attempts to build an 'anti-Stellato' caucus . . . will defeat everyone but Stellato. Such a fatal mistake was made by the Addes, Thomas, Leonard group in 1946 after Walter Reuther won the presidency without winning the International Executive Board. Workers are disgusted with factionalism.[77]

This analysis was remarkable for several reasons. It made clear the emergence of yet another "revisionist" line within the CP. When the Addes, Thomas, Leonard group died in late 1947, Saul Wellman had expressed relief because it liberated the CP to embrace a more militant position. The lesson learned at that time was certainly not that Reuther should not have been opposed. In 1950, however, the CP had begun to return to its wartime posture, embracing a minimum program as the basis for alliances with compromised incumbents.

The revisionist analysis also drew an unusual conclusion from the election. In late 1949 and early 1950, the CP had made overtures to the "do-nothing," unpopular administration of Tommy Thompson. This shift to the center had led to a rank-and-file rejection of such compromising labor politics. For the CP, however, the lesson learned was not the urgency of moving closer to the rank and file, but the necessity of compromising in order to build alliances with new incumbents. Schatz concluded that

> the united front from below remains the main base for all activities. In the new situation, however, the united front from below takes on a new aspect. It becomes a front of struggle in support of activities of progressive leaders, instead of a front of struggle to initiate activities to move and pressure leaders.[78]

Rather than initiating activities to move and pressure Stellato, the CP scaled back its agenda in search of his support rather than the support of the rank and file. In fact, there was now very little on the CP labor agenda, apart from unity with the Stellato administration. Reuther was to be attacked for his anti-Communism within the UAW, his support for Truman's reactionary war program, and his hostility toward the Soviet Union.[79] There was, however, no critique of Reuther's labor policies. The CP had begun a process of retreat.

The earlier call for a militant trade union program had been little more than a last gasp before the Michigan party went underground. Wellman recalled, "We had a Ford Party section office ... By 1950 we abandoned all that. We abandoned it not because we were rejected but because of the attacks on us and the political line we had."[80] Party leaders were tried and convicted of advocating the overthrow of the government. In defense, the Communist leadership disavowed any earlier demand for a new militancy after 1946 and claimed that the wartime policies of the party had continued throughout the post-war period.[81]

The CP did not abandon Local 600—far from it. The Party did abandon its quest for support from the rank and file and replaced it with a search for friends in high places who would use their status to defend the CP and oppose the Cold War. These issues, more than rank-and-file militancy on the shop floor, became the nearly exclusive measure used by the CP to guide its strategy of top-level alliances. An earlier period of self-criticism had discerned that this bureaucratically centered strategy had prepared the way for the convention defeat to Reuther in 1947, but the CP had returned to this strategy at Local 600.

Stellato was an opportunist looking to unburden himself of the Communists while trying to maintain rank-and-file support. His first move was to make sure he had the support of the rank and file. In his presidential acceptance speech before the General Council of Local 600, Stellato announced that he favored a six-hour day with eight hours' pay. Stellato's embrace of the 30-40 program was a dangerous venture. Undoubtedly aware, both of the program's support among Local 600 militants and its repudiation by Reuther, he nevertheless decided that, for the moment, his reputation among the membership was more precarious than his relationship with Reuther. He made 30 for 40 a centerpiece of his program for fighting unemployment. In an extraordinary show of unity for the Rouge, the 30 for 40 program was endorsed by all but two members of Local 600's ruling body, the General Council.[82]

Almost immediately, the Communists started to cuddle up to Stellato. The "Old-Timer" conjured up some wishful thinking when he described "a reported conversation" between Carl Stellato and *Detroit Times* labor reporter, Jack Crellin.

> **Crellin:** Is Paul Boatin . . . a card carrying member of the Communist Party?
> **Stellato:** I don't know.
> **Crellin:** Will you work with him?
> **Stellato:** The workers in the Motor Building elected Boatin. They elected me. Yes. I will work with him.[83]

Stellato may have even played along for a month. Not long after his election victory, however, Stellato shifted gears dramatically and attacked the CP activists at Local 600. Perhaps he could smell their fear. It was, however, a fateful mistake. Stellato's assault on the Communists revitalized the local CP activists at the Rouge and gave new life to the factional fires and the political culture within Local 600, despite the conciliatory intentions of the CP leadership.

In July 1950, Stellato launched his red-baiting campaign. The Cold War heated up considerably in the summer of 1950 as Truman ordered an escalation of the conflict in Korea. When the Communists at Local 600 distributed leaflets opposing Truman's policy, Stellato ordered a non-Communist loyalty pledge and managed to win approval for the pledge from the General Council. Sixty-two delegates voted against the pledge, but it passed by twelve votes. The pledge was distributed and Stellato called on the rank and file to urge officers to make the pledge or resign. Perhaps Stellato expected the CP activists to resign from office, but the Communists simply signed the pledge.[84]

Stellato became even more aggressive. In August, he proceeded to prefer charges against five officers. He took careful aim and named many of the leading CP activists at the Rouge: John Gallo, Paul Boatin, and Ed Lock, along with Dave Moore and Nelson Davis, two of the most militant and popular African-American unit leaders at the Rouge.[85]

Stellato scheduled a trial to begin in early October 1950. The five accused Communists launched a militant campaign that aimed, not exclusively or even primarily at a defense of civil liberties for CP members, but at an attack on the 1949 contract between Ford and the UAW. The left-wing activists turned the tables on Stellato and put him on the defensive, demanding that he do something to remedy the weakness of the 1949 contract. That contract was originally set to run until April of 1952, but the accused agitated for an immediate renegotiation of the terms. If Stellato was going to purge Local 600 of its Communists, then the accused were going to make sure he was forced to do so under intense scrutiny of his performance at the bargaining table.

The strategy began to pay dividends even before the start of the trial. The revitalized left wing at Local 600 effectively pressed the Local 600 General Council to vote for strike action against Ford if the corporation refused to meet the members' contract demands. When the company rejected the Council's demand for a review of the contract, the Reuther administration stepped in to formally request that Ford agree to reopen the 1949 contract. As the *Wall Street Journal* noted, "Behind the union's request ... is believed to be an intra-union squabble between right and left wing factions. The left-wingers are expected to make a demand for wage increases soon and the right-wing elements in control of the U.A.W. want to obtain an increase to take the ball away from their opponents."[86]

The left-wing faction continued to mobilize around a fighting program at Local 600. The campaign for reopening the contract yielded a series of wildcat strikes and, ultimately, negotiations among Stellato, Reuther, and the company did produce a tentative deal that included a significant wage hike. However, the new Ford contract also included an extraordinary provision that barred any additional renegotiation of settlement terms until 1955. Reuther predicted that he would have no trouble winning ratification of the new contract, but this prediction proved to be somewhat optimistic. Although Stellato persuaded eight of the ten Local 600 Executive Board members—including Bill Johnson, the African-American unit leader who had been serving as the attorney for the defense—to endorse the five-year contract, an unprecedented 40 percent of the rank and file at Local 600 voted against the new contract. The contract was ratified, but not without some trouble.[87]

The strength of the CP position was confirmed during the course of the trial. An election of delegates to the General Council had staggering results. Stellato went into the election with a slim majority of support on the Council, but when the votes were finally counted, his support had dropped from approximately 60 percent to approximately 48 percent, with a net loss of at least twenty-eight seats. Stellato would later recall, "We took a terrific shellacking."[88] The *Wage Earner* ran an exasperated headline, "Rank and File Stupidity."[89] Four of the five accused elected to the Council, and all but one of the trial committee members were defeated. Stellato and the trial committee prolonged the trial process by refusing to report their findings to the General Council. Stellato was clearly hoping that with the upcoming round of Local elections in March 1951, he would be able to swing support back to his own camp.[90]

In December 1950, former president Tommy Thompson announced that he would attempt to make the leap from his "new" job, working the midnight shift, back to his "old" job, as president of Local 600. Thompson quickly tried to enlist the support of Pat Rice, whom he hoped would run as vice-president on his ticket.[91] The CP had been promoting Rice for president, but once Thompson entered, word spread that Rice was expected to team up with Thompson on a coalition ticket.[92]

Trotskyists and independent progressives at the Rouge once again attacked the Communists for embracing Thompson. The *Militant* branded the idea of a Thompson-CP coalition "unprincipled opportunism." The pact risked splitting the progressives again.[93] In an effort to appease the independent progressives, the CP agreed to support Joe Hogan, a relatively unknown, independent, left-wing unit leader, to run against Stellato and Thompson for president of the Local.[94] The CP strategy was to emerge from the primaries with Thompson and Stellato facing each other for president. The CP did not expect Hogan to survive the primary.[95]

Hogan, who had been a part of the defense committee in the trial, ran a campaign that continued to hammer away at all the themes which had led to electoral success in the October 1950 General Council election. Indeed, the five accused officers issued election leaflets in support of Hogan's slate. Hogan attacked the "war program for full employment that Stellato and Reuther are advocating" and proposed "a guaranteed annual wage and a six-hour day with no reduction in pay" along with increased unemployment compensation. Hogan also argued that the recently negotiated pension plan would "make slaves of the workers" because it left them "tied to the same company for their complete period of employment." He proposed to fight for Government administration of the pension rather than company administration.[96]

Stellato continued to attack the CP. He used *Ford Facts* as a vehicle for defending his anti-Communist crusade, describing himself as "engaged in a death struggle with international Communism. We did not seek this struggle; the Communists sought it."[97] However, Stellato recognized that he also required a positive labor movement program. He did not run on his contract negotiation record from the 1950 round. He did not even try to name any past negotiating successes. Instead, he began promoting the 30-hour week. In an effort to appeal to the rank and file without alienating the Reutherites, Stellato walked a tight rope. His

words were carefully chosen in an almost explicit attempt to reconcile his position with Reuther's, especially in light of Reuther's
1949 attack on the shorter hours program.

> The goals of our Union are not pie-in-the-sky ... Our first aim is the
> guaranteed annual wage. Our next aim is the 6-hour work day, or the
> 30-hour week. Both these objectives are as practical and feasible as the
> present social security system and unemployment compensation pro-
> grams, and the 8-hour day. Only a few short years back these objectives
> of Labor were considered communistic and anti-American. However,
> every American ... now accepts these institutions as American ... It
> is not the intention of our Union to wage war against the American
> people to accomplish these objectives. We recognize the exactions of a
> war-time economy and the need of sacrifice by all.[98]

Stellato and Hogan ran on shorter-hour platforms, although
Stellato projected his plan into the future, after the expiration of
the 1950, five-year contract. Hogan, in contrast to Stellato, accused
Reuther of using war as a full-employment program and proposed
shorter hours as an "alternative labor strategy" in opposition to military Keynesianism.

In preparation for the thirteenth UAW convention, set to open
in Cleveland on the first of April, 1951, the Reuther administration
had made clear its intent to amend the UAW constitution in order
to increase membership dues from $1.50 per month to a $2.50 per
month minimum. This created some difficulties for Stellato at Local
600. As a faithful member of Reuther's caucus, Stellato was
expected to do everything he could to facilitate the passage of the
dues increase. But after the October 1950 General Council election
demonstrated the strength of the opposition within the Local,
Stellato was understandably wary of selling an unpopular dues hike.
Stellato's solution was to initiate a rank-and-file referendum on the
question of the dues increase. The referendum would provide

Stellato with a mandate from the membership that would insulate him from criticism from the left-wing faction at Local 600.

Hogan and the other left-wing officers at Local 600 opposed the dues increase. Hogan posed sharp questions about the dues increase and issued a leaflet that characterized the dues increase as little more than a fund for building Reuther's bureaucratic machine. Strike preparation, Hogan argued, hardly seemed urgent after Reuther had just negotiated a five-year contract.[99]

Nevertheless, Hogan seemed to agree with Stellato's calculation that the rank and file, if asked, would support the requested dues increase. When Stellato proposed to the Local 600 executive board that the question be submitted to a referendum vote of the membership, Hogan, Pat Rice, Ed Lock, Bill Johnson, and other left-wing officers campaigned against the idea of a referendum. The Executive Board voted in favor of a referendum, however, and scheduled the vote to coincide with the election of Local officers and convention delegates.[100]

Ahead of the 1951 vote, the CP conceded that "Thompson was favored . . . to be a cinch to meet Stellato in the finals."[101] But it did not happen that way. Stellato topped the other two, winning an impressive 16,205 votes. Hogan, however, won an impressive 9,010 votes, whereas Thompson received only 7,784. Hogan had upset Thompson and was set to meet Stellato in the finals. *Labor Action*, sympathetic to Stellato and the Reuther administration, declared that Stellato "established himself as an up-and-coming figure in the UAW by his triumph," but also noted that Thompson's poor showing was a "surprise." Moreover, the article noted, "Hogan's 8,000-odd votes [sic] were more than Reuther forces conceded he would obtain."[102] The *Militant* called Hogan's showing "a big surprise," whereas the *Worker*, somewhat awkwardly, scoffed at the way other newspapers celebrated the "amazing results" signaled by the high vote for Hogan.[103] The CP played down Hogan's triumph.[104] Its election coverage emphasized, instead, the fact that each of the five accused Communist officers won the highest number of votes in the primary election, and that only Gallo faced a run-off election. The other four were re-elected outright.[105] Independent progressive, anti-Stellato candidates also won the presidency in several units.[106]

The Stellato administration was not without electoral success in this primary round; however, he was repudiated on several important fronts. First, the easy re-election of four of the five accused officers demonstrated that his red-baiting campaign had backfired. Second, the referendum had backfired, much to the surprise of Stellato and the progressives, both of whom significantly underestimated the anti-administration sentiment within the rank and file. The Ford workers turned down the dues increase by a vote of 23,000 to 9,000.[107] The anti-dues vote was significant because it put Stellato in the extremely uncomfortable position of attending the UAW convention as the leader of a delegation opposed to Reuther's convention agenda.

But Stellato faced additional hurdles as the convention approached. The run-off election was scheduled for March 13–15, 1951. Hogan his militant campaign, calling for abrogation of a contract provision that granted the company the right to establish, maintain, and enforce the speed of production. Hogan proposed that the speed of production be cut 20 percent. "Ford workers can't wait for the 5 year Company Security Contract to expire. Negotiations . . . must take place now. The workers want action and improvements now!"[108]

Stellato shot back with his most vicious red-baiting campaign to date, dashing CP hopes that he would warm up to the Communists. He used a major, front-page article in *Ford Facts* to launch an anti-Communist tirade in which he claimed that he was being persecuted by the Communists who, he said, were sending their "best organizers into Dearborn to defeat me in this election." Stellato asked the membership to choose between trade unionists and "persons in our local who are being supported by a political organization which owes its allegiance to a foreign country."[109] He even went so far as to reproduce a copy of Victor Riesel's "Inside Labor" column from the *Sunday Mirror* in which Riesel complained,

> One of the gimmicks the Commie comrades called for in this massive poll . . . was a demand for 20 percent more leisure in the plants. They simply ran on a platform saying let Ford slow down the work by 20 percent. This would make more jobs—and then there wouldn't be the need for war production, no war. Peace, it's wonderful . . . the old Bolsheviks from New York are in to plot the smearing of the anti-Communists.[110]

Stellato did, in fact, face a threat from the local activists at the Rouge, if not from the CP leadership. As Riesel noted, however, Stellato was vulnerable, not because his opponents were Bolsheviks but instead because the left-wing at Local 600 was promoting a fighting labor program that embraced leisure and an equitably distributed reduction of work.[111] Stellato did not directly attack the program of his factional opponents. His strategy was either to ignore these trade union issues or to appropriate the progressive position, as in the case of his endorsement of the shorter workweek.

Stellato won the run-off election. But when the votes were tallied, Stellato was stunned to learn that he had come within about 450 votes of losing the presidency to Hogan.[112] The results were all the more upsetting to Stellato because Hogan was an unknown outside of his unit building, had announced his candidacy no more than a couple of weeks before the primary election, and had run for the presidency without ever having held any local-wide office. The unruly rank and file of Local 600 had, once again, caught Stellato by surprise. And although he had managed to hold on to his office, Stellato had also been handed an undeniable mandate from the rank and file that he use that office to lead a fight against Reuther's dues increase at the upcoming convention.[113] Stellato also emerged from the election without firm control of either the General Council of Local 600 or its Executive Board.[114]

Stellato's first post-election comments were somewhat conciliatory to Local 600's potent left wing. "Now that the elections are over," he wrote, "it is our duty to try to effect the program which we ran for election on. But it is also the duty of those who were defeated to try to bring to realization those parts of their program which are good for our membership."[115] In a sign of respect for the support demonstrated for Hogan's program, Stellato conceded that "parts of their program" would be "good for our membership." But Stellato was not yet clear which parts he considered powerful enough, given the militant climate of Local 600, to warrant appropriation.

Stellato's first piece of business, coming only one week after the local election was to try to find a way to get through the UAW convention in Cleveland. The issue of *Ford Facts*, published the day before the convention, included a massive, front-page, banner headline, "Local 600 Pushes Fight Against Dues Increase."[116] This fighting line was in direct opposition to Reuther, who made the dues increase his top convention priority.[117] The headline was certainly intended to appeal to the anti-Reuther rank and file, but when Stellato arrived in Cleveland, he attended a pre-convention meeting of the Reuther caucus, reportedly as "a Reuther supporter."[118] He announced the referendum results from Local 600, made clear his intention to carry out the wishes of the membership, and argued for a rank-and-file referendum on the issue. His suggestion was met with boos and jeers from the Reutherites. Stellato kept pleading that he was a right-winger and belonged in the Reuther caucus.[119]

During the convention discussion of the dues increase, secretary-treasurer Emil Mazey initiated a ferocious attack on Local 600. Mazey declared,

> I am a little sick and tired of seeing cheap politicians come to this Convention who have a one-point program against dues, not in favor

of organizing or political action or other things. All they are in favor of is getting re-elected. And I say that I am ashamed of some of the leadership of the Ford Local because, by God, your organization was made possible by people sitting in this room today.[120]

Stellato may have wanted to use Mazey's attack on "some" of the Local 600 leadership in order to distance himself from the so-called "cheap politicians," but he calculated that his precarious position at home was more dangerous than the wrath of Mazey or Reuther.

Having incurred that wrath at the convention, however, Stellato was determined to cash in some chips with the militants when he arrived back home. He used the first post-convention issue of *Ford Facts* to demonstrate his fidelity to the membership by contrasting his own opposition to the dues increase with those convention delegates from other locals who had promised their membership opposition only to switch at the convention. Formally, at least, it was to these delegates that Stellato was referring when he ran a banner headline, "Betrayal," on the cover of *Ford Facts*. The article, however, discussed Reuther's pressure tactics in convincing such delegates to support the increase and clearly hinted that it was Reuther who had betrayed the membership.[121]

Stellato was almost certainly a reluctant dissident within the UAW. He had done Reuther's bidding at Local 600 throughout his difficult first year in office. He had tried to maneuver around the left-wing officers on the dues increase, but the membership forced his hand. He had gone to the Reuther caucus in search of some sympathy for his uncomfortable circumstances, but the caucus did not show Stellato sympathy—the caucus showed Stellato the door. He was, after all, doing the work of the opposition now, whether he wanted to or not.

The rank and file at Local 600 had not elected an opposition figure; they had created one. And although Stellato may have been a reluctant militant, he was not a stupid one. Stellato had been part of the Reuther caucus and was well aware of Reuther's Achilles heel:

the shorter workweek. It was, as Reuther had once acknowledged in 1949, an enormously popular program. Stellato had recognized the widespread support for the shorter workweek when he campaigned for office in 1950 and 1951, but had soft-peddled the issue at that time for fear of losing Reuther's support. After the dues fight, however, his bridge to the Reuther administration had been burned; if he was going to withstand a challenge from the International, he would have to rally the rank and file. The 30-40 program was an obvious choice. Reuther's strongest argument against the program in 1949 had been its association with the CP, but Stellato had developed a reputation as a right-wing, red-baiting anti-Communist. Who could be better insulated from the charge of Communism?[122]

Reutherites within the Rouge felt betrayed by Stellato's new oppositional relationship with Reuther. James Ryan, a self-described "old-timer" who had known Walter Reuther "from the time he was an apprentice tool & die maker" at the Rouge, was highly critical of Stellato's opportunism. "The time has come when the rank and file of Local 600 woke up to the fact that you are no longer the man we thought you were when they elected you at the last election."[123]

The summer of 1951 marked the tenth anniversary of the historic 1941 strike that had forced Ford to recognize Local 600. Stellato decided to use the occasion to inaugurate his new life as a born-again labor union militant, to launch an attack on the Reuther administration, and to initiate a high-profile campaign for the shorter workweek. The June 23, 1951 celebration was to be an enormous rally, with John L. Lewis as the featured guest speaker. The selection of Lewis was infused with meaning at the Rouge. As the founding president of the CIO, Lewis had initiated the CIO organizing drive that led to the 1941 victory at Ford. Lewis had subsequently emerged as third force in organized labor, independent and critical of both the AFL and the CIO. Even as the rival federations prepared to inaugurate a no-raiding pact, Lewis threatened to disrupt plans for labor unity by inviting units from both the AFL and the CIO to consider joining him in the formation of a new, independent labor federation.[124] The Reuther administration decided to boycott the celebration, not only refusing to accept an invitation to speak, but also forbidding attendance by UAW staff members and advising other allies that the UAW opposed the event. The Reuther administration publicly charged that the event was a Communist plot against him.[125]

The Anniversary Celebration was an enormous affair.[126] The Local purchased advertisements in Detroit's daily newspapers and on local radio stations. Lewis, who had not stepped foot in Detroit for more than ten years, arrived by train and was greeted by an enthusiastic crowd. He was escorted by Local 600's flying squadron in a caravan that traveled from Detroit to a huge rally in Dearborn.[127] One Reuther supporter lamented, in the pages of *Labor Action*, the stark contrast between the massive rally at Ford Local 600 and another big labor event of that June, the invitation-only dedication of the new UAW headquarters, Solidarity House. Although some autoworkers had tried to attend the Solidarity House celebration, they were reportedly denied admittance. However, "the ceremonies at which Lewis spoke were truly a working-class rally: auto workers with their wives [sic] and kids by the thousands, like the CIO picnics and rallies of old times."[128]

Stellato's rally speech launched his campaign to build a dissident challenge to Reuther within the UAW. He set forth a "Fighting Program for the Auto Workers" that soon became known in labor circles as the "Ford Program." At the center of the Ford Program was, not surprisingly, the 30-40 program. The idea of shorter hours and higher pay, which Lewis heartily endorsed in his remarks, was proposed as a basic trade union strategy for tightening labor markets, increasing bargaining strength, and giving workers added freedom from the burdens of work life. Stellato shed the caution that had nearly cost him the 1951 election. Gone was the acquiescence to Reuther's Korean War "Equality of Sacrifice" rhetoric. He called out, before a crowd of at least

50,000 people, for the 30-hour week for 40 hours' pay and the guaranteed annual wage. But this time he did not adopt Reuther's delaying tactics, which postponed such demands until some perfect moment, always just over the ever-receding horizon. Stellato demanded that the program be pursued, not in 1955, but "Now!" The crowd echoed the call for action as Stellato demanded new contract talks and a national UAW emergency conference to combat unemployment.[129]

With this speech and rally, Stellato emerged as a leading opposition figure within the UAW. *Business Week* interpreted the strength of the opposition at Local 600 as a troubling sign, noting that the factionalism hit just as the UAW was "beginning to win a reputation for being a responsible organization ... UAW's employers, though far from loving Reuther, watch with some dread the efforts of an opposition to organize. Such an opposition invariably tries to outdo Reuther in being tough toward management."[130] As the summer of 1951 turned to autumn, Stellato worked to enhance his profile, not only at home in Local 600, but also within a larger movement of 30 for 40 supporters in the largest UAW locals. Other leaders, tempted by the prospect of a successful challenge to Reuther's administration of the UAW, began to rally support for a dissident movement. In August, support arrived from Buick Local 599 in Flint. "Ford Local 600 has called for a shorter workweek, a 30-hour week so that more men [sic] will be employed. BUT it must be 30 hours work with 40 hours pay. The workers today cannot afford to draw a smaller pay check than a 40-hour pay week ... We join with the Ford Local Executive Board in this demand for all labor."[131]

The most immediate demand from Stellato was his call for an emergency UAW conference to consider labor responses to unemployment. When the International did not respond to this demand, locals began to propose conferences without International sponsorship. In mid-July, Stellato began threatening that, if the International did not respond to the demand for an unemployment conference, Local 600 would serve as host for such an event.[132] A meeting of Chrysler stewards, representing 60,000 Chrysler workers, quickly picked up the conference call. They agreed to demand an unemployment conference and threatened to take matters into their own hands if the International did not take some action. An even bolder move was announced when Chevrolet assembly plant workers took the unusual step of announcing that eleven Chevrolet locals had already agreed to sponsor such an independent conference, to be held in St. Louis on September 1, 1951. Local 600, as the initiator of the demand, was invited to send representatives to the event.[133]

In response, Reuther moved to take the wind out of the Chevrolet locals' sails by calling an unemployment conference of all GM locals, to be held in Detroit on September 28, 1951.[134] This was quickly followed by the announcement of a Ford conference, scheduled for October 11–12, 1951, and the promise of a Chrysler conference.[135]

As preparation for the conferences proceeded, Local 600 produced and distributed a booklet, commemorating the Anniversary Celebration and reproducing the new "Fighting Program for the Auto Workers."[136] The booklet identified the program as one supported "unanimously" (if only ceremonially) by the Local 600 workers at the Anniversary Celebration, and endorsed by a "state-wide meeting of auto workers" in Flint, Saginaw, Pontiac, Bay City, and Detroit. In addition to promoting the 30 for 40 program, the booklet included an extraordinarily harsh attack on Reuther's recent bargaining strategy. Ignoring his own complicity in the 1950 round, Stellato now disavowed the entire affair. The most striking element of the "Fighting Program" was its charge that Reuther's corporatism entangled him in the unseemly logic of war-dependent job creation.

Some top leadership in labor were influenced by the government's pronouncements of abundant defense employment for the automobile industry over a period of the next five years. These glittering promises, dangled before the eyes of this top labor leadership, lulled them into a false sense of economic security and induced them to sign five-year contracts ... It is apparent to all of us that these five-year contracts mean economic security only for Big Business, while on the other hand, labor was no longer to rely on its economic strength as its chief bargaining power, but was to await the shower of blessings that were to come from Government, Big Business, and labor and government politicians.[137]

The "Fighting Program" became the basis for a new caucus within the UAW. The Committee for a Democratic UAW met for the first time during the weekend of the GM unemployment conference in Detroit. The caucus meeting, held at the Fort Wayne Hotel, drew approximately 200 participants. Stellato served as chair of the new group, with additional leadership emerging from Coburn Walker, president of Flint Chevrolet Local 659. The inclusion of Local 659, one of the large locals at the heart of the 1936–37 sit-down strikes, was a major coup for Stellato's new caucus. Although Local 600 was a thorn in Reuther's side, he never considered Ford to be his "base" of operation. As UAW vice-president, Reuther had led the GM department, although even within GM, his support was greater in Detroit than in Flint.[138] Not withstanding his early experience as a Rouge worker, Reuther had always been known as a GM man. Now, the giant Ford local combined with Flint's finest and rallied around the "Fighting Program" as the basis for a new insurgent movement.[139] The group distributed a leaflet at the GM conference, urging support for the 30 for 40 program.[140]

At the start of the GM conference, Reuther addresssed the 350 delegates who gathered to discuss responses to unemployment, explaining the current unemployment crisis and attacking the Ford "Fighting Program." Reuther explained that a temporary shortage of metals, the "bread and butter problem of today ... is the issue."[141]

Reuther knew, however, that the delegates had come to talk about something more than metal shortages. Reuther needed to confront the challenge presented by Ford Local 600. Reuther made no concessions to the popular 30-40 program. Using many of the arguments he had formulated in 1949, Reuther began by identifying the shorter workweek proposal as "unrealistic," if popular. His second line of attack was to impugn the motives of those who would advocate the shorter hours program, arguing that the demand was aimed at "dissipating the power of our union." His attack focused on John L. Lewis, the Communists, and the leadership of Ford Local 600.

After this assault, Reuther disparaged the demand by misrepresenting it as a call for more leisure and less pay. Reuther then boldy asserted that the real struggle was for more goods, not more leisure. Finally, Reuther moved to dismiss the entire notion of an employment crisis, promising that war production would soon create labor shortages.[142]

During the week or so between the GM conference and the meeting of the Ford delegates, Stellato spoke to Rouge workers during lunchtime rallies of each of the three shifts (11:00 A.M., 7:30 P.M., and 3:30 A.M.). He told the workers that the Rouge delegation to the Ford conference would introduce a motion to open negotiations immediately for a 30-hour week with 40 hours' pay.[143] The conference began on Thursday, October 12, 1951, with speeches by Reuther and Mazey. Stellato rose to introduce a resolution for a 30-hour week at 40 hours' pay. The chair of the Ford Council, a member of the Reuther caucus, ruled that the resolution was out of order because contract demands were not on the agenda.[144]

After the conference, Reuther called Stellato and vice-president Pat Rice to appear immediately for questioning before the entire IEB to explain statements "detrimental to the interests of the International Union."[145] Stellato and Rice presented themselves at Solidarity House later that day, accompanied by Local 600 executive board members and many rank-and-file workers. Some building officers, unable to join the Solidarity House visit, sent telegrams to the IEB. One telegram, from the Gear and Axle Building, proclaimed,

> We strongly protest your action in demanding that brothers Stellato and Rice appear before the international executive board today at four p.m. for asking for the 30-hour work week at 40 hours pay for Ford workers. We also strongly protest your action in ruling Brother Stellato out of order when he attempted to put this vital issue before the Ford Council for consideration and action.[146]

The leadership of Local 600 went on the offensive. Stellato refused to answer questions until specific charges were provided in writing. Furthermore, Stellato and Rice used the occasion to speak out in defense of their 30 for 40 program. According to one observer, Stellato "ridiculed the five-year contracts" and "renewed his demand for a 30-hour week with 40-hour pay."[147] The Rouge militants put Reuther on the defensive, demanding to know what program he advocated in response to the growing pool of unemployed autoworkers. Reuther responded by ridiculing the 30 for 40 demand, saying that war production would soon create labor shortages.[148]

On Sunday, October 14, 1951, a meeting was called of the 200-member General Council of Ford Local 600. At this meeting Stellato introduced the "Fighting Program," including the 30 for 40 demand, and called upon the International officers to cease attacking Local 600 and adopt the "Fighting Program" as their own. The General Council voted overwhelmingly in favor of the program. In a powerful sign of the support Stellato's program had won at the Rouge, the Council vote was nearly unanimous, with only seven Council members, all of them members of the Reuther caucus, voting against the program.[149] This was followed, a month later, by a massive membership meeting that also voted for the program, including a call for abrogation of the five-year contract in order to make the 30 for 40 demand. Several thousand members reportedly roared with approval as Stellato mocked C. E. Wilson and Walter Reuther, both of whom had been predicting labor shortages for more than a year. Responding to new Ford company plans for "revolutionary" new production technologies for 1952, Stellato proposed the 30 for 40 demand as a progressive answer to the labor movement difficulties caused by the threat of technological unemployment.[150]

Reuther did not budge in his opposition to the 30 for 40 demand. On November 7, during the 1951 CIO convention, Reuther received a telegram from Stellato.[151] The telegram, addressed to Reuther as "Chairman, Resolutions Committee, CIO Convention," was a copy of the message Stellato had sent to Ed Lohre of the CIO Woodworkers Union. Lohre, a member of the Resolutions Committee, had drafted a 30-hour week resolution for the convention. In his message to Lohre, Stellato recalled:

> Recently Local 600 UAW CIO raised a demand for a 30 hour week with 40 hours pay ... We feel that only through a shorter workweek without any reductions in take home pay can we guarantee employment to our members, 20,000 of whom are now laid off and seeking employment. We are aware that your International Union is confronted with the same problems and is prepared to introduce a resolution to the CIO Convention calling upon the Convention to fight for the establishment of the 30 hour work week.
>
> We hope that your fight to put the CIO squarely behind the demand for a 30 hour week will receive the support of the overwhelming majority of the delegates present. It represents a basic need for all workers in all segments of organized labor and is a fight that must be waged with the combined strength of all labor.
>
> Within our Local union we shall continue the demand for a 30 hour week with 40 hours pay and extend our full support to any union seeking the establishment of this same program.[152]

In the copy sent to Reuther, Stellato concluded, "We urge you, as Chairman of the Resolutions Committee, to support the resolution proposed by the CIO Woodworkers Union." The Resolution never got beyond Reuther's Resolutions Committee. None of the resolutions brought forth from the Committee mentioned the shorter workweek demand, and there was no discussion of the issue at the CIO convention. Reuther used the occasion to expound upon the complexity of metal shortages.[153]

Reuther reportedly began making speeches that included sarcastic remarks about the 30 for 40 program. In particular, Reuther, trying to pin the demand on opportunistic and ambitious officers at Local 600, declared that he had never received a request from the rank and file for a 30-hour week. In response, the opportunistic and ambitious officers at Local 600 collected between 30,000 and 40,000 cards, signed by members of Local 600. Each card asked Reuther to join the rank and file in demanding immediate negotiations for a 30-hour week with 40 hours' pay. The public statement also addressed itself directly to Reuther: "Walter, your position does not help the auto workers. It helps the Fords, Chryslers, and GM . . . We repeat. Don't help industry. Join with us in our fight for our membership."[154] On November 19, 1951, a delegation of fourteen Local 600 members crafted a brilliant piece of political theater when they carried the thousands of cards to Solidarity House in order to present the demand to Reuther. Dave Moore and William Johnson, both prominent African-American leaders at Local 600, led the delegation and asked to meet with Reuther.[155] One of Reuther's assistants told the delegation that they could not see Reuther or talk to him on the phone. A heated exchange followed as more members of the Solidarity House "palace guard" blocked the doors to the building. Finally, several members of the delegation angrily dumped the cards on the floor. The event, a rare high-stakes intra-union protest action, appeared in the headlines of the Detroit press, and the photo of the scattered cards made the front page of the *Detroit News*. *Fortune* reported the incident, including the Local 600 demand that Reuther "tear up existing auto contracts and ask for a 'thirty-hour-week at forty hours' pay,'" and dubbed the event "the opening round of a new war in the still turbulent union." The 30 for 40 demand had moved to center stage.[156]

2.

THE MOST DANGEROUS
MAN IN DETROIT

Walter Reuther had a problem. He was celebrated within liberal
circles as the leading labor statesman of the postwar era, but the
compromises expected of a statesman made for rough relations
within the ranks of his own union. Reuther had not yet secured the
authority upon which a statesman depends. Many of the pieces
were in place, but he had not yet managed to build a united, sin-
gle-party union bureaucracy. Until unity was established, Reuther
remained vulnerable to factionalist forces that criticized Reuther's
brand of responsible unionism.

Reuther's right-wing allies within the Association of Catholic
Trade Unionists acknowledged the predicament created by
Stellato's factional campaign for a shorter workweek. The ACTists
newspaper, *Wage Earner*, cautioned against support for the 30-40
program. "Thinking members," they suggested, "will see the 30-
hour-week demand as pie-in-the-sky, and recognize the reasoning of
Reuther who declared this is not the time for a 30-hour week with
40-hour pay." Stellato, however, had hit a nerve. "That Stellato is
militant is an obvious fact ... Honest veteran unionists admit that

Stellato, even with his wild roundhouse swings against top UAW officers, has won much popular support by his demands . . ."[1]

Within two weeks of the Local 600 shorter hours protest at Solidarity House, the International took action to defuse the growing restlessness within the union and the emerging interest in the Ford Program of Local 600. On December 12, 1951 the IEB answered Carl Stellato's call for a national unemployment conference and announced that approximately 600 to 800 delegates would be invited to Washington for a January meeting about unemployment.

When the conference opened, on Sunday, January 13, 1952, it was not difficult to discern Reuther's intentions. Rather than a "strategy" session to craft a labor movement response to unemployment, the conference was instead a publicity event to pressure the government to take action on behalf of the unemployed. On one wall, an enormous banner announced, "Congress Has Acted to Protect Corporations During Defense Emergency . . . It Must Act to Protect Workers' Families Against Hardship." But the banner at the front of the room, hanging over the podium, was even more indicative of Reuther's agenda: "Unemployment *Weakens* Democracy—*Strengthens* Communism."[2]

Although much of the conference time was devoted to visiting Congressional leaders on Capitol Hill, the conference proceedings also included a speech by Reuther in which he discussed the problem of metal shortages and the unwillingness of the auto industry to fight aggressively for defense work. Reuther complained, "the big companies in the auto industry proper haven't got a large enough volume of defense work to take up the slack of the unemployment . . . but we have got to get more defense work . . . they still have too little, if we are going to absorb the unemployment."[3]

Reuther devoted a considerable amount of energy to attacking the 30 for 40 movement. Rather than wait for Stellato to make another shorter hours motion, as he had at the Ford conference, the administration introduced an unemployment resolution that included an eight-point program for fighting unemployment, and a one-point program for fighting the 30 for 40 movement.[4] The administration resolution, entitled "UAW-CIO Practical Program to Keep America Strong—To Keep America at Work," began its attack on the shorter workweek with Reuther's familiar red-baiting strategy. "Certain forces outside our union are again attempting to seize upon the feeling of insecurity and uncertainty that unemployment has created, in an effort to make political capital of the present problems by raising the impractical and unrealistic demand for a 30-hour week with 40 hours' pay at this time . . . in order to weaken our defense mobilization program."[5]

Next, Reuther returned to an older theme that had won him the UAW presidency in 1946—i.e., the CP productivity drives during World War II. It was, after all, the CP shift to the right wing of the political spectrum that had provided Reuther with the opportunity to position himself as a militant. "These are the same political forces who . . . following . . . the invasion of Russia by Hitler . . . were then willing to put every hard-earned trade-union gain on the altar of sacrifice in their complete desire to serve the Soviet Union. The Communist Party . . . launched a campaign to put piecework in every shop." Rhetorically, at least, Reuther had once again reconstructed the old political landscape that had positioned him to the left of the CP. Reuther's resolution jumped seamlessly to the contemporary situation in order to make its central claim: "A careful study of the *Communist Daily Worker* and other Communist publications will show conclusively that the demand for a 30-hour week with 40 hours' pay was engineered at this time by the Communists for the purpose of creating discontent and confusion and to weaken the efforts of the union to carry out its practical program to deal with unemployment and at the same time to strengthen the mobilization effort."[6]

Firing in many directions at once, the resolution also advanced Reuther's idea that the 30 for 40 demand was, on its own terms, a legitimate demand, but one that awaited more perfect timing. The program would have to await a time "when our technological productive capacity has advanced to the point which enables us to create sufficient wealth to guarantee a higher living standard than we currently have on the basis of a shorter workweek." At present, the resolution argued, such a program would be "dangerously unrealistic" and "irresponsible," especially at a time "when employment levels are high, due to defense production and the increasing requirements of the Armed Services."[7]

The printed record of the proceedings, published by the International, included a full-page chart, along with explanatory text, which asked, "When is the Strategic Moment?" for the 30-hour week. The chart showed labor force employment rates dating back to 1929 and projected through 1953 in order to contrast the high unemployment of the 1930s with the relatively low unemployment of 1952, and the even lower unemployment predicted for 1953. The accompanying text said, "This chart shows that a 30-hour week is an absurd and a false solution to the unemployment problem now ... The drain of men into the armed forces plus the increased defense production requirements make a 30-hour week impractical and unrealistic at this time."[8] A similar caption beneath a photograph of Reuther declared, "Talk of a Thirty-Hour Week is Untimely and Irrelevant" due to "(1) obvious Communist inspiration; (2) failure ... to recognize the actual causes of defense unemployment (the lack of coordination between civilian curtailment and defense production); and (3) recognition that a 30-hour week now would only multiply the roadblocks which stand in the way of re-employment for laid off workers."[9]

Finally, Reuther spoke to the issue of Communist inspiration.

There is a fundamental difference between believing in a 30-hour week, which we believe in—some day we are going to make that fight—and raising that as a practical immediate trade-union demand at a time like this ... this thing was engineered at this time by the

Communist Party. We can document that. We can document by the *Daily Worker* and other Communist publications that this originated at this time—not the idea, not this long-range goal with labor to get a shorter workweek, but this demand was raised by the Communist Party, and that can be documented.[10]

The 30 for 40 demand at Local 600 had originated with the CP. After 1950, however, it was Stellato who had recognized the opportunities for capturing rank-and-file support by pushing the 30-40 demand. The leadership of the CP had, in fact, begun to chastise local militants for pressing the demand. Nevertheless, even without evidence of CP inspiration for the 1952 campaign, Reuther did show the conferees two articles. One article from *Ford Facts*, the official newspaper of Local 600, quoted a Communist magazine that called for "Unity among the big five for world peace."[11] The article did not even mention shorter hours. The other article was taken, not from a Communist newspaper, but from the *Detroit News*. It was the article about the November 1952 30-40 card protest at Solidarity House. Nobody in the audience could have doubted that this article demonstrated the existence of a dissident 30 for 40 movement within the UAW. Although the article did not mention Communists, the perceived link between the CP and the shorter hours movement was certainly plausible. Reuther did acknowledge that Carl Stellato was not himself a Communist. "I think that temporarily for reasons of opportunism, he has permitted himself to be seduced by them ... And I say, Brother Stellato—your slip is showing."[12]

Bill Hood, the African-American recording secretary of Local 600, did introduce an alternative conference resolution crafted by the Committee for a Democratic UAW-CIO.[13] The resolution included the demand for 30-hour week with 40 hours' pay, but it was mixed in with several other proposals. The proposal did not include the earlier stinging critique of those labor leaders who depended upon the shower of blessings from the defense establishment.[14]

When Stellato took the floor to speak, however, he did not challenge Reuther. He did not challenge Reuther on the issue of Communist inspiration, nor did he defend the campaign as a product of his own presidency at Local 600. He did not challenge Reuther's claim that a lack of coordination was responsible for unemployment or the suggestion that the formation of a technical task force to address metal shortages was equivalent to a fighting program to confront unemployment. Nor did he question how defense unemployment could simultaneously be so serious that it could lead people in their "insecurity and uncertainty" to embrace a Communist-inspired plot, and yet so minimal that the 30 for 40 demand was irrelevant. Rather, Stellato defensively asserted that "[We] did not come down here to engage in any debate or political squabble with President Reuther or anyone else . . . We believe, in Local 600, that President Reuther has done a good job in trying to avoid the unemployment. There is no question." He then reminded the delegates of his 1950 program.

> In 1950 . . . Local 600 adopted a program along the same lines that you see up there on that board here today.[15] We went further. We asked that the automobile industry be completely diverted to defense and that one automobile manufacturer be allowed to build cars for the purpose of transportation.[16]

Stellato completely retreated from the militant critique of Reuther's military Keynesianism, and took the extra step of disavowing the entire period of his opportunistic radicalism by returning to his 1950, pro-Reuther days.[17]

Why, at this moment, did Stellato abandon the "Fighting Program" of Local 600? Stellato had always been a reluctant militant, of course, but pressure from the rank and file had forced him either to lead or get out of the way. Stellato opted to lead rather than leave. Having begun the high-profile work of organizing an opposition caucus within the UAW, many of the likely costs of challenging Reuther and already been incurred. Why would Stellato put his dissident status at risk by abandoning the "Fighting Program" that had so united the rank and file in support of his presidency?

Stellato may have feared losing his job at the hands of the militant Local 600 membership, but in late 1951, Stellato had something else to fear: the House Un-American Activities Committee (HUAC). In November 1951, shortly before Local 600's 30-40 post-card protest at Solidarity House, news arrived in Dearborn that the HUAC was preparing to hold public hearings to investigate the influence of Communism in Detroit. The hearings, to be held locally, targeted Local 600 and, reportedly, an agent for the committee had already visited Solidarity House for a meeting about the Ford Local.[18]

Stellato had supported the initiation of the post-card protest, but once the news of the HUAC hearings broke, he had quietly retreated from participation in the publicity stunt. He allowed the postcard signing to proceed, thus avoiding a direct confrontation with left-wing militants, but did not show his face at Solidarity House.[19] Thus, as early as November 1951, the threatened HUAC inquisition had curbed Stellato's appetite for confrontation.[20] By early January, it had become clear that the hearings were intended to make a big splash in Detroit: the HUAC staff made the highly unusual announcement that the entire committee would travel to Detroit to participate in the hearings.[21]

The hearings themselves were, by most accounts, quite effective in transporting the red scare to the motor city.[22] Militants from Local 600 protested the hearings, but no resistance was forthcoming from the UAW International. Reuther was briefly caught in the crossfire of the red scare when the local press quoted W. H. Hall, secretary of the Board of Commerce, accusing Reuther of leading the country toward "the socialistic state."[23] Nevertheless, observers of all political stripes noted that Reuther seemed quite pleased with the HUAC attack on Local 600. Reuther instructed several members of his

International staff to testify as cooperative witnesses before the Committee. *Business Week* noted that in the past Reuther had denounced the HUAC members as "witch-hunters," but "this week Reuther and the committee were working together on the UAW like a well-rehearsed vaudeville team."[24]

The most important testimony came from Lee Romano, formerly a CP activist at the Rouge, vice-president of Local 600 during the Thompson years, and now a member of Reuther's staff. Romano testified that the Communists and their supporters controlled Local 600. Romano also tried to follow Reuther's example from the Washington unemployment conference by using the witch-hunt, not merely to expose the existence of Communists at the Rouge, but to crush the 30 for 40 movement, linking it with the CP and the Soviet Union. Referring to the old World War II alignment of the United States and the Soviet Union, Romano noted,

> In that day, [the Communists] were waving two flags. In one hand they were waving the American flag and in the other hand the Soviet flag. Today, they are only waving the Soviet flag. They have dropped the American flag for the 30-hour week, because everybody knows in America that although we may have a problem in Detroit, in most of the key centers of industry there is a shortage of manpower.[25]

But when Congressman Walter of Pennsylvania asked how successful the CP had been in bringing about a shorter workweek, Romano answered in two distinct ways. First, following Reuther's now-familiar refrain, Romano suggested that the CP activists "have not been successful in that because the people objected to that themselves, with the high cost of living and everything concerned, the more hours you put in, the much better and much easier it is to buy the commodities and necessities of life." But the Congressman asked a follow-up question: "Because of that resistance, did the Communist Party abandon its program of the shorter week?" In answering this question, Romano forgot his scripted response. "No," Romano recalled.

> They asked for a 30-hour week with 40 hours' pay. That is something everybody desires. Every worker in America desires it. I desire it and I imagine you gentlemen desire it—to work less hours, if possible, and still maintain an equilibrium insofar as your living is concerned, your standards are concerned. Everybody wants that and we know that ... The only thing is, they point up these things and fan this hysteria ... They know that by creating this hysteria, which meets the needs and desires of the people, that they are able to drum up enough agitation for this particular program. They don't say they want a 30-hour week with 30 hours' pay. No, they are for 30 hours a week with 40 hours' pay.[26]

The Committee's counsel, Frank Tavenner, quickly interrupted that line of inquiry and moved the discussion to safer ground. Romano's description of a 30 for 40 "hysteria" provided some indication of the depth of the program's popular appeal, as well as the difficulties Reuther was having keeping a popular demand down.

Reuther, however, was about to act decisively to overcome these difficulties. The hearings into Local 600's affairs ended on Wednesday, March 12, 1952. Within four hours of the Committee's concluding questions, Reuther initiated a new campaign against his opponents at Local 600.[27] In a daring power play, Reuther ordered the officers of Local 600 to appear, once again, before the IEB, this time challenged to "show cause why an administrator should not be appointed to take charge of the local union."[28]

On Thursday, March 13, the General Council of Local 600 met in a special session and voted overwhelmingly to support the local officers in their fight against an administrator. The officers of Local 600 released a statement condemning Reuther and the IEB for joining forces with the HUAC. "We reiterate our previous statement that your actions have been conceived in a desire to destroy the most democratic union in the UAW-CIO since you have failed in every effort to take control of Local 600 through your cohorts and paid international representatives."[29]

Reuther, acting as prosecutor, began a one-day hearing on Friday, March 14, inviting thirty-nine local union presidents to sit in on his homemade un-American activities trial. The key charge made by Reuther was that "the manipulation of a small, but well-disciplined communist group ... was able to subvert the policies, programs, and publications of Local 600 to their own ends and against the best interests of the union membership."[30] In the early morning hours of March 15, after listening to prosecutorial accusations for thirteen hours, the IEB made its decision and issued a press release claiming that Local 600's leadership had become completely subservient to the foreign policy needs of the Soviet Union.

Reuther seized control of Local 600. On Sunday, March 16, an Administrative Board met to announce that five unit officers had been removed from office, accused of being either members of or subservient to the Communist Party line. Reuther was warmly praised by the HUAC for acting on the committee's findings and for assisting in the ongoing war against subversives in the United States.[31]

The five deposed officers were the same five that Stellato had accused in 1950. In addition to supervising the "purge" of these five elected officers, the Reuther administration also took control of the Local 600 newspaper, *Ford Facts*. This was a significant step because *Ford Facts* was not only the newspaper of the Rouge workers, but had, after the creation of the fighting "Ford Program," become a widely distributed dissident newspaper and the most important independent labor publication willing to challenge the publicity of the Reuther machine. Indeed, Reuther cited the role of the newspaper as one of the reasons for taking control of the local. Without explicitly mentioning the influence of the 30-40 movement, Reuther did mention irresponsible action by the local that was harming the entire union.[32] When the Reuther administration began publishing its own version of *Ford Facts*, it immediately took aim at the 30 for 40 program, recalling for the membership how a "minority group" put forward a program of their own at the Washington Unemployment Conference instead of supporting the "realistic" official program of the UAW.[33]

The four top officers—Stellato, Pat Rice, Bill Hood, and Bill Grant—were not actually removed from office. They were stripped of all responsibilities, and all normal functions of the local were suspended (i.e., meetings of the local's Executive Board, the General Council, etc.), but at least formally, the top officers remained in office.[34] Fred Collins, a *Time-Life* reporter, called this move "some first class politics . . . This, of course, gives the appearance of a 'soft hand' on local matters and is obviously designed to prevent any great unrest in the local."[35]

Many wondered how the leadership, and the membership, of Local 600 would respond to the administratorship. In a private report to his editors, Fred Collins observed that the hearings may have created a "break" between the four top officers. Collins suggested that Stellato and Pat Rice may have made a deal with Reuther. Stellato, it was alleged, had "changed his defiant manner from the 'we will not let them take over the local' to 'when this is over I will take the issue to the convention.'" Rice reportedly "spoke, in a cheerful manner, with Reuther in the hall." In contrast, Bill Hood "said little, left hurriedly" and Bill Grant was "still defiant."[36] It is not clear that Collins correctly identified the nature of the split, but all observers knew that Stellato would, at the very least, be tempted to sit quietly as Reuther tried to accomplish what Stellato had failed to do at the start of his presidency: extinguish factionanlism at Ford Local 600.

There was reason to believe that Reuther might succeed where Stellato had failed, if only because he was a more sophisticated political operative. Few believed that Reuther would have taken such a bold step unless he was certain of victory when, after sixty days of rule, he would have to hold an election. "The stakes for Walter P. Reuther are high," wrote B. J. Widick. "A defeat for his faction in the Ford Local 600 elections, after these drastic measures to win control of the local, would be a major blow to his reputation and influence in the UAW as well as nationally. Reuther is now in a position where he must have a victory at any cost!"[37] *Business Week* added that "Reuther has only two months in which to destroy the majority support [the local's officers] have had, or face the most serious setback he will have had since he took over the union's helm."[38] Second, even militant left-wing observers of the HUAC hearings acknowledged that Reuther's "cooperation" during the hearings "gave the witch-hunt a certain appearance of 'legitimacy' in the minds of many workers."[39] Finally, because Stellato had been so acquiescent during the Washington Unemployment Conference, and Reuther had given him such a tongue lashing, there was every reason to expect that Stellato would now gladly return to the Reuther fold. Reuther's decision to leave Stellato in office clearly reflected this expectation.[40]

Reuther had, in fact, miscalculated. Communists and anti-Communist witch-hunters had accepted that the HUAC hearings were about CP activity. The CP had been active at Local 600 and everybody knew it. But Reuther's dictatorial imposition shifted attention from Communism to Reutherism. The membership of Local 600 was well aware that the fighting "Ford Program" had been a thorn in Reuther's side. Moreover, the "Ford Program" was a militant labor union program and its shorter hours demand was a decisive challenge to Reuther's corporatism. By seizing control of the local, Reuther instantly turned the battle into a war between the shorter hours program of the dissidents at Local 600 and the bureaucratic dictatorship of Reuther. Reuther provided an occasion for activists at Local 600 to rally around democracy and militancy in a unified campaign against Reuther.

Moreover, the local CP activists adopted a far more militant position than the national CP leadership had been promoting. Immediately following the imposition of the administratorship, the State Committee of the Communist Party of Michigan began producing editions of the *Michigan Party Forum* that were far more militant than the standard CP line. The *Party Forum* hailed the development of an organized caucus devoted to "a return to militant trade unionism," including the "30 hour week with 40 hours pay."[41] Moreover, the five officers accused of being Communists publicly campaigned, not with a defensive and formalist civil liberties program, but with a substantive fighting program, to restore the independent fighting spirit of Local 600. In a clear message to Stellato and others, one pamphlet issued by "the five" reported,

> Many rumors are floating around. The anti-labor press happily predicts that President Stellato is about to break with the Progressives of Local 600 . . . Unless the Coalition is maintained, there is a great danger of division and disunity and a Reuther victory. Whoever splits this unity for pork chop deals, will stand exposed and branded forever with the hatred and disgust of the Ford workers. Ford workers want a continuation of the solidarity and struggle which has won such popular support amongst the auto workers throughout the country.[42]

If there were splits in the unity, these were not evident at an extraordinary "special" Local 600 meeting, held only a week after the administratorship was imposed. Because the Reuther administration controlled the Local 600 building, a meeting was called at Dearborn's Club Supino, where "more than a thousand workers" reportedly jammed the hall to rally for a fight against the Reuther dictatorship. All four top officers were said to have made "fiery speeches" with Stellato taking the lead. Stellato charged Reuther with using the "Communist" issue to hide his real target: the militant program of Local 600. In particular, Stellato pointed to the significance of Reuther's opposition to the demand for a 30-hour week with 40 hours' pay. Moreover, Stellato began the process of mobilizing against Reuther's seizure. Committees were established for publicity and finance, and $4,000 was collected at the meeting itself. The fight for Local 600 had begun. Within a month, the local leadership was producing its own independent newspaper—*Local 600 Union Facts*—as an alternative to Reuther's edition of *Ford Facts*.

The *Wage Earner* conceded that the seizure of the Local had pressed Stellato to once again adopt a militant pose. The Local 600 president had initiated "a campaign to confuse the rank and file" with demands that "included . . . such legitimate UAW long range, but-not-now objectives as the 30-hour week."[43]

Reuther appointed his most trusted aide, Jack Conway, as the administrator of the local. Conway, who received national attention for this role, faced the enormous challenge of building support for Reuther and pro-Reuther candidates, even as he continued to remove popular, democratically elected officers from power. After the Administrative Board removed the initial group of five accused Communists, Conway dismissed many more officers. In these cases, Conway did not even use the pretext of Communism to take action. Rather, the reasons given included "reorganization on a more efficient basis" and providing "the workers . . . better representation."[44] Leaving resentment in his wake, Conway nevertheless tried to build a Reutherite base of support. An effort was made to build up the right-wing caucus associated with the Association of Catholic Trade Unionists, but without a positive program, the caucus had fallen on hard times. The *Wage Earner* acknowledged that the "difficulties ahead are obvious. Veteran right-wingers point out that the only remaining capable members available are men over 60—too old to face the rough 'gaff' ahead." In addition to general decline, the caucus also had to concede that when, in the past, its leaders had been defeated in elections, Reuther saved them from "the shop" by giving them staff jobs at Solidarity House. The *Wage Earner* confessed, with sadness, that "the rank and file looks at International staffers as pork choppers interested strictly in politics" rather than programs.[45]

Conway and Reuther kept close tabs on all of the Rouge buildings, trying to keep a careful watch on the political mood. But the reconnaissance simply confirmed the bad news. In April, Reuther sat down with a list of unit names and membership numbers. Next to seven of the larger units, Reuther marked "CP problem," meaning that he was in trouble. Next to one building, a frustrated Reuther wrote, "workers don't understand *issues*." Next to another building, Reuther had scrawled, "in BAD shape ... will support Stellato." Finally the page included two urgent notes: *Don't hold* election too quick—" and "CALL JACK C."[46] Shortly thereafter, the IEB announced that there would be no election at Local 600. Since the top officers had not been formally removed, no election was required.

Even as Reuther's campaign for control proceeded to crumble, opposition at Local 600 grew increasingly united. When the Administrative Committee denied a request to convene a General Council meeting, Stellato issued a call for a massive "private" meeting of all Unit Officers, Committeemen, and General Council Delegates to be held at the Salina School gymnasium on May 3, 1952.[47] Resistance grew and the idea of a more or less "permanent" administrator infuriated even the most staunch right-wingers.[48] According to one report, Rouge workers may have protested in front of Solidarity, demanding elections.[49] With resistance on the rise, and right-wing activists forced to support calls for democratic elections, there was no way the Administrative Committee could sustain its decision to deny the call for elections. Stellato, who had agreed not to violate any of the orders of the International, announced that this "cooperative" posture would not continue if the sixty-day mark passed with no election date set. After May fifteenth, Stellato suggested, "the gloves will be off."[50]

Finally, after stalling as long as possible, Reuther capitulated five days before the deadline. As one leaflet proclaimed, the rank-and-file fight for elections "finally penetrated the sound proof walls of Solidarity House."[51] Unit elections were scheduled for June and July and local-wide elections were scheduled for September 9–11, 1952.

Once again, the political alignments at Local 600 were in flux. Where did Stellato belong? If Stellato thought that the time was right for him to rejoin the Reuther caucus, and if Reuther agreed, then the right wing would have to resist the temptation to offer a challenge to Stellato from the right. The ACTist *Wage Earner* argued that if at all possible, the right wing should "bide their time, and adopt CP maneuvers: drive a wedge between Stellato and the Communists."[52]

If, on the other hand, Stellato still felt compelled to maintain his militant, anti-Reuther program in order to keep the support of the rank and file, then the right wing would have to do everything in its power to challenge Stellato. Indeed, some right-wingers were quite anxious to renounce the top officers altogether and create a viable, trustworthy, independent right-wing slate. Motivated by the desire for such a principled approach, several right-wing leaders at Local 600 wired a caucus resolution to Solidarity House on May 4, 1952. The telegram threatened, "we will not pardon or condone any deal or private agreement by any one man or group in the International UAW with the present top four Local 600 officers."[53]

Similarly, the left wing (including those still close to the CP and other independent militants aligned with the SWP) faced the prospect that their erstwhile ally, Stellato, would double-cross the left as he had once double-crossed Reuther. Stellato's performance at the Washington Unemployment Conference certainly signaled that, without pressure from the membership, Stellato would once again drift back toward the Reuther caucus.

Finally, Stellato himself undoubtedly was in search of safe passage through the election. He was not about to begin making decisions on the basis of ideological principles and was, therefore, as eager as anyone else to test the winds in order to gauge the political climate at the Rouge. Immediately after Reuther announced the scheduling of elections, Stellato issued a leaflet in which his picture appeared alone, without his fellow officers, Pat Rice, William Hood, and W. G. Grant. The leaflet announced Stellato's intention to seek re-election as "an independent candidate." Over his own picture, he had printed, "Local 600 Belongs to the Membership, Not Reuther—Not Ford—Not the Communist Party." Stellato acknowledged, "Yes, there have been many rumors circulated in the daily press and in the Rouge Plant about Stellato making a deal with Reuther, and Stellato making a deal with the Communist Party ... These two rumors are deliberate lies." Stellato's triple negative campaign theme—not Reuther, not Ford, not the Communist Party—did not include a positive program. Stellato recalled the memory of his position against the dues increase, but the demand for a 30-hour week for 40 hours' pay was listed as a sub-category within a larger pledge of unity within Local 600 and more generally within the UAW. In one final hedge, undoubtedly designed to appease the left, the final demand was for "peace."[54]

At first, there were rumors that Stellato had actually visited Solidarity House to meet with UAW "top brass." But, when Stellato distributed a new leaflet, adorned with the photographs of all four top officers, the right-wingers concluded that Stellato "had not met with success" in his outreach to Solidarity House. The *Wage Earner* took comfort in this development. "So long as Stellato remains teamed with the other three well-tagged officers as a member of the slate, the right wing has hopes. Should Stellato run alone, a belligerent, autonomous-loving, top echelon-suspicious rank and file might vote him back."[55]

Stellato's second leaflet did show signs that Stellato was trying to gain support from the most militant workers at the Rouge, even as he and his "well-tagged" officers asserted, "We are independents ... We are independent of Reuther, We are independent of the Communist Party." But the leaflet did make clear that Stellato was not going to dump the left wing of his slate. "As Independents, we are united as officers because . . . [we] agree that cooperative action is in the best interest of the membership."[56] The leaflet went even further. Its program included a call to "fight speed up" (missing from Stellato's solo-leaflet) and 30 for 40 was prominently displayed as the primary demand of Local 600. The Administrative Board had announced that the five officers accused of being Communists would not be permitted to campaign for office in their units.[57] The Stellato leaflet, in an unmistakable reference to the five CP-aligned officers asserted, "we believe that any member in good standing of Local 600, who is not specifically prohibited from doing so by trial of his own peers, should be permitted to run for office."[58]

Stellato's opportunism was exceeded only by his political sensitivity. The membership of Local 600 had been united behind Stellato and his militant "Ford Program" and Reuther's dictatorial actions had only strengthened the independent resolve of the membership. Stellato opted to maintain his independence from the administration in order to insure that he would not be abandoned by the membership.

In the unit elections, Stellato-slate candidates ran with full force on the 1951 "Ford Program," highlighting the demand for a 30-hour work week at 40 hours' pay.[59] In one building, a unit president who had been removed by the Administrator without charges of Communist conspiracy was replaced by a pro-Reuther officer. The ousted president ran with the 30-40 program displayed prominently, the support of respected militants like Joe Hogan, and the righteous indignation of one who had been undemocratically removed from office.

Pro-Reuther candidates ran a campaign "under the overall direction of International appointed administrators."[60] ACTU leader John Fitzpatrick produced *The Score*, "the official UAW administration publication for the right wing." The *Wage Earner* itself found the newspaper disappointing and feared that its tone did not particularly cater to the militant Rouge workers. "We doubt . . .

[it will] sway many Local 600 workers into a frenzy of right wing devotion."[61] The Reuther slate produced leaflets with the slogan "Support UAW Program; Full Employment—Guaranteed Annual Wage." These leaflets were primarily filled with accusations that "the Commies, Stellato and the 2,000 Club (pro-Communists)" had made "the Communist Party Program . . . the Program of Local 600, and the records don't lie."[62] There was no demand for formal independence from the International.

While the right wing was attacking Stellato for his "Commie" labor program of shorter hours and higher wages, the national CP was doing its best to undermine the local CP activists at the Rouge who had rallied behind Stellato's militant "Ford Program." Beginning in April of 1952, an author identified as John Swift[63] crafted a series of four articles addressed to "Problems of Work in Right-led Unions," in general, and then "Reuther's Seizure of the Ford Local," in particular. These articles marked a final rift between the local militants of Local 600 and the CP. As the CP prepared to make peace with Reuther, the party launched a campaign to remove the 30 for 40 program from the discourse of CP activists.

In order to shift the Party to the right of the Local 600 militants, the articles invoked the authority of Lenin's "brilliant" polemic in which left-wing Communism was dismissed as an "infantile disorder."[64] The first direct attack was against local CP enthusiasm for Stellato's Committee for a Democratic UAW. Back in October 1951, George Morris had warned of the influence of pro-Reuther "Trotskyites" within the group, but had vigorously promoted the *program* of the Committee. Swift, however, argued that the group was too anti-Reuther, too factional, and lacked a viable program. Swift denounced as "unfortunate" and "inaccurate," the headline "over a story in an outstanding [CP] progressive labor magazine" because it reported that "Anti-Reuther Forces Unite to Fight Lay-Offs, Speed-Up." "The rank-and-file movement," Swift suggested, "cuts across the pro- and anti-Reuther lines."[65]

What "program" cut across the pro- and anti-Reuther lines? Surely it was not the 30 for 40 program. Although the demand for a shorter workweek at full pay might have been popular with the membership, it was not popular with the Reuther administration. Reuther had made it clear on several occasions that he opposed this program and he demonstrated his commitment to the destruction of the movement that promoted the demand. In a dramatic retreat, the CP argued that whatever positive program would ultimately serve as the basis for unity with Reuther, shorter hours would not be that program. The 30-40 program had become an obstacle to unity with Reuther and would have to be abandoned.

In an article written after Reuther's seizure of Local 600, but before the elections, Swift publicly criticized the local militants' emphasis on the 30 for 40 demand. In an incredible rebuke to "gross illusions" among "certain Michigan Party leaders," Swift discussed "a number of weaknesses which had developed" at Local 600. While acknowledging that "the Ford Local did distribute its local paper to other plants," Swift asked, "Did it not ... frequently leave the impression of seeking close contact only with locals whose leaders shared its general outlook?" Still, this criticism was too abstract. "Let us take, for example, the issue of unemployment." Swift acknowledged that it was "to the credit of the Ford Local leadership that it was among the very first to recognize the serious consequences of this problem" and that it "raised sharply the demand for immediate attention ... to alleviate the hardships caused by the unemployment which everybody admitted existed in large numbers."[66] But this line of credit was quickly and dramatically withdrawn.

> And yet ... Reuther was able to put the Local 600 leadership on the defensive ... Reuther launched his main attack upon Local 600's proposal to make the 30-hour week slogan a demand for immediate action. At a conference in which the overwhelming majority of the delegates were from locals in which there was no acute unemployment problem,

Reuther was demagogically able to make it appear that the 30-hour-week demand at this time would jeopardize the earnings of those working full time and over-time ... The delegates of Local 600 to this conference defended their local program, but did not call for the unity of all locals around that on which they could all agree ... Thus, those in the Ford Local leadership ... forgot ... that workers judge leadership on the basis not of who *demands* more, but of who helps them to get more.[67]

Swift had dropped the demand for a full 40 hours' pay when mentioning the demand for a 30-hour week. Local 600 stood accused of foolishly making excessively bold demands for a shorter workweek. Why excessive? Why did Local 600 deserve the whipping it got from Reuther? Because for the most part "there was no acute unemployment problem." This was one of Reuther's own twisted lines of defense at the Washington Unemployment Conference. The previously mentioned "hardships caused by the unemployment that everybody admitted existed in large numbers" were completely forgotten.

Although the internal coherence of Swift's article was questionable, his message to Local 600's CP activists was altogether clear: drop the shorter workweek demand. Should Stellato choose to press forward with his factional struggle for the 30 for 40 program, then the CP would be forced to break with Stellato. Having made deal after deal with compromised administrations at Local 600, the CP was suddenly prepared to declare its principled independence of any Local 600 president, if only to push the Local closer to Reuther. Swift characterized recent events at Local 600 by suggesting, "Reuther spread the lie that the leadership of the Local was subservient to the Communist Party." In fact, Swift argued, the CP had become too subservient to the Local. "Actually the Communists felt so keenly the need for supporting the progressive coalition, that they actually remained silent on points of disagreement, remaining silent, in particular, on the danger of factionalism." Swift attacked "the failure of the Left to take an independent position and to partake openly in constructive criticism," that is, criticism of Stellato and his factional campaign for a shorter workweek.[68]

What explains this strategic shift within the CP? What possible reason could the Party have for walking away from an issue that had allowed local CP activists to retain a base of support at Local 600? The CP had spent most of the early Cold War years sniffing around Local 600 trying to pick up the scent of any program that would win the support of the rank and file. The 30 for 40 program had been successful at Local 600 and had created sufficient heat to force an ex-Reutherite like Stellato to appropriate the demand in order to stay in office. Now the CP was walking away from a winning issue. What could move the CP to abandon the rank and file in this manner?

Swift insisted that personal attacks on Reuther should give way to a more programmatic emphasis, letting individuals be judged based upon substantive positions. But if the shorter workweek was not to be the positive program by which all leaders would be judged, then what would be the CP criterion? "Our basic evaluation," Swift asserted, "must rest on a solid foundation."

> This today is determined by the central issue, the issue of war and peace. A labor leader is a progressive to the degree that he stands for peace, not abstractly, but concretely—that is, for peace and co-existence with the Soviet Union. He is a reactionary to the extent that he stands for war—that is, supports the war drive of US imperialism and its anti-Soviet foreign policy.[69]

Thus, CP priorities were made clear and explicit. All labor union issues would be subordinated to the service of the Soviet Union. The subordination of the CP to the imperatives of the Soviets, however, was nothing new. Why the new friendliness toward an old Cold Warrior like Reuther? After all, Reuther's original sin in the eyes of the CP had been precisely his support for the war drive of US imperialism and its anti-Soviet foreign policy. The answer to this mystery became clear during the March 1953 UAW convention. Headlines from the *Worker* tell the story: "Auto Workers Urge Government to Accept Malenkov Peace Bid," "Reuther Plan for Peace Economy," and "Reuther Talks Peace."[70] Reuther had agreed to introduce a so-called "peace" resolution at the convention. The post-convention *Worker* article celebrated the fact that "the resolution noted Malenkov's recent declaration that there are no issues which cannot be settled peacefully." The same article called it "unfortunate" that the Reuther leadership "larded the peace resolution with the same Cold War red-baiting line that Washington uses" even as it "recognizes the great peace sentiment among the workers ... The important thing, however, is that at long last labor is officially talking up for peace."[71] In a later article, the CP quoted with delight another Reuther proclamation: "We must find a way to get together not because of hatred and fear of something but for hopes and aspirations, for a peaceful world of the brotherhood of man."[72]

If Reuther was willing to carry water for the Soviets, then the CP was more than willing to join hands with Reuther. The CP moved to shift attention from Local 600's demand for shorter hours and higher wages toward the demand for peace and trade with Communist-led countries. "Not increasing war production, but increasing production for peace is what the workers want and need," Swift reported. "They will want work, and work without war. While the demand of the local for a six hour day is one plank of such a program, it does not answer how the Rouge and the rest of the auto-air-craft industry can avoid shutdown when a crash comes." Swift suggested that "trade with China and with other Communist-led countries may make all the difference in the world in determining whether the workers in the Rouge have jobs or not."[73]

Reuther never openly welcomed the CP into his caucus. Indeed, even as the CP heaped praise on Reuther's new "peace" policy, the *Worker* noted with regret that Reuther never completely abandoned his red-baiting Cold War language.[74] Nevertheless, many former CP militants now joined Reuther and his bureaucracy. As a result,

Reuther had moved one step closer to disarming factionalism and dissent within the UAW. The seeds of future tranquility had been sewn. In time, Reuther's triumph would be complete.

In the latter part of 1952, and early 1953, even as Reuther was continuing his persecution of Communists at Local 600, the CP abandoned its critical posture. For the first time, the *Worker* featured news stories about Reuther and his labor policies, but included none of the biting commentary that had consistently hammered away at Reuther's own internal union publicity machine. Now the *Worker* became merely one more outlet for that machine.[75]

In a long, detailed article by Saul Wellman and Nat Ganley, published several weeks before the March 1953 UAW convention, the CP argued for unity within the UAW and called on CP activists to set aside "all other considerations, all divisions which weaken the union, all personal ambitions and group bitterness produced by the years of inner factionalism." What it also set aside was the 30 for 40 demand. The article included a long section devoted exclusively to collective bargaining demands, but almost no mention of the shorter workweek demand. Buried on the final page of the article, after extensive commentary about the need for peacetime jobs, etc., the article suggested "moving towards the eventual realization of the longer-range economic goals of the UAW, such as the 30 hour week with 40 hours pay."[76] In an article about Local 600's own convention resolution submissions, the *Worker* reported that one resolution had affirmed the 30 for 40 demand. In its commentary on "some of the top resolutions," however, there was no mention of the 30 for 40 demand.[77]

A review of the Party's historical positions, written in 1955, confirmed the strategic shift in the relations between the CP and Local 600.

> From 1947 to 1951 ... we placed, correctly, great emphasis, though of a schematic and mechanical nature, in the development of the tactic of the united front of struggle from below and for special attention to

the development of single issue struggles . . . In 1951, at Ford Local 600, old hard and fast factional lines were broken by the emergence of the Carl Stellato middle-road position (neither in the 'war' or 'peace' camp) and which coalesced with the left. While welcoming this new unity development, some Left and Communist forces. . . saw it primarily as a blow at the Reuther machine. We said, "Ford workers have found the Achilles heel of Walter Reuther."[78]

The review recalled the events of 1952 and the Party's changed relation to Reuther.

We called for a shift in tactics . . . The Reuther policy has gradually changed . . . his foreign policy stand has progressed from the 1953 convention policy favoring US-Soviet peace talks at the summit."[79]

Even as the Party itself explained its shift in terms of changes in Reuther's policies, there were significant external factors that may have propelled the Communists into Reuther's arms. In September 1952, Saul Wellman, Nat Ganley, William Allan, and Phil Schatz—in short, the leaders of the Michigan Party—were indicted and subsequently convicted for conspiring to advocate the overthrow of the government by force and violence. Although the Party may have tried to retain its fighting spirit under these circumstances, the pressure of state repression undoubtedly took a major toll on the Party and its outlook.[80]

After this shift, the CP became increasingly pro-Reuther in its labor movement orientation. If the rank-and-file fight for the shorter workweek in the UAW was going to survive, it was going to have to do so without the factional support of the Communists. However, Cold War fissures—especially the vehement campaigns by anti-Communists to identify and destroy any vestiges of Communism within the labor movement—continued to fan the flames of UAW factionalism and to influence the fate of the 30 for 40 movement, even after the Communists had abandoned the factional battlefield within the UAW.

3.

THE COLLAPSE
OF COMMUNISM

The 1952 Local 600 election turned out to be a terrible loss for Reuther and a triumph for the coalition of Local 600 leadership who had rallied around the demand for union democracy and the 30 for 40 program. With or without Communist support, the shorter workweek demand remained popular at the Rouge. Moreover, the right wing offered no alternative, positive program, apart from anti-Communism. As the initial unit election returns piled in, ACTU's *Wage Earner* headline acknowledged not only the sad news, but also the lack of a viable right-wing program: "Admitting Poor Early Strategy Ford Right-Wingers Race Time to Hammer Out Slate, Program." "While unit elections already held may not be added up to a Progressive or Communist sweep since victories included those of independents, anti-Reuther and anti-Commie slates, nevertheless straight right-wing caucus losses are admitted."[1] The Trotskyist SWP was considerably more up-beat in its newspaper coverage.

Campaigning on the basis of clear-cut opposition to red-baiting and dictatorial intervention in the affairs of Local 600 and for a program that included demands for a six-hour day and breaking of the five-year contract, the Unity forces grouped around the four top officers of the Local won a heartening election victory and the Reuther machine suffered the most crushing defeat since it came to power in the CIO United Automobile Workers Union ... Of the 19 units, 15 put into office opponents of the Reuther machine.[2]

These victories included not only the return of anti-Reuther incumbents, but also the success of pro-Stellato insurgents against Reuther incumbents and the return of officers removed by the Administrative Board.[3]

The building unit elections were fiercely contested and the competition helped to maintain the accountability of Stellato-aligned candidates. One incumbent who may have been hoping to curry favor with Conway and the Administrative Board dropped the 30 for 40 program from a "Unity" campaign leaflet. A group of relatively unknown right-wing activists promptly published their own leaflet, calling attention to the omission: "missing in his program printed on his leaflet is the 30 hours work for 40 hours pay plus cost-of-living allowance for pensioners. Well the $120.00 question now is: IS OUR PRESIDENT ALSO TRYING TO DOUBLE CROSS CARL STELLATO AND HIS PROGRAM?" Although not supporters of factional fights against Reuther, the local right-wing challengers kept the factional battle alive and forced the incumbent to restore the 30-40 program as a part of his campaign. The Reutherites mobilized that the *Militant* called a "major concentration of administrators in an attempt to defeat him," but the incumbent was returned to the presidency.[4]

Bill Johnson, one of the two African Americans who led the 30-40 protest at Solidary House, beat the right-wing candidate in a building unit presidential race. As one CP observer noted, the right-wing candidate "received 500 and some votes or 16% of the total, the most devastating rejection of Reuther by this great concentration of Negro workers."[5] As Stellato himself declared, "The Reuther dictatorship received a shellacking of major proportions."[6]

The upset was so significant that even relatively obscure unit elections received national press attention. *Fortune* announced that Reuther's "men from headquarters" were "continuing to have difficulties" at Local 600. "The unit elections held in July and August appear to have resulted in a number of victories for left wingers and other anti-Reutherites."[7] Although local-wide elections had not yet been held, there was no doubt that Reuther had failed to gain control of the secondary leadership. This meant that any presidential candidate would in all likelihood face an Executive Board and General Council controlled by officers who had run on programs that were explicitly opposed to Reuther's administrative policies.

Fortune took note of "insistent rumors that Carl Stellato . . . has made a compromise of sorts with the UAW administration," but this in no way altered *Fortune*'s analysis of the fundamental significance of the unit election outcomes. "In any case," *Fortune* predicted, "the control over the volatile membership that Reuther expected to attain when he sent in administrators is still a long way off."[8]

Rumors of deal making spread quickly after the unit elections, but the nature of the compromise was in dispute. The *Wage Earner* reported, "In winning units piecemeal the CP and Progressives have much of an advantage. Right-wingers believe that President Stellato can capitalize on the situation today and successfully run on a Progressive slate or engage in an International compromise."[9] The Local 600 ACTU right wingers considered all talk of compromise as evidence that Reuther was preparing to concede the election to Stellato. Despite these rumors, the right wing supported Edgar Lee, a veteran right winger, as its candidate to oppose Stellato in the Local-wide elections. Although Lee had served as an International representative and staff member for the Education department, his was an independent candidacy, developed without the permission of the International. According to Local 600 right-wing caucus members, "his 'independence' did not make him a popular selection with the UAW International."[10] Reuther and Conway let Lee continue to talk about running, but it did not take long for Lee and others to recognize that the International was backing down from its offensive against Stellato. Lee remarked, "I was going to be a candidate for local president, but I don't know now if the right wing or the International wants anyone."[11]

The right wing publicly criticized Reuther for failing to support the independent right wingers at Local 600. By early August, one member of the publicity committee for Lee's campaign admitted that the caucus was considering withdrawing its right-wing slate.[12] In late August, the caucus very publicly announced to Detroit's daily newspapers that they had been abandoned by Reuther and would therefore no longer run against Stellato's slate. In two separate, front-page stories, the *Wage Earner* announced, "Right Wing Charges 'Whitewash' as UAW Administrators Concede Local 600 to Stellato Machine," and, still more dramatically, "End of UAW-Reuther Era Seen in Events at 600."[13] One article suggested that "when Reuther failed to meet with right wing caucus leaders after their nominations, they recognized certain facts . . . [and refused] to let candidates be sacrificed in what we knew would be a defeat."[14]

The right-wing retreat applied only to the case of Stellato, who ran unopposed in the election and was elected with 19,678 votes.[15] The other three incumbent officers, however, all faced right-wing challengers. The incumbent officers beat their Reutherite challengers by powerful 3-to-1 ratios and reinforced the significance of the earlier unit elections. In the General Council elections, anti-Reuther forces were elected to almost 80 percent of the delegate seats. As the *Wage Earner* bluntly asserted, "Local 600's right wing caucus failed to function . . . A last minute attempt to plunker for right-wingers in vital building elections for delegates to the local's powerful general council failed . . . [and] the right wing suffered a near total defeat."[16]

The fact that Stellato himself was allowed to run unopposed signaled that a compromise had, in fact, been reached between Stellato and Reuther. One pre-election article in *Business Week* announced, "Backstage Agreement at Ford."

> At first glance it looks like defeat in advance for the forces of UAW president Walter Reuther ... One theory has it that Reuther simply didn't want to take a sure beating ... Recently, however, it has begun to look as though Reuther may be winning after all—behind the scenes ... Reuther seems to have gained an agreement from his opposition that they will put a damper on their anti-Reuther campaign.[17]

What did Reuther offer his opponents in order to secure this alleged agreement? One right-wing caucus member suggested, somewhat cryptically, "It looks now as though the International's slip is showing ... A right wing caucus just isn't wanted because votes for the International—no matter what the price of compromise—are needed when men are ambitious."[18] Reuther, it appeared, had jettisoned his own right-wing caucus at Local 600 as the specific price that the International had paid for compromise with Stellato.

Stellato may have been promised something more than a Reutherite retreat from support for Edgar Lee. After all, Stellato was set to win the presidency, with or without opposition for Lee. The *Worker*'s gossip column, "Autotown Alley," announced that Stellato would definitely be making a run for Joe McCusker's position as regional director when the delegates voted at the upcoming 1953 UAW convention. The directorship, which included a seat on the IEB, offered Stellato an escape from pressure of the Local 600 presidency and his precarious status as a UAW dissident. He could run with the backing of Local 600 and, once elected, quietly make his way back into the Reuther caucus.[19]

Something went wrong. The alleged peace pact between Reuther and Stellato failed to materialize. *Business Week* reported, "There was talk of a 'deal' between Reutherites and Stellato. If there was one, it didn't last."[20] By the start of 1953, the factional lines were drawn and the demand for a shorter workweek had once again emerged as the crucial battleground in a bitter contest between Reuther and Stellato.

What kept the factional fires burning between Stellato and Reuther, even after the Communists had abandoned their fight against Reuther? It was almost certainly Reuther, not Stellato, who ultimately upset the compromise, although both men probably would have preferred to preserve their mutual security pact. Reuther, however, came under considerable pressure from his own erstwhile anti-Communist allies to keep the heat on Stellato and Local 600.

Within the UAW, Reuther's ACTist supporters were reported to be "bitter at Reuther's action in 'ditching' them and giving 'his blessing by innuendo' to erratic president Carl Stellato, who intermittently travels the party line."[21] According to *Business Week*, Reuther had lost face because of his abandonment of the right-wing caucus. The *Wage Earner* went so far as to suggest that the event marked the end of the heyday of the UAW and even suggested that the future belonged to such unions as the chemical workers union. Once the Reutherites decided to stick with McCusker, however, the *Wage Earner* suggested the move would "remove Mr. Reuther from an embarrassing clash" that might otherwise have had "serious reverberations on the higher and more important national CIO level" where Reuther was "trying to solidify his power" as the new CIO president.[22]

The implicit threat from Reuther's ACTist friends was that a clash with right-wing anti-Communists over Stellato's bid to oust McCusker at the 1953 convention could be used by anti-Communist forces outside the UAW to smear Reuther. The UAW president had, in fact, already come under attack for his deal making at Local 600. In September 1952, as the Reutherites agreed to let Stellato run unopposed for the Local 600 presidency, the

International officially declared the Ford local free of Communist and subversive forces. In December, however, Reuther was publicly chastised by the HUAC for his failure to effectively purge the local of Communists and for his attempt to conceal their continuing influence in the affairs of the union. The HUAC legislators charged that Local 600 was still Communist dominated.[23]

Reuther responded with a high-profile initiative to eliminate Communist influence within the UAW and with a retreat from his earlier compromises with Stellato. Although Reuther might have wanted find a way to distinguish between Stellato and the Communists, his ACTists allies had effectively barred this pathway to compromise. The Reuther administration prepared to challenge Carl Stellato's leadership of Local 600.

Stellato was forced to renew his campaign as a leader of the anti-Reuther opposition. He used *Ford Facts* to launch a militant defense of the 30 for 40 program and to denounce, with full force, the 1950 five-year contract. On the front page of *Ford Facts* Stellato proclaimed, "We in Local 600 have, for almost two years, recognized the complete failure of the 5-year contract ... At the National Ford Conference in 1951 and again in 1952, we in Local 600 have insisted on action from our International Union."

> It is history now that in 1951 at the National Ford Conference, THE DELEGATES FROM LOCAL 600 WERE SEVERELY CRITICIZED AND CASTIGATED BECAUSE THEY DARED TO SUGGEST CHANGES IN THE CONTRACT. Yes, we were called disrupters, Communists and what have you. We were accused of being out of line with the rest of the UAW which we readily admitted.[24]

While Stellato was busy reconstructing his credentials as a union militant, Reuther was preparing a frontal assault on Communists, Local 600, and the movement for a shorter workweek. By late March 1953, as delegates began arriving for the fourteenth UAW convention, dissidents at the Rouge had been hammering away at the shorter hours issue for more than five years. As the convention began, the Reutherites introduced a resolution in favor of a Guaranteed Annual Wage (GAW). The idea of an annual wage for autoworkers had become a standard element within Reuther's program.[25] As the years went by, Reuther kept the annual wage idea alive and rehabilitated it at most meetings. The proposal was first adopted as a resolution at the 1951 convention and had become Reuther's standard response to the problem of cyclical and seasonal unemployment. Moreover, insofar as the distinction between the hourly wage and the annual salary had become a mark of distinction, Reuther introduced a kind of class status politics into the mix by suggesting that autoworkers deserved the same annualized compensation as salaried white-collar workers.

At the 1953 convention, Reuther had moved the GAW demand to center stage. As delegates entered the convention hall, a massive banner over the rostrum pledged, "Next Step Forward: Guaranteed Annual Wage ... Full Employment, Full Distribution, Full Production ... Peace, Abundance, Progress, Freedom ... UAW-CIO, 1 1/3 Million Strong."[26]

In its earliest incarnations, the discourse of the GAW aimed at short-term, recurring problems long associated with the auto industry: temporary layoffs and "short work weeks" caused by model changes, and cyclical production dips associated with weakness in the consumer market. In 1952, however, Ford engineers coined and publicized the term "automation" in reference to the company's new Cleveland, Ohio engine plant. Union leaders were forced to confront the "technology" problem.[27] Reuther's GAW resolution ominously warned

> Despite tremendous technological progress in the last decade, still greater and more revolutionary technological developments are on the way ... Today's dream of the completely automatic factory is moving rapidly to become tomorrow's reality ... The more we learn how to produce with lessened human effort, the greater becomes our need to

find the means of keeping our vast productive power at work by maintaining and increasing mass purchasing power and mass distribution of the goods we are able to produce. Unless we solve that problem today's technology will become the cause of tomorrow's bread lines.[28]

Following the swift adoption of the GAW resolution, Resolutions Committee member Charlie Groves approached the microphone and presented "Resolution #26: Thirty-Hour Week." The resolution was an attack on the 30-40 demand.[29]

The resolution included an assault on the reputations and intentions of those who favored the shorter workweek program: 30-40 advocates were either fools or knaves.[30] The knaves were the Communists. "Certain political forces outside our Union choose to inject into the councils of the UAW-CIO the impractical and unrealistic demand for a 30-hour week now ... A careful study of the Communist *Daily Worker* and other Communist publications will show conclusively that the demand for a 30-hour week with 40 hours' pay now was engineered and directed by the Communists for the purpose of creating discontent and confusion and to weaken the national defense effort."[31] No Reutherite red-baiting episode would have been complete without a rehearsal of the role of the CP during World War II, including its "campaign to put piecework into every shop and, before the party line shifted ... a no-strike pledge for five years after the war."[32] The fools were the rank-and-file numskulls who fell for the plan. "Some local unions and sincere and conscientious local leaders have taken up the demand ... because they have not fully understood the facts of the present situation."[33]

Although Reuther's own GAW resolution had capitalized on the rank-and-file fear of potential "bread lines" caused by technological unemployment, the "Thirty-Hour Week" resolution argued that a shorter hours demand was unnecessary during the alleged war "boom." As Reuther had argued during the January 1952 Unemployment Conference in Washington, labor markets were already tight, rendering unnecessary any fight for a shorter work-week. "With our economy going full blast . . . unemployment is near historic lows and millions of workers are working overtime. We are operating at close to the limits of our present capacity in terms of human as well as material resources."[34] But just in case some dele-gates in the convention hall were uncomfortable with this charac-terization, the resolution simultaneously proposed that the shorter workweek was equally inopportune during economic slumps.

> The winning of the 40-hour week, while representing a monumental achievement for American labor, did not, however, deal with the fun-damental problem of unemployment. In the dark days of the depres-sion, reduced hours provided jobs for some by spreading the available work over a large number of workers. This represented a sharing of hunger to reduce outright starvation. But the 40-hour week was of lit-tle consolation or benefit to the millions of unemployed who contin-ued to walk to the streets of America without work and without hope.[35]

Thus, according to the proposed convention resolution, the shorter hours movement was worthless during periods of high unem-ployment and superfluous during boom times when labor shortages provide unions with the market leverage to make robust demands.

The resolution also argued that the 30-40 program was undesir-able. Advocates of the shorter workweek at higher pay were lamen-tably ignorant of the fundamental, economic facts of life. "The size of the economic pie that determines living standards," the resolu-tion instructed, "can be no bigger than total production. With less work there is less produced and less to enjoy . . . [and] the most com-pelling need is not for more leisure but for more goods to satisfy the unfilled needs and wants of millions of workers' families . . . Forty hours' pay for 30 hours' work will not buy more if only 30 hours' out-put is available . . . The membership," it was predicted, "will have no difficulty making its choice between an immediate 30-hour week with a reduced living standard and the security and high living standards that will come from a guarantee that they will enjoy a week's pay or a week's income 52 weeks in the year."[36]

Although the resolution endorsed the idea of a trade-off between time and money, the resolution also addressed itself to those who affirmed the possibility of a growing economic pie and shorter hours of work. Perhaps it was possible to imagine greater output with less work, as suggested by the description of technological innovation highlighted in Reuther's GAW resolution. The "Thirty-Hour Week" resolution, however, did not support the notion that organized labor might anticipate or even induce such technological changes by pressing for an immediate reduction in the duration of the workweek.

> The time will come when satisfactory living standards can be provided out of a 30-hour work week just as surely as the time came when hours could be cut from 12 a day to 10 a day, to 8 a day and then from 6 days to 5 days a week ... [and] the reduction of the work week remains a basic objective of the UAW-CIO to be fought for with all the strength and militancy of the Union as soon as and whenever the productive capacity of our national economy makes it possible to maintain high and satisfactory living standards with fewer hours of work.[37]

The resolution, however, "rejects and repudiates the demand for a 30-hour week with 40 hours' pay *at this time* ... as an attack on the hopes of workers' families for higher living standards."[38]

The resolution included one final argument that conceded almost everything to the 30-40 advocates. The shorter hours demand—even if it is assumed to be extremely desirable—was nevertheless excessively ambitious from a collective bargaining perspective. The 30-40 program "is unsound, impractical, unrealistic, and irresponsible." The resolution attacked "[t]he opportunists who call for the 30-hour week with 40 hours' pay ... This is a demand for a 50 percent increase in wages—an easy demand to make, provided someone else has the responsibility for winning it in negotiations."[39]

After the resolution was presented, Reuther led the delegates through one of the most contentious convention-floor discussions since the 1947 consolidation of Reuther's rule within the UAW. Reuther's temper was short and he tightly controlled the back-and-forth of the discussion. Indeed, one 30-40 advocate complained that delegates were limited to short, strictly-timed comments whereas, "Brother Chairman, it seems that you manage to speak on everything that comes up even when debate is closed." Reuther shot back with a caustic response. "Whenever I think it is necessary to raise my voice to help protect this Union against elements that I think are working for somebody other than the Union I am going to raise my voice."[40] Nevertheless, the opposition held its own and Reuther's appropriation of presidential privileges did little to effectively curb the debate.

The Reutherites who spoke in favor of the "repudiation" of the shorter workweek demand pursued many of the arguments developed in the resolution, although few actually took up the red-baiting line. As Emil Mazey, secretary-treasurer of the UAW, noted, "I think it is unfortunate that the tone has been set that everyone who opposes [this resolution] is an opportunist, Communist or fits in some other category, because I believe that there are some delegates who may be confused on this matter, who may be mixed up on this subject, and who believe in the 30-hour work week but don't fit in the category of the opportunists or the Communists." In order to make clear that it was Stellato, and not merely the Communists, in the Administration's cross hairs, Mazey added, "I think in the case of Brother Stellato that when we use the word 'opportunist' in the resolution we were dealing specifically with him . . . Carl made a political deal . . . He picked up the Communist party slogan of the 30-hour week."[41]

Mazey urged delegates to have faith in Reuther, to stick with the terms of the five-year contract, and to abandon the demand for a shorter workweek.

We might feel our oats at the moment. We might feel that we have the economic power at this minute, that we have the advantage over the employers and that we can set aside a contract and fight for the opportunity to make progress. What happens when we have an economic depression in America, when there are millions of unemployed workers, and management has the upper hand? If we take the position that we set aside a contract when we are strong, what is to prevent them, the same people, when they are strong and we are in a much weaker position, from taking advantage of us?[42]

Mazey's plea for restraint was consistent with the central themes of Reuther's corporatist labor philosophy. "I think if we view all of the arguments," Mazey suggested in reference to the 30-40 demand, "you will find it just doesn't make sense."[43]

Roger Smithey, president of Tulsa, Oklahoma's Local 1093, argued, "I put in work hours of 60 to 70 hours a week, and I personally don't think that is too much. If you are a good union member you won't think so yourselves ... A 30-hour work week at this time is ridiculous. Surely industry will resist our demand for a full living standard, because it calls for more money and more stock and shares out of their business profits ... We in the UAW should set an example and not shorten the work week for avarice ... Let us not kill the hen that lays the golden egg."[44]

Resolutions Committee Chairman Ken Morris explained, "One of the main reasons this issue is being presented to the Convention is that a number of elements within our local unions have been raising the matter of a 30-hour week with 40-hour pay ... We received a few resolutions that dealt with this specific subject and made this specific demand. In those resolutions the request in almost every case was this be done now."[45] During the discussion, Reutherites repeatedly referred to the challenge from below, mentioning details about resolutions that the Committee had refused to present to the delegates. Mazey, for example, described a resolution that the delegates would never see. "Local 600's resolution, Stellato's resolution is that we scrap our contracts and that we fight for a 30-hour week with 40-hour pay now."[46]

Morris acknowledged the popularity of the 30 for 40 program. He was clearly attempting to impugn the character of Stellato and other "opportunists," but in the process he revealed a great deal more.

> In many of our large plants . . . we have those political opportunists, and that is what I think they are and nothing else, who for political expediency advocate a 30-hour week with 40-hour pay. Many times, sure, our membership will be for these things. There are none of you sitting in this room who, in all probability, if you could see the possibility of having a 30-hour week with 40-hour pay tomorrow, if you could see that possibility, wouldn't feel that it is necessary. The same applies to our rank and file in the shop. These issues, though, are presented to some of our rank and file . . . and they are given the idea that this is one of the things UAW is fighting for now.[47]

Why would it be "politically expedient" for "opportunists" to advocate a 30-hour week with 40-hours' pay? Morris had simply confirmed the popularity of the demand. "I think we can all recognize that if our unions were to take on the task of securing now a 30-hour week with 40-hour pay we would have one of the damnedest fights on our hands we could imagine."[48]

A number of 30-40 advocates tried to help the UAW imagine making this damnedest of fights. Stellato himself took the floor to make the case.

> It is my impression today the UAW is the most militant fighting force in the United States for the working man, and today we hear speeches on the rostrum saying we would have an awful time if we vote for a 30-hour work week with 40 hours' pay. Well, maybe the officers are afraid to fight, but the membership of the UAW is not afraid to fight. You are giving aid and comfort to industry by saying here today everyone in favor of a 30-hour work week with 40 hours' pay is a Communist. The

speeches made from the rostrum sometimes should be made in a NAM conference.[49]

Other delegates condemned the resolution's red-baiting. Martin Greenberg, a delegate from Bristol, Connecticut's Amalgamated Local 626, suggested, "I think we are getting worse than McCarthyism in our International Union."[50] Stellato and Greenberg both reminded delegates of the hypocrisy in Reuther's red-baiting of the shorter hours demand. Greenberg recalled, "I would like to point out that many of us here were present in 1944 and 1945 and were willing to follow Walter Reuther down the line on the same policy of shorter workweek—not now, but years back."[51] Stellato went so far as to cite an August 26, 1944 article from the *New York Times Magazine* entitled, "A 30-Hour Week After the War? Yes, says Walter Reuther of the Auto Workers; No, say Eric Johnston and Henry J. Kaiser." Indeed, Stellato went on to recall just how effective Reuther had been at advocating the demand when he found it politically expedient in his battle to win control of the union. "In 1947, in your opening remarks to that Convention, after you had been president for one year," Stellato remembered, "you tore [C. E.] Wilson to pieces, and rightfully so, because he was talking about a 45-hour week with no overtime. You insisted we go to bat for a 30-hour work week with 40 hours' pay."[52]

Martin Greenberg attacked the resolution's economic analysis insofar as it suggested that the shorter hours movement represented an attack on the hopes of workers' families for higher living standards. "What reduction of hours," Greenberg asked, "has harmed our progress, when we went from 56 to 48 to 40 hours, leaving the implication that if we go to 30 hours there is harm going to be done?"[53]

There were also challenges to the resolution's assumptions about technology and labor markets. First, Stellato noted that new technological innovations were providing management with new weapons for breaking labor's back and destroying its postwar market leverage. The labor movement needed an immediate response to management's demonstration that it could increase production while diminishing its relative dependence on living labor. "Let me tell you brothers ... industry is bragging about the technological improvements and automation." He referred delegates to a February 23, 1953 article from the *Detroit News* entitled, "Where 41 Men Do the Work of 117." Industry, Stellato warned, was "doing everything automatically, and eliminating workers."[54]

Finally, Louis Ciccone, a delegate from South Gate, California's Amalgamated Local 216, spoke against the resolution, asserting simply, "It contains false propositions, things which in effect challenge the dream of the American labor movement for a shorter work day and week without the reduction in take-home pay."[55] After a delegate moved to close debate, Reuther called for a vote on the resolution. The anti–30-40 resolution was adopted by a show of hands.[56]

Later in the same day's proceedings, the delegates returned from dinner to consider the case of the five officers who were originally accused, by Stellato, of being Communists. The trial was Reuther's response to HUAC charges that he had been insufficiently ruthless in his dealing with Communists in the UAW. The IEB had prohibited the five members "from holding any position, either elective or appointive, in Local 600 or its Units."[57] The five appealed the case, and the convention's "Grievance Committee," chaired by Paul Schrade, recommended that the convention delegates support the IEB's action. This entire prosecutorial drama was facilitated by a new constitutional amendment, adopted earlier in the convention, that provided the international union with the power to review decisions of local union trial committees and to keep Communists out of leadership positions.[58]

The convention delegates were treated to a courtroom spectacle lasting five hours. Reuther asked vice-president Livingston to "present the case of the International Executive Board" and allowed Local 600 to be represented by Carl Stellato and Dave Moore, one of the accused. Livingston presented evidence that the five officers were members of the CP and mapped out Carl Stellato's political flip-flops, showing that Stellato changed his tune after the 1951 dues increase and that the CP was, from that day forward, an enthusiastic supporter of Stellato's administration.[59]

The International's attack on the five officers was more straightforward than its attack on Stellato. When Livingston read aloud headlines from the post-dues increase issues of *Ford Facts*, he acknowledged that such headlines demonstrated what everybody already knew: Stellato had moved into the opposition, to the Reuther camp. "Naturally such [critical] articles started hurting our Union and our organizational drives throughout the country ... Now, it is important that we once again call your attention to ... the kind treatment that [Stellato] received [in the Communist press] after he mad his peace with them. I want to make it clear Stellato is not on trial. This is important only because of his actions, his actions that clearly show the price of compromise with the [Communist] party, what the price is."[60]

Moore's defense was simple. He did not speak to the question of CP membership. He did, however, charge that the IEB's decision threatened internal union democracy because it overturned a legitimate decision of the General Council of Local 600 and did so "without offering a shred of proof" that the General Council's decision was "a political deal engineered by the Communist Party within the General Council of Local 600." Moore also pointed to Reuther's hypocrisy as a red-baiter—and, perhaps implicitly, to Reuther's own vulnerability in the face of HUAC investigations—insofar as Reuther himself had once revealed a keen interest in the idea that "we must Sovietize America."[61]

When Moore finished speaking, Reuther called upon Carl Stellato. Reuther had not accused Stellato of being a Communist, but he was called to the microphone all the same. What could Stellato say under such circumstances? If he simply denounced the five officers, he would have appeared to be capitulating to Reuther. In so doing, he would have alienated his base at Local 600, knowing full well that Reuther was either unwilling or unable to welcome Stellato back into the fold so long as the HUAC legislators were watching Reuther's every move at Local 600.

Instead, Stellato shifted the ground on Reuther. He provided an entirely different rationale for the entire prosecutorial circus. He took the microphone and proceeded to present himself to the delegates as the persecuted, but militant, defender of the movement for 30 hours' work and 40 hours' pay. As a preface, he recounted the fact that he had, in fact, preferred charges against the alleged Communists. He even noted that in the "elections that took place while the trials were going on . . . we took a terrific shellacking . . . Every single member of the Trial Committee except one was defeated." He recalled that the new General Council had voted against the report of the Trial Committee, but also went out of his way to note that, "For the record Brother Carl Stellato voted in favor of the Trial Committee."[62]

All of this was, according to Stellato, beside the point. The Trial Committee report was thrown out in the spring of 1951. "Now, we did not hear from the International Union until October 12, 1951, when it is true we were asked to appear in front of the Executive Board."[63] Stellato hit his stride as he rehearsed the story of Reuther's seizure of the great Ford Local. He described the events leading up to the takeover of Local 600, including the HUAC hearings.[64]

Why were the administrators moved in? If it was because of Communist control in Local 600 why did they have to wait from August, 1950, to March 1952? . . . I can tell you what the real reason was . . . Detroit News, October 12, 1951, "Stellato Loses at the Ford Council." Detroit Times, October 11, 1951.[65] "A 30-hour Work Week Out of Order. UAW Board Blocks Stellato Proposal." The 30-hour week was no Stellato proposal. The labor movement in this country and part of our [Union] Constitution, by the way, calls for the shortening of the work hours for the working man. It is not a Stellato proposal, but at that particular time it was a proposal coming out of Stellato's mouth being shoved in there by the Communists. Well, this, by the way, is a fight that Local 600 put on in the National Ford Conference . . . Those are the reasons why the administrators didn't move in until 1952. And we kept saying that we were for a 30-hour work week. There was nothing wrong with being for a 30-hour work week. I tried to point out this morning to the Convention of the automation, the technological improvements. Yes, as I said before, today there is a war on, there is all kinds of work. But unless this Union prepares or starts working toward a goal of a shorter workweek with the same pay, we are going to be faced with that economic collapse.[66]

Stellato could not resist one final jab. Without ever mentioning the specific circumstances of Local 600's highly publicized 30-40 postcard delivery, Stellato recalled, "We went to the International Union. You are going to see a lot more copies of Ford Facts here today, I imagine, but these are some that you are not going to see. Here is one: 'UAW-CIO Turns Down Union Delegation.' You will be surprised how hard it is to get into Solidarity House if you are from Local 600. But we have seen [Ford Industrial Relations director] John Bugas walk in without signing his name."[67]

When Stellato finished speaking, Reuther took the microphone "to correct the record on a number of things."[68] Reuther could not let stand Stellato's dig about the 30-40 post-card campaign. Instead, he decided to tell his own version of the story.

He said he couldn't get into the headquarters of the International Union, but that John Bugas can get in . . . [They] put a picket line around the International office . . . They had sound trucks and pickets around the International Headquarters . . . And they sent around a delegation into the International Union with boxes of cards that they said were signed by the Ford workers . . . They took these cards, scattered them all over the lobby of the International Union … That is why we went out there and that is why we put an administratorship over the Local and we had the authority under the Constitution we said, "O.K., we are going to step up to these five fellows who we think are Communists, and we are going to take you out of office … Every delegate in this Convention is going to get a copy mailed to your home address … of the front page of the *Detroit News* showing the International lobby with boxes and postcards on the floor with Stellato's boys kicking the boxes around … These are the things that went on. These are the things that made us move in.[69]

Reuther had taken the bait. Stellato had drawn Reuther into the debate about Local 600's substantive, alternative labor strategies. Stellato had charged that the administratorship was not about Communism, but instead about Local 600's militant challenge to Reuther and his repudiation of the 30 for 40 demand. And in his fury, Reuther conceded that it was precisely on this basis that he had decided to seize control of the Local.[70] The charges of Communist infiltration of Local 600 were merely a belated rationale crafted to justify the move against the Rouge workers and their elected leaders.

Reuther had been beat and he knew it. Reuther scrambled through his past to find evidence of his own credentials as a militant leader. Perhaps it was Stellato who had sparked his memory. During his speech, Stellato made much of this past. "I couldn't help but be interested," chuckled Stellato, "in the copy of *Ammunition* that all of you have on your tables. It shows a picture on Page 13 of Brother Reuther with the marks of 'Battle of the Overpass' at Ford. Alongside of that is a copy of a picture of a leaflet that Brother Reuther was passing out before the goons beat him up. 'Ford Workers—Unionism not Fordism … —join now in the march and win higher wages and better working conditions—stop speed-up by union supervision—six-hour day."[71] Reuther's response did little to shift the debate back in his favor.

Now these fellows would have you believe that the leadership of your Union has gotten soft and flabby; has got a dictatorship policy comparable to the Kremlin. I also was a Ford worker. I worked six years in the Ford Motor Company. I got beat up on Gate 4. I had my office blown up when I was the president of Local 174. I had my home broken into and shot into. These fellows don't have a monopoly on the will to fight.[72]

Reuther must have recognized that his defensiveness was not helping his cause. He turned the microphone over to Paul Schrade who brought the issue back to the specific question of the five accused officers. Schrade rehearsed all of the charges, and after a few more delegates made brief remarks, the debate was closed. The delegates voted overwhelmingly (Reuther ruled that it "carried by 96 percent or 97 percent") to support the Committee's recommendation, deny the appeal, and bar the five from holding office at Local 600.[73]

4.

FUTURE PERFECT

After the 1953 convention, all eyes turned to the Rouge in antici-
pation of Local 600 elections. The HUAC legislators had challenged Reuther's claim that Local 600 was no longer Communist
dominated. Reuther responded with renewed anti-Communist vigor
at the convention and had put himself on a collision course with
Local 600 president, Carl Stellato. This time, there would be no
deals or compromises with Stellato. The election would be
Reuther's best chance to win control of the local. The Reutherites
could compete on a level playing field without the disadvantage of
being tainted as administratorship dictators and power-hungry
bureaucrats.

In preparation for his campaign to win control of Local 600, the
Reuther caucus put together a full slate of candidates. For the top
slot, Reuther chose his own on-staff ACTist, Gene Prato. Prato took
a leave from the Reuther staff in order to return to Local 600.
Business Week declared that Prato was "backed by all the power and
influence the international union could throw into the fight."[1]
Reuther persuaded recording secretary William Hood, to switch

sides and join the Reutherite slate. Hood—the founding president of the left-wing National Negro Labor Council (NNLC)—was welcomed aboard the Reuther ship, even as Reuther attacked the NNLC as a "Communist-dominated, dual unionist organization" that [had] as its sole objective the disruption and wrecking of the American labor movement."[2]

Faced with the defection of Hood, Stellato selected William Johnson, the prominent African-American Rouge leader who had trounced a Reutherite incumbent in the October 1952 building unit elections. With a full slate of candidates challenging the Stellato slate, Reuther had once again launched a high-profile, high-stakes offensive to try to capture Local 600. *Business Week* called it a "showdown" destined to "decide [the] stormy battle between Reutherites and left-wingers."[3]

After the election, the *Wage Earner* was blunt: "The right-wing slate, headed by three candidates on leave from the International UAW payroll, took a drubbing at the giant Ford Local 600, UAW-CIO election completed May 7."[4] Stellato was returned to office by an extraordinary margin, winning with 18,767 votes compared to 7,930 for Prato and 2,393 for Rice.[5] As *Business Week* admitted, "The one-sidedness of the victory surprised everyone. Reutherites expected that Stellato would lead in this vote but pinned their plans to a belief that he might not obtain a majority, and that the run-off would give them time to overtake their opposition."[6]

Pat Rice—the potential "left-wing" spoiler in the first round—made no dent and Stellato was able to win an outright majority. Stellato did not lose any of the votes that he had received in 1952 when Reuther agreed to let him run unopposed for president. The *Wall Street Journal* called Stellato's victory "a blow to Mr. Reuther's prestige" because Prato's campaign program "went down the line in support of Reuther policies," whereas "Mr. Stellato, on the other hand, plumped for a 'more aggressive attitude'" and "continued his stand for a 30-hour week on a 40-hour pay basis. He told Ford Local

600 members the international union should urge this policy on auto makers."[7]

Stellato's entire local-wide slate prevailed.[8] Bill Johnson beat incumbent Bill Hood in the race for the recording secretary job. The *Wage Earner* acknowledged that Hood had been picked up as a Reutherite candidate and called Hood "the surprise loser in this contest."[9]

Actually, the surprise of the contest may have been the one unit-based Reutherite victory of the election round. Horace Sheffield, the African-American maverick aligned with the Reutherite caucus, won Bill Johnson's vacated unit presidency.[10] *Business Week* concluded, nonetheless, that "the Stellato slate triumphed generally from major offices down to building units."[11] The implication was clear. "Stellato with popular support from the rank and file, from the left wing and apparently from at least a few anti-Reuther factionalists, will call the tune from here on Ford local politics."[12]

The election marked a kind of turning point for the 30-40 movement at the Rouge. By all accounts, Stellato's enormous victory established—at least for a while—that he could use his strong showing at Local 600 to continue his factional fight with Reuther and to press the demand for a shorter workweek. Stellato had cemented his place as the leader of opposition forces within the UAW. It was also generally assumed that Reuther, having played his hand and lost, would be "abandoning the battlefield in Local 600, for a time at least."[13] Nobody, least of all Stellato, was certain when Reuther would renew his campaign for control of Local 600, but Stellato had emerged victorious in one major battle of the ongoing war.

During the summer of 1953, Walter Reuther was very much on the defensive. In July, Stellato began to reach out to potential allies outside Local 600 in an effort to expand the 30-40 program and move it to the top of the UAW bargaining agenda. According to *Fortune* magazine, "Ford Local president Carl Stellato, ever eager for a political issue, began loudly demanding a thirty-hour week . . . [and] raised a new bug-bear for union men to worry about: 'automation.'"[14]

First stop for the newly confirmed opposition leader was, appropriately enough, the installation of an anti-Reuther slate of officers at Chevrolet Local 659. Back in 1951, during his previous caucus-building effort, Stellato had reached out to Local 659 for the founding of his Committee for a Democratic UAW. Having spent more than a year defending himself against Reuther's attacks on the legitimacy of his administration and its demand for a shorter workweek, Stellato was back in business. With anti-Reuther factions winning electoral victories at Local 600 and Local 659, Stellato embraced his allies and was warmly embraced by them. Stellato was invited to be the keynote speaker at the installation of officers at Local 659 where he celebrated the victory of Robert Murphy, president of the local, who had been elected on a program of 30 hours' work at 40 hours' pay.[15] The Stellato-Murphy alliance was a potent brew. The heart of the Ford and GM empires within the UAW were now crawling with anti-Reuther factionalists and shorter hours advocates.[16]

Stellato's speech at Local 659 explicitly contrasted the syndicalism of the shorter workweek demand with the dangers of Reutherite corporatism, taking aim at Emil Mazey's effort to promote military spending as a cure for joblessness. In a high-profile trip to Washington, Mazey was reported to have "stormed into the Capitol to protest the Kaiser [defense department contract] cancellations. Mazey warned that 'the $500-million cutback in tank and truck production means the end of jobs and hardships for many thousands of workers.'"[17] Stellato did not disagree that an end to the war economy would threaten auto jobs. He added that, in addition to military cutbacks, autoworkers also faced the challenge of responding to the introduction of labor-saving technologies. Recalling Reuther's UAW convention attacks on the 30-40 demand, Stellato threatened to build a dissident rank-and-file movement in support of the shorter workweek and prophesied that "Brother Reuther will have to change his position in the near future."[18]

After the defeat at Local 600 in the spring, a summer of wildcat strikes in Detroit, and months of emboldened 30-40 campaigning from within Local 600, the Reuther caucus had reason to fear losing control of the rank and file during the autumn and early winter of 1953. Reuther's opposition to the popular shorter workweek made him vulnerable to all those willing to challenge his authority and don for themselves the mantle of militancy.

Robert Murphy, the opposition president of Local 659, used his local's independent newspaper *The Searchlight* as an important voice for the 30-40 drive and the Local 659 membership proclaimed the 30-40 demand as its number one priority going into the new round of UAW negotiations.[19]

In November 1953, the General Council of Local 600 met to discuss the current state of the movement and to fully articulate its substantive program for action within the UAW and beyond. Reuther had tried to portray the shorter workweek movement as a movement in support of greater leisure at the expense of higher wages. Local 600 responded by emphasizing the demand for pay hikes and shorter hours: "MAINTAIN AND RAISE THE LIVING STANDARDS OF ALL WORKERS AND ALL PEOPLE."[20] Local 600 called for "substantial wage increases, not only to offset the high cost of living, but to raise living standards."[21] In 1953, such a position was considerably to the left of Reuther, who confirmed that he was "not disturbed" when rising "escalator contracts" produced de-escalating nominal wage cuts in a deflationary economic environment.[22]

The Local 600 program explicitly linked the syndicalist demands that provided the foundation for the challenge to Reuther: "the fight for substantial wage increases, against speed-up and for the shorter workweek."[23] The General Council proposed "a 30-hour week, with no reduction in pay, so that workers share the fruits of automation, instead of becoming victims of it. THIS IS THE KEY

TO ENLIGHTENED LABOR UNIONS WELCOMING TECHNOLOGICAL IMPROVEMENTS."[24]

Once again, the program was linked with a critique of the Reuther administration's military Keynesianism. "We vigorously reject the concept that war or preparations for war offer any permanent solution to unemployment or any other economic problems."[25] The Council also demanded an end to "all differentials in the wages of men and women . . . a model anti-discrimination clause in all contracts" and an end to discrimination against foreign-born workers.[26]

With Local 659 and Local 600 in full-scale revolt, Reuther was compelled to respond to the rumblings of discontent. He announced that the UAW would hold a two-day unemployment conference in Washington, DC on December 6 and 7, 1953. Stellato promptly shot off a letter announcing to Reuther that "Local 600 hails the calling" of the conference. "Seeing the handwriting on the wall, the officers of Local 600 have devoted considerable thought to a program to combat unemployment and provide full employment. After considerable discussion at our last General Council meeting, the enclosed program was adopted unanimously."[27] Stellato not only enclosed the Local 600 program in his letter, but he made certain that both the program and the letter were widely distributed and discussed in advance of the conference. By the time of the conference, it was well known that Local 600 had presented a complete program for consideration at the conference. Local 600 had effectively put the 30-40 demand on the agenda.[28] Eight months after the 1953 convention, the movement remained strong, despite Reuther's persistent attacks on its legitimacy. Indeed, it was in preparation for the December unemployment conference in Washington that the Reuther administration began a careful retreat.

The director of Reuther's research department, Nat Weinberg, was given the task of drafting a new, more accommodating stance. The Reuther administration was still unwilling to adopt the program as its own, and it still attacked the leaders of Local 600, but it backed away from head-on opposition to the demand itself, at least in the abstract.[29]

Weinberg's draft for Reuther's conference statement began with an embrace rather than a repudiation of the shorter workweek. "I believe we will win the 30-hour week. When it comes, I hope we will work four 7 1/2-hour days or three 10-hour days a week and not five 6-hour days as proposed by the top officers of Local 600."[30]

Of the five arguments used in the 1953 UAW convention resolution to repudiate the shorter workweek demand, a few were missing from Weinberg's draft. The "Kremlin" talk and red-baiting that had challenged the patriotism of anyone who supported the shorter workweek had been jettisoned, as had CP leadership of the shorter hours movement. Although the Weinberg document expressed some skepticism about the motives of the leaders of Local 600, the charge was one of irresponsible union campaigning more than anti-American subversive activity. Under pressure from the HUAC crowd, but unable to win control of Local 600, Reuther was no longer eager to call attention to the role of Communists in the UAW.

The 1953 convention resolution had also downplayed the likelihood of significant unemployment. This position no longer seemed viable, especially in light of the increasingly obvious threat posed, not only by cyclical recession and a post-Korea economic slump, but also by automation.

The Reutherites, however, still opposed the shorter workweek demand. The primary reason given at the unemployment conference was that the UAW was already too weak to impose serious demands upon employers. Weinberg concluded that "the arithmetic on that one is out of this world."

> If I thought they could bring back even a sizable fraction of such a package, I would be in favor of putting them on the national negotiating committee. But I would want them first to put up or shut up. I would want them to agree that if they didn't bring back what they now

so freely promise, they would resign their local union offices, keep quiet, and get out of the way to let the rest of us take care of the serious business of trade unionism—advancing and protecting the workers' interests on a sound basis that makes sense.[31]

Simple opposition to the 30-40 demand, however, was becoming increasingly unsustainable for the Reuther administration. There was, however, the possibility of refuge in delay. The Weinberg document asserted, "I am in favor of launching the fight for a shorter workweek as soon as it makes sense to do so. To me, that means *after* we have won the guaranteed annual wage."[32]

By the time of the December meeting in Washington, the Reutherite line had become even more accommodating. "We are prepared to say," conceded Reuther, "that while the Guaranteed Annual Wage is first, it does not preclude a shorter workweek. You can mark it down for the 1955 pre-negotiations conference. We will be out front leading the fight for a shorter workweek when the factors are right."[33] After the Washington event, one commentator observed,

> Reuther has been compelled to make a tactical shift at the recent Washington conference. Rather than take the proponents of 30-40 head on, Reuther retreated from the position of [March 1953] and proposed that the question of a shorter workweek with no cut in take home pay be discussed in a 'Pre-Negotiations Conference in 1955.' Reuther now treated the shorter workweek demand as legitimate and assured the conference that 'we will be out in front leading the fight for a shorter workweek when the factors are right.'[34]

According to the same observer, the Local 600 leadership and other 30-40 advocates were quite stunned by Reuther's reversal. After the assault of the UAW convention in March, Reuther's concession was undoubtedly somewhat disarming, precisely because it was a straightforward promise to put the shorter workweek on the collective bargaining discussion agenda in preparation for the 1955 round. Stellato's report to the rank and file of Local 600 was quite optimistic. Although Local 600 had always argued that the demand was an urgent one, and nobody could doubt that Reuther's postponement was still a sign of resistance to the 30-40 campaign, Reuther had, for all intents and purposes, yelled for mercy.

Stellato explained to his members, "When Brother Reuther took the position that the question of a shorter workweek would be re-evaluated in a collective bargaining conference to be held in the latter part of 1954—just prior to the '55 contract negotiations—we were completely satisfied."[35] Local 600's agenda, which was after all a collective bargaining demand rather than a legislative proposal, was now officially on the agenda for discussions of the next contract round. Reuther's concession was a substantial victory for Stellato and the 30-40 movement. Reuther, it appeared, had lost control of his most prized possession: the union's agenda.

Reuther had not been converted to the shorter hours movement. But he had been moved to recognize its power within the rank and file. Reuther's maneuver represented a retreat from direct confrontation with Stellato and the movement for a shorter workweek.

In Detroit, the shorter hours movement continued to gain momentum. Each week, the pages of *Ford Facts* were filled with arguments and comments in support of the 30-40 movement. Many of the columns written by the unit leaders spoke to the urgency of the issue. Writers balked at Reuther's suggestion that the shorter workweek would have to wait until a time "when the factors are right."

> We are of the opinion that that time has arrived. Industry has made tremendous strides in installing automation which resulted in thousands of workers being laid off every day. We are concerned with jobs for all—not a guaranteed wage for the few who will be lucky enough to remain at work. We believe that now is the time to begin preparing for the fight for the 30-hour week with 40 hours' pay because we believe that is the only foreseeable solution to create jobs for the jobless . . . We call on the

International Union officers to change their position and join with Local 600 in fighting for a better life for all Americans—Now.[36]

Local 659's paper, the *Searchlight*, concurred. "We in Local 659 are not waiting until our people are in dire need of assistance to take action," the newspaper announced. Robert Murphy, president of Local 659, recalled for readers, "I advocated a thirty-two hour work week with forty hours' pay because the handwriting was on the wall at that time that we were going to go on short work weeks or mass layoffs."[37] "We are now faced with a 32 hour work week with only 32-hours pay . . . For the past fifteen years our nation's economy has been fed by billions upon billions spent on war materials. This also provided work on a temporary basis . . . We must take positive action . . . to forestall the elimination of our jobs and the security from which we have received some solace since late 1939."[38]

In May 1954, however, HUAC took an interest in the big Flint local. Reuther once again joined his anti-Communist allies in a coordinated assault on Local 659. HUAC investigations of Local 659 provided the backdrop for Reuther's bureaucratic power grab in Flint. On May 9, just before local elections, the Reuther administration suspended all further publication of the *Searchlight* and placed an administrator over the big Chevy local. The International charged that Local 659 had refused to make the local's publication conform to international policies. Fourteen officers and members of the local—including the president, Robert Murphy—were charged and put on trial by the UAW Executive Board.[39]

In his remarks before delegates at the December 1953 unemployment conference, Reuther had acknowledged that the campaign for a GAW in 1955 did not preclude a shorter workweek. He told the delegates that they could mark it down for the pre-negotiations conference in advance of 1955 contract negotiations. In November 1954, delegates assembled for the promised discussion of the shorter-workweek demand.

The pre-negotiations conference met at the Masonic Temple in Detroit with 1,100 delegates in attendance. The entire first day of the conference was devoted to selling and discussing Reuther's GAW, which was endorsed as a demand for 1955 negotiations. Everyone knew, however, that the real drama of the conference was reserved for the second day of the two-day meeting, when the delegates were scheduled to discuss a UAW report on automation and the shorter workweek.

The report marked an impressive victory for shorter hours advocates. In it, the Reuther administration promised that the shorter workweek and higher living standards would take its place at the top of the union's collective bargaining agenda. "At the coming Convention ... we are prepared to commit our Union ... by a Convention mandate, that the next basic demand beyond the guaranteed annual wage ... should be the historic struggle for a shorter work week."[40]

In the discussion that followed, not one delegate spoke out against the shorter workweek. Some delegates, however, protested the delay and advocated immediate action in 1955 on the shorter workweek demand. Reuther admonished the unruly delegates.

> I would like that thirty hour week with forty hours pay. I would like to even go them one better. As a matter of fact, I'd like a twenty hour week. But I know damn well we are not going to get it in 1955, and I don't want to make any worker believe that we are even going to try, because we can't.[41]

Reuther's proclamation was hardly a ringing endorsement of the power of the UAW. Nevertheless, he once again affirmed that the union would commit itself to a drive for the shorter workweek in 1957, a pledge, Reuther insisted, "made in good faith."[42] Although many of the delegates seemed inclined to view Reuther's capitulation as a victory for the 30-40 movement, the *Wall Street Journal* was more impressed by Reuther's ability to get the delegates to delay action on the shorter hours demand. Employers, the *Journal* suggested, could take "solace" from the fact that "the union will not press for a shorter work-week in next year's contract talks."[43]

Back at Local 600, Stellato celebrated what victory there was to declare and asked the rank and file to do the same. "We in Local 600 feel that even though our program was not adopted in its entirety, the conference was held in a democratic manner, allowing full voice and expression to all shades of opinion, and that it now behooves each of us to solidly close ranks behind the majority thinking on the 1955 economic demands."[44] Stellato could have pressed for more, but he did not. With a concession in hand, Stellato declared victory and dropped his dissident posture.

Either formally or informally, Stellato and Reuther had, at long last, come to an understanding involving mutual concessions. Stellato had been ready for peace with Reuther late in 1952, but Reuther had turned his back on the deal. In 1954, however, with his anti-Communist credentials bolstered by the attack on Local 659, Reuther could afford to deal with Stellato. Moreover, Reuther had failed in his bid to unseat Stellato during the 1953 local elections. He had no choice but to deal with Stellato. Finally, 1955 was contract time. Reuther needed Stellato's support in order to get a new contract ratified by the union membership.

As Reuther had learned in 1950, contract ratification votes could be a potential source of trouble at Local 600, even with Stellato's endorsement. Compared to contract ratification votes, the minefield of UAW convention politics seemed relatively tame. Convention elections had become a mere formality. Reuther had been elected by acclamation, without any challenger, since the late 1940s. The rank and file had no direct vote in convention elections and Reuther had long since established powerful political machines in the many small locals that sent delegations to the UAW conventions. Few delegates had prior contact with other local officers from around the country and fewer still felt compelled to initiate rebellions.[45]

The contract ratification process, however, was an entirely different matter within the UAW. The rank and file of each local voted to either ratify or reject all tentative contract deals.[46] In contract votes, members were asked to ratify immediately something relevant to everyday life: the agreement governing wages, hours, and working conditions.

Reuther's five-year contracts had provided him with five years in which he could establish himself as a statesman, without a direct confrontation with the membership of his union. His fear of the role of the rank and file in the upcoming 1955 contract negotiations undoubtedly contributed to his decision to make a concession on the shorter workweek. It was, after all, a substantive—if only partial—concession. But it was only one of the two concessions Reuther made in preparation for negotiations. The other was a concession to Carl Stellato.

Reuther needed Stellato. Any tentative Ford contract would have to win the approval of the National Ford Negotiating Committee. Because of its size, Local 600 was given three seats on this thirteen-member Committee. Formally, the Committee was governed by majority rule and dissenters were required to sign a contract in accordance with the will of the majority.[47] But a divided Committee nevertheless could create enormous difficulties, especially if a portion of the Committee refused to endorse a tentative settlement. Stellato's popularity with the Local 600 membership was at an all-time high, and it seemed plausible to fear that he could torpedo any tentative settlement if he chose to do so. As the *Wall Street Journal* subsequently noted, Reuther was dependent on Local 600 for successful ratification votes. "The local can almost dictate the terms of any contract settlement with Ford—or at least reject whatever agreement is brought in by Mr. Reuther."[48]

Stellato and Reuther had to navigate two significant political events on their way to the 1955 contract negotiations: the 1955

UAW convention and elections at Local 600. Both events reinforced the early signs of a thaw in the relations between Stellato and
Solidarity House.

One of the items on the 1955 convention agenda was the
administration's decision to increase the number of International
vice-presidents from two to four.[49] The administration had desig-
nated its own, hand-picked candidates for the spot. The Reuther
caucus printed posters and signs with its slogan, "Solidarity in the
Rank, Teamwork in Leadership," and its slate: Reuther, Mazey,
Gosser, and Livingston (the incumbents) and Leonard Woodcock
and Norman Matthews, the new vice-presidential candidates.[50]

In a surprise disruption of the smooth-running Reutherite tradition of election-by-acclamation, Pat Quinn—the vice-president of
Dodge Local 3—took the microphone and nominated Carl Stellato.
In a further rebuke to the administration, Nathaniel Turner, an
African-American delegate from Flint Buick Local 599, was nominated for the other new vice-presidential spot. His election would
have integrated the all-white IEB, a move persistently resisted by
the Reutherites.[51]

Turner accepted his nomination and gave a compelling speech
in which he intimated that the UAW could never move industry on
racial discrimination so long as the union remained a lagging indi-
cator on race questions. In contrast, Stellato was clearly reluctant to
play the dissident and had to be pushed to accept the nomination.
When Quinn nominated Stellato, "a spontaneous demonstration
began, participated in by at least half the convention, that literally
forced the latter to accept the nomination. It was the most enthusiastic demonstration seen in any UAW convention since 1947, and
was, by all odds, larger and more spirited than the one received by
Reuther."[52]

Stellato did give a decent speech. On the question of collective
bargaining, he recalled the 1953 convention attack on his leadership and the 30-40 movement.

Did you notice what the position is on the shorter workweek today? Two years ago some of us were called tools of the Kremlin or opportunists. Today, thank God, the International, I hope, will go on record in this Convention that our next major objective is going to be a 30-hour work week for 40 hours' pay. Quite frankly I am still of the opinion as an individual that that should be our major objective in this set of negotiations. However, the majority of this International Union has decided that the Guaranteed Annual Wage is our major objective and we are for it and with it 100 per cent.[53]

This reconciliation rhetoric had been his position since November 1954. As the *Militant* reported with obvious disappointment and frustration, "The truth was that the Local 600 leadership had decided several months ago that they would not fight Reutherism at this convention."[54] But Stellato went even further, signaling his willingness to behave, and explicitly giving a nod to the terms of his peace pact with Reuther in advance of the Local 600 elections. "I did not come into this Convention to challenge anybody and I was not seeking anyone to challenge me or challenge my Local Union."[55]

Nevertheless, Stellato seemed surprised and even moved by the unexpected show of support for Quinn's nomination speech.

Quite frankly I want to thank all of the delegates that have urged me to accept. I want to thank those of you that engaged in the demonstration. I don't know how to put it. It makes an individual feel mighty fine when fellows who have never seen you before come up to you and say, "Carl, I believe in the things you stand for, I believe in the things you have been fighting for."[56]

He cleverly put his most factional comment in the words of nameless "other" delegates who had said to him, "Many of us think it is not fair . . . that we should wake up one day in January and see across the headlines of the Detroit newspapers that the Executive

Board of our great Union has selected this individual or that individual to become vice-president. We don't think that demonstrates democracy." And, in his own voice, he also suggested that the IEB could use "some honest, constructive objection" from someone who would "once in a while raise a voice" for some alternative proposals. He even went so far as to accept the nomination, saying "I would like to be that someone." But even this was embedded within accommodating suggestions. "I want to repeat," Stellato said in his concluding remarks, "I didn't come in here to fight anyone."[57]

Notwithstanding all of his hesitancy, Stellato's acceptance speech "unloosed another ovation." It also provoked attacks by Woodcock and Matthews, both of whom told the delegates that they "resent very greatly" Stellato's remarks. Matthews began to suggest, "If Brother Stellato could only sit in—," but he was shouted down.[58]

In a procedure more reminiscent of proceedings of the 1940s, the convention actually had to schedule a roll-call vote—rather than a simple voice vote—for an International election. Although the Reuther caucus had made its position clear, there were a large number of defections—especially impressive in light of Stellato's reluctance to campaigned for the position.[59]

Stellato and Turner surprised most observers. Turner got about 10 percent of the votes cast. Stellato polled 31 percent of the total vote.[60]

Reuther moved to guard against such unfortunate dissent by appeasing his opportunistic friend. Stellato went into Local 600 elections at peace with the Reuther administration. In 1953, the anti-Stellato candidate was Gene Prato, a high-level UAW official within the Reuther caucus, who ran with enormous support from Solidarity House. In 1955, Stellato faced Frank Thorpe, Jr., an unknown figure with no discernible institutional support from the International.[61] When the election results were tabulated in mid-May, Stellato had trounced Thorpe. Stellato won 24,490 votes to Thorpe's 4,235—by far the widest margin of Stellato's tenure at Local 600. His entire slate of union-wide candidates won office.[62]

Stellato would almost certainly have been able to beat back any challenge Reuther could have sponsored. The Local 600 president was justifiably popular in his own right, and his electoral triumph in 1953 undoubtedly made Reuther reluctant to come back for more embarrassing defeats in 1955. Timing also aided Stellato's electoral effort. He sailed into office just a few weeks prior to the completion of contract negotiations and, thus, did not have to run on his accomplishments as a responsible negotiator at the bargaining table. Rather, he could run on his four-year record as a militant and effective dissident agitator within the UAW.

When the contract negotiations actually began, the Stellato-Reuther team had their hands full trying to satisfy the demands of the Ford workers in 1955. The Ford membership voted in favor of a request by the Ford negotiators for strike authorization, and a strike deadline was set for 12:01 A.M. on Thursday, June 2. At the last minute, on Wednesday, June 1, Stellato spoke before a huge rally at Local 600. He announced that the strike deadline would be pushed back four days, to Monday, June 6. The *Militant* reported, however, that he met with enthusiastic cheers when he "promised to keep fighting for their demands and to call a strike . . . if a satisfactory settlement wasn't reached" by Monday.[63]

On Monday, Stellato emerged from negotiations in time to tell a noontime gathering of 15,000 Rouge workers that negotiators had reached a settlement. As Stellato reported the results to the enormous crowd of workers, his explanation fell flat. At several points in his presentation, Stellato was roundly booed. Stellato tried to build some enthusiasm for the deal, calling on workers to ratify the contract in two weeks (June 20–21) when the vote would be conducted. His suggestion met with little enthusiasm. He then told the assembled members to return to work. But instead, the rally turned into a wildcat strike. Fewer than 5,000 of the 30,000 day-shift workers returned to work and the plant shut down.[64] *Fortune* reported, "workers' resentments spilled over into a series of wildcat strikes" throughout the Ford empire.[65] By Tuesday and Wednesday, there were strikes in thirty-seven of Ford's sixty-seven plants, and 74,000 of Ford's 140,000 workers were idle.[66]

Fortune was puzzled by the "paradoxical fact" that "Reuther was having trouble selling the Ford and General Motors contracts to his own membership."[67] The *Detroit News* noted that labor leaders hailed the agreement, but "the people who pin on badges each morning, punch a time clock and turn out the cars . . . They are not impressed."[68] Even the *American Socialist*, which considered the settlement "the best contract obtainable without a strike," was compelled to ask, "Why is there then such widespread dissatisfaction with it in the union ranks?" As a general response, the journal concluded,

> After a five-year wait [workers] simply do not think that enough has been won in the new contract . . . The auto workers, it has been commonly accepted, have been conservatized in recent years because of steady work and improved living conditions . . . but as the rash of strikes at GM and Ford demonstrates, these evaluations should not be pressed too far. Beneath the surface of complacency, great dissatisfactions are building up and . . . the latent militancy of the ranks comes to the fore, the many suppressed grievances are brought to light, and satisfaction for them is demanded . . . It was not fortuitous that . . . [Stellato's] stock went down when he decided to drop his previous manner and to do a "salesmanship job" for the new contract.[69]

More specifically, the contract included many elements that were troubling to the membership. Even if, as the *American Socialist* suggested, the workers were "never particularly excited or even very much interested in the supplementary jobless-pay proposition," the settlement fell far short of Reuther's Guaranteed Annual Wage. Reuther had demanded that the benefits last for one year following a layoff. The settlement cut the unemployment supplement from the proposed fifty-two weeks to half that, a maximum of twenty-six weeks. In its proposed form, the supplement was supposed to begin immediately after a layoff and was supposed to bring unemployment compensation up to the worker's full wage. The settlement included no benefits until the second week of a layoff, benefits equal to 65 percent of take-home pay for four weeks, and then only 60 percent of take-home for the remaining twenty-two weeks. Finally, low-seniority workers—the most vulnerable to layoffs—would have to work for approximately three and one-third years before becoming eligible for the maximum 26-week layoff supplement.[70]

In general, there was also a sense of betrayal in the fact that the tentative contract deal was a three-year agreement, which—shorter than the five-year deal of 1950—was nevertheless in direct violation of a union convention mandate for contracts not more than two years in duration.[71] The contract retained an unpopular clause from earlier Ford contracts, allowing that "Employees participating in unauthorized work stoppages or slowdowns . . . shall be subject to discharge."[72] The contract did deliver a sizable increase in monthly pension benefits.[73] However, even the CP's George Morris—hardly Reuther's toughest critic—noted that the UAW rank and file was "already quite handicapped by the pension system that requires a worker to have [30] years service with the same company . . . at age 65, to qualify. Many workers nearing the pension deadline are inclined to be submissive, and even drop union activity, to 'safeguard their pension.'"[74]

But the greatest anger came from the skilled workers. A skilled trades revolt led by John Orr (Local 600 vice-president) was based upon the fact that by 1955, Ford skilled tradesmen earned seventy cents an hour below the maximum rate for comparable work in independent shops. The demand, going into negotiations, had been for a raise of thirty cents per hour. The settlement included an additional eight cents per hour. Having withdrawn the shorter workweek as a contract demand—a demand that would have signaled commitment to enhancing the leverage of production workers— Reuther and Stellato had opted, instead, for a strategy that used the leverage of skilled workers in the Big Three to subsidize the more precarious market position of production workers. When informed of the contract terms, the skilled trades leaders recommended that skilled workers stay out of the plant, even as others began to return to work.

Stellato denounced the walkout and the skilled trades leadership, and ordered the wildcat strikers back to work. The denunciation provoked a further walkout from additional skilled trades workers.[75] On Wednesday, June 8, the workers called off the strike but simultaneously voted to conduct a campaign to reject the new contract.[76] With a week and a half between the agreement to mobilize a "No" vote and the scheduled dates of the ratification vote, the workers were able to muster 8,236 votes against the contract. This represented 32 percent of the votes cast in the ratification process.[77] *Fortune* almost certainly understated the sentiment of the rank and file when it characterized the "No" vote as representative of a "coolness" toward the contract.[78]

Stellato's clash with the Local 600 membership created an opportunity for challengers who were willing to champion the cause of the ranks. In the summer of 1955, however, the "cause" that motivated the most serious rebellion was not a progressive demand for shorter hours, but a reactionary demand for the protection of skilled trades privileges. The skilled trades revolt represented a kind of return of the repressed within the labor movement. Skilled tradesmen had been instrumental in helping organize production workers during the formation of the UAW. And the shorter workweek movement had been led by skilled tradesman, drawing on a long history of shorter hours agitation within craft unionism. But they did so in an effort to increase the autonomous leverage of the production workers so that industrial unionism would be based on something other than the willingness of skilled trades workers to subsidize production workers. The skilled tradesmen who helped build industrial unionism had been agitating within the auto union since the early 1930s in the hope of moving toward a broad-based shorter hours movement for skilled trades workers and production workers alike. After twenty years, the shorter workweek was still a distant promise. In the intervening years, a more reactionary, exclusive and hierarchical tradition began to fill the vacuum left behind by Reuther's resistance to shorter hours.

5.

FALSE PROMISES

In the spring of 1957, there were signs that Reuther did not intend to make the shorter workweek fight in 1958. On April 7–12, 1957, ten years after Reuther had consolidated his presidential power, the UAW convention returned to Atlantic City. In his opening remarks to the convention, Reuther asked that the delegates delay a full discussion of collective bargaining demands until January 1958 when the International would convene a "Special Convention" for the development of the 1958 demands.[1] It was yet another delay. Nevertheless, Reuther did promise the delegates,

> When we go to the bargaining table in 1958 we need to strike a blow, a powerful blow, to begin to shorten the work week, but we are not going to fight for a shorter workweek with the same take-home pay. We want a shorter workweek with more take-home pay, because we need more purchasing power.[2]

Reuther knew how to compete for the support of the rank and file when he thought he needed to do so. In his new capacity as an advocate of the shorter workweek, he got all the rhetoric right. He did not to try to sell the delegates on the shorter workweek as a demand for more leisure at the expense of higher pay. Rather, he promoted the shorter workweek as a "win-win" demand—simultaneously a means for tightening labor markets, raising wages, and affording greater leisure. "The only realistic alternative to the involuntary and barren idleness of widespread unemployment is the voluntary and constructive leisure that flows from rational reduction in the hours of work."[3]

The proposed Collective Bargaining Resolution—which provided the mandate for the January 1958 Special Convention—suggested that because the "foundations of guaranteed employment have been laid ... we reaffirm the decision of the 1955 convention to make the shorter workweek with increased take-home pay ... the next major collective bargaining objective of our union."[4] The only argument during the discussion of the resolution came from delegate Tony Dallesandro of Chicago's International Harvester Local 1307, who announced, "I am glad to hear that this Convention is coming out for a shorter workweek, but I believe that when we started organizing the CIO back in the '30s our goal at that time was for 30 hours. It seems like we are about 24 years behind ... we should come out with a 24-hour week." The resolution was adopted with little additional discussion.[5] During the election of officers, a delegate from Dodge Local 3 nominated for president of the International "a man that has put the life back into the 30 for 40 ... Carl Stellato." But Stellato declined the nomination and refused to challenge Reuther.[6] *Business Week* called it "perhaps the quietest, most obedient UAW convention on record."[7]

Stellato was clearly finished playing factionalist games. With Reuther supporting the 30-40 demand, he could avoid alienating Reuther and still appear loyal to his own members at Local 600. When a so-called "Stellato" caucus meeting was held at the UAW convention, a crowd of approximately 400 delegates jammed into a room designed to hold about 250 people. But, as the *Militant* reported, neither Stellato nor Pat Quinn "made proposals for voting on particular resolutions or outlined a strategy for the convention floor." Stellato did little more than recount the history of the 30-40 fight at Local 600. When one delegate proposed forming a formal dissident caucus, the chair of the meeting responded, "That's just what we want to do. Everyone take down the address of Local 600 and write in when you get home." Rather than begin organizing a caucus while everyone was in the room, Stellato promptly ended the meeting.[8]

After the convention, Stellato returned home to face another local-wide election. Once again, Stellato was allowed to run without the interference of the International. With the Reuther caucus neutral and most of the other 1955 conditions unchanged, Stellato beat five minor challengers, winning with 21,233 votes—more than 80 percent of the votes cast.[9]

In early May 1957, Reuther took his first step toward negotiations for a shorter workweek. Reuther invited the auto industry to join the UAW in the formation of labor-management committees to study "the many phases of the problems related to the reduction of the work week." The call for cooperation suggested, "we have always believed that collective bargaining should be based on economic and technological facts rather than upon economic force."[10] General Motors and Ford swiftly rejected Reuther's study proposal. Apparently, the industry was well aware of "the problems" related to the shorter workweek, required no further study of the "economic and technological facts," and was ready to move on to the question of "economic force."[11]

As late as June 1957, however, Reuther seemed on track to demand the shorter workweek. In an address to the Industrial Union Department of the recently merged AFL-CIO he declared, "Soon, we of organized labor will take up the cudgels for a shorter workweek." Responding to the industry's rejection of his cooperative labor-management committees, Reuther suggested, "Already, the men of little faith are pulling their hair and gnashing their teeth ... They say, as they have always said, it can't be done." Now, as a 30-40 advocate, Reuther even demonstrated that he had understood all along that the shorter workweek could both spur and provide labor's response to productivity growth and technological innovation. "We got the 8-hour day and living standards rose more than we ever dreamed of with a 16-hour day."[12]

Soon after this address, however, stories began to emerge suggesting that Reuther was preparing to retreat from his shorter workweek commitment. The first public indication came in the form of a rumor circulated by Victor Riesel. On July 8, 1957, Riesel told a radio audience that GM had secretly "offered to make a terrific money settlement to get Walter Reuther to quit the fight for the four-day week at five day's pay. It has offered to put down ... an unprecedented 25 cents an hour wage increase ... It has been reported that Walter Reuther is considering taking this."[13]

About six weeks later, on August 18, Reuther dropped what newspapers called "a bombshell."[14] Ignoring the UAW convention mandate for a shorter workweek and the official UAW bargaining program adopted there, Reuther sent a letter to GM, Ford, and Chrysler suggesting that the UAW would reduce its contract demands if the auto companies would cut auto prices an average of $100 per car. Reuther's price-cut proposal was a bold attempt to divert attention from the shorter workweek demand.[15] Notwithstanding Reuther's willingness to restrain UAW demands, Ford, Chrysler, and GM all immediately rejected Reuther's price cut proposal.

Reuther's price-cut plan received mixed reviews, even among his closest allies. Writing in the Reuther-friendly journal Labor Action, B. J. Widick suggested that, should the proposal have been accepted, "Reuther would have been behind the eight ball in terms of the politics within the UAW, for any scaling down of UAW demands for the 1958 negotiations in advance of them would have been rather unpopular with the ranks." Moreover, he worried that

Reuther was, "in effect, proposing to arbitrate the 1958 contract" by proposing that, should the International and the industry fail to agree on a contract package, "an impartial three man committee would be set up to review the bargaining proposals of both sides."[16]

Labor Action also published a more enthusiastic review of the price-cut proposal, entitled "UAW Leads Cause of Whole People," written by Herman Benson.[17] Benson noted that Reuther had written to Eisenhower suggesting that if industry profits fell below a "reasonable" level in the aftermath of a price cut, "then our proposal irrevocably commits us to scaling down our collective bargaining demands."[18] In agreeing to reduce UAW demands, Benson claimed, Reuther's proposal "raises collective bargaining into a dramatic struggle between two classes over price control and into a fierce competition for the loyalty of millions victimized by inflation." This constituted "a step forward in labor's great struggle to curb the antisocial power, the 'prerogatives,' of monopoly capitalism."[19]

Benson was correct in suggesting that Reuther sought to use his proposal to make peace with American consumers. Ford and the other auto companies quickly exploited Reuther's offer to subordinate UAW demands to the demands of consumers. Ford simply took Reuther's thinking to its logical conclusion: if wage cuts could deliver price cuts, then it was reasonable to blame high car prices on the high wages of autoworkers. Similarly, Chrysler simply asked, "Would it not be just as logical for the automobile industry to ask members of the UAW to take an immediate and sizable wage cut?"[20]

Close observers of internal UAW politics noted that the real aim of the price-cut proposal was to displace the shorter workweek demand. *Business Week* noted, "Bit by bit, the major area of conflict between the United Auto Workers and the automobile industry . . . is being narrowed down . . . [as] this week the trend setting issue of the shorter workweek [was] lost in the running fight over whether wages push up prices or vice-versa."[21] *Fortune*, like Widick, suggested that "if any of the companies had evinced serious interest in the [price-cutting] scheme, Reuther might well have faced some embarrassments within his union."

> For in the past year, after prolonged public discussion, the Ford, Chrysler and GM divisions of the UAW had all gone on record overwhelmingly in favor of heavy wage and fringe-benefits increases and substantial reductions in hours ... there was no mention of automobile prices in any of the union's statements of objectives. When Reuther ... replaced these objectives ... [he] did so without consulting the members.[22]

The question was not *why*, but instead *how* Reuther would drop the shorter workweek demand without risking rank-and-file rebellion within the UAW, or, if Reuther had already secured the cooperation of Carl Stellato, then how would Stellato survive? Rumors circulated that Stellato had aligned himself with Reuther in the retreat from shorter hours. Herman Benson's *Labor Action* article suggested that, in a recent issue of Ford Facts, "Stellato solidarize[d] himself with Reuther."[23] Benson was right about the emergent alliance between Stellato and Reuhter, but this alliance was far from explicit in the pages of *Ford Facts*. Stellato had used the Local 600 newspaper to respond to Reuther's proposal, but he was hardly prepared to unite himself with Reuther on the front page of *Ford Facts*.

> *This is Our Position!!! We want to make it crystal clear where we in Local 600 stand. Whether prices are raised, lowered or remain the same we will be seeking the fulfillment of our contract demands as adopted by the General Council and the membership of Local 600. We in Local 600 are prepared to stand firm on the [1958 Collective Bargaining] resolution ... in which the delegates made it clear that the shorter workweek with increased take-home pay will be the key demand for 1958.[24]*

Stellato was playing the militant for his restless rank and file; he had no choice. Nevertheless, Stellato's administration simultaneously did try to cultivate a new relationship between Local 600 and

Solidarity House. Stellato, for example, wrote an article in *Ford Facts* encouraging Local 600 members to attend a mass meeting to hear UAW vice-president Leonard Woodcock. Woodcock was described as "a dynamic speaker who knows the score and is dedicated to the labor movement."[25] James Watts, the editor of *Ford Facts*, later reported that the mass meeting had been "very good" even though "the turnout was disappointing."[26]

By November, as the special collective bargaining convention drew near, Stellato was clearly struggling with the tension between his militant posture at Local 600 and the thaw in his relations with Solidarity House. "We in Local 600 who were the first to feel layoffs due to automation, technological improvements and decentralization, and who were the first to raise the cry for a shorter workweek with increased take home pay," Stellato declared in his most militant tone, "[we] will have to assume our responsibilities in the battle . . ." The "battle" in question, however, was not the battle for 30-40, but "the battle against inflation."[27] Still, *Ford Facts* continued to promise the membership that "the 1957 Convention had already finalized the demand for a substantial wage increase combined with a shorter workweek."[28]

In preparation for the upcoming January 22 Special Convention, where bargaining plans would be finalized, Reuther spent the weekend of January 10–12, 1958 meeting with his Steering Committee, the top brass of the Reuther caucus.[29] On Monday, January 13, Reuther emerged with a press release and a strategy for extricating himself from his commitment to the shorter workweek. *Deus ex machina!* Reuther had found his salvation in the "little moon" that the Soviets had launched into orbit on October 4, 1957.

Every thinking American and Canadian concerned with the security of his country and the future of human freedom recognizes today that the problem symbolized by the Russian earth satellites has drastically changed what appeared to be the situation at the time of the 1957 UAW convention. The launching of the sputniks has revealed and dramatized the true dimensions of the challenge of Communist tyranny and has emphasized the necessity for us to make the fullest possible use of our human and material resources to meet that challenge. As responsible citizens and in conformity with established UAW policy in relation to the timing of the introduction of the shorter workweek, the leadership of the UAW recommends that the delegates to the Special Convention temporarily defer the implementation of the shorter work-week in 1958 in the light of the realities of the world situation.[30]

Reuther also suggested that the nations slumping economy—which would, in fact, turn out to be the first serious postwar recession—was another factor that rendered untimely the demand for a shorter workweek. Reuther returned to his old money-leisure trade-off rap, as though the 30-40 demand had no relation to the question of unemployment. "We believe that … the real need is to get the unemployed back to work and to get those on short work weeks back on a full work week and that greater leisure, for the time being, can wait."[31] In the question and answer session that followed the issuance of the press release, Reuther used the U.S.-Soviet space race to justify his abandonment of the shorter workweek demand. "I am an American first and a union member second," Reuther declared.[32]

Reuther had, in many respects, always been "an American first." Reuther's primary response to the movement for the shorter work-week had always been couched in terms of Cold War patriotism. In 1953, the shorter hours demand was subordinated in the name of production requirements for the fight against the Kremlin. In 1958, even in the midst of growing unemployment and recession, it was the same story. America's manpower needs would trump labor's desire for shorter hours.

Having postponed action on the shorter workweek for at least eleven years, the Reuther administration had effectively squandered the labor shortages of the postwar economy. Finally, in 1958, with a significant recession at hand, Reuther suggested that the shorter workweek, previously undesirable, was now unattainable. It was too late for labor market strategies. The time had come for concession bargaining.

Reuther was not so foolish as to leave the press with nothing but "Reuther Retreats" for the morning headlines. Instead, he used the press conference to propose a profit-sharing plan. Reuther introduced a scheme for dividing up any profits beyond 10 percent of invested capital whereby the company would keep the entire 10 percent, plus half of anything more. The other half of any so-called "excess profits" would be split: one-quarter going to employees and one-quarter going to consumers as year-end rebates.[33] The auto executives unanimously opposed the plan.[34]

The *American Socialist* suggested that Reuther's profit-sharing plan "has to be viewed as a public-relations job ... an attempt to retreat under cover of a synthetically ferocious struggle."[35] Reuther played the game well. The headlines in Detroit on Tuesday, January 14 led with the Big Three attack on Reuther and his profit-sharing plan, making him appear to be an audacious David taunting the Goliaths of industry. The *Detroit Times*, for example, ran a huge, splashy headline, "Big 3 Tells UAW: No." The *Detroit Free Press* announced, "Auto Executives Assail UAW Profit-Split Plan." The *Detroit News* similarly put the emphasis on corporate hostility toward the radical Reuther, declaring, "Big 3 To Fight UAW Profit Plan."[36]

The battle to watch was with Reuther's labor left, not his corporate right. The profit-sharing idea was met with serious criticism from within the union, but opposition within the UAW centered on the fact that Reuther had scrapped the shorter workweek. Headlines aside, the newspapers did take note of the 30-40 reversal. "In a startling about-face on the four-day week," the *Detroit Free Press* reported, "The UAW Monday pigeonholed its long-standing demand for a shorter workweek in the auto industry."[37] In a small front-page article the day after the press conference, the *Free Press* predicted that Reuther would face "stout opposition" from Stellato, the "fiery leader" of Local 600.[38] "I don't think he'll get away with it," Stellato warned. "I don't know what he can be thinking about … I'm deeply disappointed and I'm sure there are thousands of other UAW members who are just as disappointed."[39]

In his own press release, issued on Tuesday, Stellato declared that he was "astounded," not so much by the reversal itself, but by the fact that the IEB recommendations "were released to the public press before being submitted to the Special UAW Convention." Stellato went on to recount the history of the 30-40 movement at Local 600, including a General Council meeting held January 12, 1958, at which the shorter workweek demand was unanimously reaffirmed by the Council delegates. Distancing himself from Reuther, Stellato suggested, "The establishment of a shorter work-week will not deter any [Sputnik-related] defense effort for assuredly at the present time the unemployed are not in a position to help either themselves or the defense effort."[40]

On Wednesday, January 15, Stellato initiated a widely antici-pated campaign to salvage the 30-40 movement. During the day, he called a series of meetings with Local 600's full-time staff represen-tatives to take the pulse of the rank and file. He told the newspa-pers, "While no official action was taken, they really raised h---. I received a telegram signed by 2,063 workers in the Dearborn assem-bly plant pledging me their support."[41] Then, on Wednesday night, Stellato and other Detroit-area supporters of the 30-40 demand met to discuss plans for the upcoming Special Convention.[42] Stellato gathered together with presidents of several locals including the two big Chrysler locals in Detroit, Local 7 and Dodge Local 3.[43] On Friday, the twenty or so union officials dubbed a "Rebel" group by the *Free Press* told reporters that they would meet again on Friday night for a second strategy session.[44]

On Saturday, January 18, the new issue of *Ford Facts* was published. The front page included a banner headline in red ink, "Local 600's Position: On a Shorter Workweek with Increased Take-home Pay!"[45] An editorial called the IEB reversal a "violation of the faith and trust" of the rank and file. "We cannot see the connection between the Sputnik and dropping the fight for a shorter workweek ... Let us repeat, so there is no room for misunderstanding, the economic conditions which have developed since the April ['57] Convention have made even more imperative the struggle for a shorter workweek ... We intend to fight at the January 22 Special Convention to retain the shorter workweek as the Number One demand for the 1958 contract negotiations."[46]

John Szluk, a right-wing unit president, published an open letter to Stellato in which he recalled, "I have been a Walter Reuther supporter all of my days in the UAW ... I am still a Walter Reuther supporter ... But I am going to stand with you in the fight for the '30-40' because ... that is the mandate of the greatest percentage of the men and women who elected me.

> We in the shop are a great deal closer to the membership than those who serve from your level ... Failure on your part, or on mine, to pursue the things they want most will certainly find them seeking new leadership on every level ... [My members are] asking why the shift in plans to go after the 30 for 40! ... Several have asked me to request that you hold special shift meetings ... so that they can get your assurance ... that you will lead the local union's delegation into the special 'crash convention' in a solid block to continue the fight for '30 for 40' ... It now promises to be a red-hot convention.[47]

Unit officers were sending a clear signal up the chain of command: our jobs are on the line if 30-40 is abandoned. Even right-wing officers like Szluk sought to publicly identify themselves with shorter hours in order to be spared the potent wrath of the rank and file.

On Wednesday, January 22, the special collective bargaining convention delegates assembled for the shorter workweek show-down. The new bargaining package, including the profit-sharing plan, was introduced as the centerpiece for debate. Reuther opened the debate with a return to the stark language of the 1953 convention attack on the shorter hours movement. He contrasted the official Resolutions committee proposal with "the other approach . . . to make the shorter workweek . . . the top basic demand."[48] Reuther warned against choosing the latter approach.

> At that point the whole recommendation here, the whole tactical approach . . . goes down the drain and therefore you can't be for this package and the shorter workweek in the basic demand because that is contrary to the whole tactical approach being suggested . . . if you say the shorter workweek is the top demand then, in effect, you are opposed to this approach and it seems to me the issue is sharply enough drawn. You are either for it or against it.[49]

Reuther offered the delegates very little in the way of explanation for dumping the shorter workweek. He spared them the sputnik speeches and found it difficult to suggest his more likely excuse, that a recession was no time to fight unemployment. Instead, Reuther tried to imply that the key to understanding the new package was its importance in the inflation wars. On the doorstep of economic recession, Reuther announced that "the whole tactical approach [was] to meet the inflationary propaganda . . . the Union will take a position before the people of America in which we say we have got a minimum economic package. That you can do without any question of inflation. That will put us in the strongest position to fight our battle"[50]

There was an extraordinary irony in Reuther's role as an inflation hawk. For ten years, Reuther had argued that the demand for leisure would have to take a backseat to the urgency of pay hikes. For ten years, Reuther had pressed for more work and higher pay while disparaging (and misrepresenting) shorter hours advocates who allegedly put leisure ahead of luxury. In 1958, with the advent of the worst recession since the Depression of the 1930s, Reuther suddenly developed the ability to correctly characterized the shorter workweek demand as an expensive and audacious demand for more pay and less work. Such a demand, he suggested, was impossible to make during an economic slowdown. It was time, Reuther proposed, not for a wage boost and an hours reduction, but instead for some humility and a "minimum economic package."[51]

Walter Reuther didn't need to work that hard to convince people that he was not an advocate of the shorter workweek. He had made that clear for years. Everyone knew that he had been forced to concede the point, not agree with it.

When Reuther had completed his remarks, Stellato rose to speak. When Reuther tried to cut off the Local 600 president, Stellato, quickly rehearsed the commitments made at the '55 and '57 conventions and concluded with a proposal for a rank-and-file referendum on the collective bargaining demands for 1958.

> Our membership expects the short workweek to be one of our major demands. It shocked us to no end when out of the Sputnik-infested skies came the substitute to a shorter workweek in the form of a profit sharing plan . . . I say we ought to put this question to a referendum vote and let the membership decide if our objective shall be a short work week or a profit sharing plan.[52]

Other Local 600 delegates, including Jesus Chantres, were even more aggressive. "We did not join this Union," Chantres told his fellow delegates, "because . . . the UAW . . . was going to fight for . . . a small group that is working and the hell with the other employees . . . I urge you to vote down this resolution and let us go on fighting in unison for a shorter workweek."[53] One older delegate, a Reuther supporter from Milwaukee Local 75 named Herman Steffes, demanded, "Let's get back and let's build this Union the way it is supposed to be . . . that is, what we formulated this organization for back in 1932:

Wages, hours, and working conditions ... Let's turn down this whole package."[54] John DeVito, a long-time dissident from Local 45, a militant Fisher Body local in Cleveland, predicted, "Now, the leadership of this Union cannot sidestep the short work week. It will keep haunting them until we put up that fight. That happens to be the dream of every American worker in this country."[55]

During the course of the discussion, approximately forty delegates spoke out in opposition to the abandonment of the shorter workweek demand.[56] Many delegates spoke out in support of the shorter workweek and in opposition to the profit-sharing proposal. Robert Lopez from GM Local 664 in Tarrytown, New York, recalled Reuther's earlier bragging about the shorter workweek and called Reuther's sputnik bluff.

> Now, I remember just from 60 days ago, when not one but two sputniks were orbiting around the earth, Brother Reuther electrified the AFL-CIO Convention by putting before them the major demands of the Auto Workers, and he included the shorter workweek ...This was in December ... This was after sputnik ... I think that, regardless of what occurs at this Convention, the shorter workweek ... will still be the major demand of the Auto Workers on the line ... We are read ... to make a fight for the shorter workweek.[57]

Referring to the profit-sharing plan, Lopez suggested, "We don't want to become silent partners and get a little hand-out from [the corporations]."[58]

The profit-sharing plan, asserted Ernest Dillard of Local 15, "seems to carry the strong suggestion that if we are to share profits we must take responsibility for seeing that there be profits ... It seems to encourage the attitude on the part of the company that we are one big family ... Regarding the shorter workweek, I would hope that we could go on record to keep that as a major demand."[59]

Lew Michener, the old, militant president of Local 406, the Ford Local in Long Beach, California, poked fun at the profit-sharing plan. He quoted Rawson Warden, national chairman of the Council of Profit Sharing Industries, who promoted such plans to employers because they "make every employee a capitalist ... they act to increase productivity without adding to the cost of the products." Michener told the delegates that he was "a little bit worried" that UAW policy now mirrored such corporate schemes.[60]

Michener's comments touched a nerve with Reuther. The UAW president took the microphone to deny any association with incentive plans. "There is as much difference as there is between day and night," Reuther asserted. But he also acknowledged an evolution in his thinking. "Going back to the old catch phrases, I could dig up some speeches I used to make but I have learned a few things along the way. If you are going back to those old phrases ... you will learn. I happen to believe that this is the most realistic way to go about this thing and I am willing to change some of my ideas because the world is changing." Reuther knew what was at issue in this debate: "I don't believe ... that we are going to have a company union. I just believe our Union is too good to degenerate into a company union."[61]

When a motion was made to close the debate, Reuther called for a show of hands in support of the resolution. Reuther ruled that "the vote in adopting the committee's report is carried by better than 90 per cent."[62] But delegates shouted out, calling for a roll-call vote. Reuther did everything he could to prevent the roll call, scolding the shouters, "You fellows never seem to learn."[63]

What these delegates never seemed to learn, in fact, was that Reuther had the convention procedures sewn up tight. Of course, the entire direction of debate and voting had already been powerfully constrained by the fact that only the Resolutions Committee could introduce resolutions for debate and voting. Resolutions Committee members were appointed by the IEB, and since 1947, Reuther could count on the support of almost every IEB member on every action. Thus, for example, Stellato's proposal—that the status of the shorter workweek demand be put before the rank and file in a referendum—was, formally, a meaningless gesture because "proposals" from the floor had no official status.

Of course, Reuther's political machine was not airtight. Delegates still had the option of voting down the official administration resolution. When delegates shouted for a roll-call vote, Reuther read from something called "Rule 12" and announced, "It shall require at least 800 regular delegates (excluding special delegates) to move a roll call vote on any question."[64] Why was a roll-call vote so important to the shorter workweek proponents? And why did Reuther invoke a rule to prevent the roll-call vote? Did the shorter hours advocates think that they had the votes to beat the Reuther machine? Had Reuther fudged when he ruled, on the basis of his quick look at raised hands, that the motion had passed by better than 90 percent?

The answer is that Reuther almost certainly did not fear—nor did he have reason to fear—that his resolution would have been repudiated by the delegates in a roll-call vote. But the record of a roll-call vote—even one documenting an enormous victory for the administration's resolution—could have been politically controversial back on the shop floor. Local officers who had demonstrated fidelity to Reuther at the expense of the shorter workweek would have to account for their actions. One loyal Reuther delegate, Harold VanAlsburg of Continental Motors Local 113 in Muskegon, seemed willing to sacrifice his reputation back home. "I heard a couple of delegates say a little while ago they were worried as to what was going to happen to them when they went back into their local unions . . . I like a little slogan I heard Loretta Young make on a program the other night when she said, 'If you want a place in the sun you have got to expect some blisters.'"[65] It is not clear how many delegates would have shared VanAlsburg's heroic spirit of self-sacrifice.

On the other hand, if Reuther could prevent a roll-call vote, then delegates would not have to pay a price for a place in the sunshine of the Reuther caucus. The delegates required some sun-blocking protection or, better still, some shadows in which to hide. No record, no accountability.

While in Detroit, delegates could remain faithful to the Reuther caucus which had helped them ascend to or remain in office. Indeed, any defections would be recorded, not for a public record, but for caucus records. Reuther made certain that the entire voting process by show of hands was transparent to him. According to the *Militant*, he placed at least one paid International staff representative with each delegation at the meeting.[66]

Conversely, in the absence of a public record, each delegate could go home to the rank and file and claim to have fought a noble crusade for the shorter workweek only to have been undermined by the majority of other delegates. When Reuther asked, "Are there 800 delegates who support the roll call vote?" he actually found "about 75 delegates with hands up" before declaring that "the motion for a roll-call vote has lost."[67]

Having secured victory by defeating the shorter workweek, Reuther moved to cover his own tracks.

> The fellows who want the 30 for 40 in the main package, they think you can make a jump and get to the top. I admire that spirit. I say we have made a decision. It wasn't my decision … You made the decision. You made it after full and democratic debate … I say that the important thing now is not the division that was expressed in debate. The important thing is the unity that we have when we sit at the bargaining table.[68]

Reuther could not end the meeting until he reminded the delegates of his glory days as an heroic militant.

> I say that the problem here is that we shouldn't have any delegate go home with the theory … the leadership just threw the unemployed to the wolves. I am concerned about the unemployed. If I weren't … I wouldn't be taking the abuse from every reactionary in the world … I am prepared to take all of the abuse that they can heap upon me, includ-

ing being vilified in the press and on the radio, and being beaten up and shot at.[69]

At Local 600, the fallout from the Special Convention was dramatic. On Saturday, January 25, 1958, the latest issue of *Ford Facts* was published. Having gone to the printer before the conclusion of the big confab, it included no coverage of the meeting itself, but was filled with shorter workweek discussions. In particular, the pages of the newspaper were filled with telegrams of support, reporting on petitions signed by thousands of workers in support of the shorter workweek and in opposition to Reuther's plan to drop 30-40 from the bargaining agenda.

Unit leaders also addressed the shorter workweek issue in their *Ford Facts* columns. One unit leader predicted that the leadership "will not be so foolish as to throw the 30-hour week . . . out the window, because the membership expects quite a bit in our next contract."[70] Arthur de la Fuente, another unit leader, was even more explicit about the stakes going into the convention fight. He reminded readers that the shorter workweek "has been Carl Stellato's dream for over eight years."

> Well, you know the rest! Sputnik has changed things . . . now we do not need a shorter workweek . . . So for the record, we want again to publicly state that our position has not changed one IOTA since 1957 . . . I'm an ambitious man. I like my present job very much . . . Moving from Local 600 to Solidarity House would be nice; but if I have to do what other fair-weather local politicians have done in the past—and some of them are doing now—to get there, you'll never catch this 'Mexican' doing the same thing.[71]

Rumors of a Stellato sell-out were running through the Rouge, even before the convention had run its course.

The red-hot tone of the January 25 *Ford Facts* had completely iced over, however, by the time the first post-convention issue was

published on February 1, 1958. There had been an abrupt reversal
of course in the immediate aftermath of the meeting. Stellato made
almost no effort to pander to the militancy of the rank and file.
"The Special UAW Convention . . . is now history," Stellato wrote.
"It is regrettable that the . . . Convention saw fit to drop the shorter
workweek . . . Nevertheless, in spite of this, much good came out of
the Convention."[72] By the March 15 issue, James Watts, the *Ford
Facts* editor, was defending the procedures by which the Special
Convention dropped the shorter workweek. He correctly noted that
the prior convention resolutions in '55 and '57 had left open the
possibility of abandoning the 30-40 demand in light of an economic
downturn or an escalation in international, Cold War tensions.[73]

The only remaining question was how Stellato thought he was
going to keep his job. The answer arrived in the March 15 issue of
Ford Facts. Stellato did not, in fact, think he would be able to stay
on as president of Local 600. He announced, instead, that he was
running for Congress.[74]

The Democratic nomination for Congressman of Michigan's
16th District was not an open race. Stellato had to win in a primary
race against the incumbent congressman, a Democrat named John
Lesinski, Jr., whose voting record was hailed by the UAW as being
"95% 'right'."[75] Stellato succeeded, with the help of CP-aligned
friends Bill Grant and Walter Dorosh, in winning the endorsement
of the "Local 600 Officers and Political Action Committee" and the
General Council of Local 600.[76]

Stellato's electoral chances, although not particularly good,
were bolstered by one other significant source of support: Solidarity
House. In advance of a new round of contract negotiations, Reuther
once again made a pact with Stellato. Endorsement from the
Reutherites arrived through the International's top emissaries,
including Ken Bannon, the ACTist director of the Ford
Department, and Joe McCusker, the UAW Regional director and
former Local 600 president.[77] The July 1958 "issue" of Stellato's

campaign newsletter, the *Challenger*, featured photographs of Stellato with the Reutherites. Not surprisingly the newsletter—which discussed Stellato's campaign program and his record as leader of Local 600—made no mention of his historic fight for the 30-40 demand, nor did it include a call for legislative action for a shorter workweek.[78]

Neither *Labor Action* nor the *Wage Earner* mentioned any *quid pro quo* in their coverage of the coincidence of Stellato's accommodating stance on the 1958 bargaining demands and the endorsement from Reuther's caucus. Herman Benson mentioned nothing about Stellato's retreat from the shorter hours fight or his new Reutherite pose at Local 600. He depicted Stellato as a champion of the rank and file, suggesting that it was on the "background of spreading unemployment and ferment among Michigan unionists that Stellato announced his candidacy."[79]

The *Wage Earner*, which had denounced Stellato for years, was downright friendly toward Stellato, referring to him as "Carl" and all but endorsing the candidacy.[80] Even the SWP was more concerned with having Stellato beat his "banker opponent, John Lesinski" than with understanding the basis for Stellato's campaign.[81] The *Wall Street Journal*, however, made a more careful study of the logic at work in the Solidarity House endorsement. "The UAW's head man, embroiled in a labor situation without precedent in the auto industry, has enough problems on his hands now without having to deal with . . . Stellato once he reaches an acceptable compromise with the companies."[82] Stellato had been bought off in exchange for assistance with his great escape. It was a reasonably fair exchange.

Unfortunately, for Reuther and Stellato, the scheme did not work. Even with the machinery of the International at his back, Stellato was unable to muster enough support from the Local 600 membership and the community to win the August 5 primary election. Having jettisoned the shorter workweek and the interracial coalition that had provided his base of support at the Rouge,

Stellato campaigned primarily in the segregated towns of Wyandotte and Dearborn. He was defeated by Lesinski, 27,842 to 21,050 votes.[83] Much to his dismay, Stellato was stranded as president of Local 600. Moreover, he would have to suffer through the humiliating and painful process of selling another Reutherite contract to the rank and file.

6.

RETREAT AND DEFEAT

The 1958 collective bargaining round prefigured, in some respects, the concession bargaining that would become common during the demise of the American labor movement in the aftermath of the Vietnam War. Having abandoned any pretense of making the fight for shorter hours, Walter Reuther entered the 1958 negotiations empty-handed in the middle of a recession. It was the beginning of the end for organized labor.

In early March, UAW Ford Department director Ken Bannon formally announced the UAW agenda in negotiations with Ford. Although Bannon tried to emphasize the demands that the UAW would make, including Reuther's profit-sharing plan, the headline in the *Wall Street Journal* focused on the demands that the UAW would not make: "UAW Won't Ask Short Work Week in Ford Talks, Union Official Says."[1] Bannon explained, "the short work week could come up in the talks only through introduction by the company."[2] That seemed unlikely.

Solidarity House, with Stellato's backing, did manage to press for one demand in response to the threat of ongoing layoffs at the

Rouge. Bannon proposed that the union was "prepared to fight for plant-wide seniority."[3] The demand for plant-wide seniority, as a substitute for the shorter workweek, signaled the end of an era at Local 600. During the heyday of the Rouge, when the payroll was growing, plant-wide seniority might have enabled African-American workers who were confined to the worst, most dangerous jobs at the Rouge to move into better units without losing seniority accumulated elsewhere. But in 1958, plant-wide seniority functioned to allow the older, more privileged white, skilled trade workers to bump production workers out of their jobs. The interracial movement for a shorter workweek had given way to an exclusive defense of privilege.

With *Ford Facts* in the hands of the Reuther-Stellato coalition, it no longer functioned as a place where workers could turn for hard-hitting challenges to the official bargaining agenda emanating from Solidarity House. Instead, Stellato used the pages of the newspaper to defend himself and Reuther from charges that negotiations were bypassing the normal procedures for consulting with elected delegates. "Last Tuesday, a top level meeting was held between the Union and the Company . . . This was not a 'secret' meeting . . . The Ford negotiations are being conducted by a well-ordered and tightly-knit team under Reuther's leadership. This is as it should be."[4]

In June, the contracts expired in the midst of widespread unemployment and Reuther came up empty-handed.[5] At the low point of the recession, more than 13,000 autoworkers in Detroit had already exhausted their unemployment compensation and their UAW supplementary unemployment benefits.[6] The GAW, designed to prevent employers from using cyclical unemployment to curb labor militancy, had broken down on its first lap around the track. "Now that the boom is over," the *Militant* charged, "Reuther is in full retreat."[7]

The Stellato-Reuther team set a strike deadline at Ford for September 17, 1958, struck on that day, and agreed to a new contract on that same day.[8] The deal was described by both sides as "non-inflationary and non-excessive."[9] "Significantly," the *Wall Street Journal* reported, "the contract made no change from the contract that expired June 1 in general automatic annual wage increases or in the cost-of-living wage adjustment formula ... Failure of the union to win a boost in the wage increase rate was regarded as a victory for Ford. John Bugas, company vice president for industrial relations, was obviously pleased with the new agreement and said the union bargained hardest on the wage point."[10]

After similar agreements were made with GM and Chrysler, the *Wall Street Journal* reported that the settlements were "much cheaper than in 1955."[11] "Labor peace in the auto industry was purchased at a relatively low price this year ... Mr. Reuther smoothly abandoned the shorter work week for a profit-sharing plan which was quickly discarded once the actual contract talks got under way. Considering ... Mr. Reuther's initial goals for the latest agreement, the car makers bought a bargain in their new three-year pact."[12] The union forfeited "its future right to bargain over increased pensions for retired workers."[13]

Skilled trade workers at the Rouge pressed the plant-wide seniority issue and refused to return to work without the right to bump lower-seniority workers.[14] The ratification process yielded the largest "no" vote in the history of the UAW, although still beneath the threshold required to sink the deal. According to the *Wall Street Journal*, the entire process seemed to prove that "the auto workers— whatever their ultimate economic goals—are not immune to the pressures of the business cycle."[15]

Stellato's career as a UAW insurgent was finished. He had become publicly identified as an ally of the Reuther administration and had smoothed the way for Solidarity House in the retreat from the 30-40 demand during the 1958 negotiations.

Rank-and-file support for renewal of the 30-40 fight at Local 600 emerged almost immediately after the 1958 battle. From now on, however, that fight would be fought without Stellato and he quickly emerged as its most immediate obstacle. Stellato not only retained the presidency of the Local, but he did so with the full support of many of the older, CP-aligned local leaders, including Walter Dorosh and Paul Boatin.[16] Boatin, who initiated the Local 600 campaign for a shorter workweek and had been found guilty of loyalty to the CP at the 1953 UAW convention, had been reinstated as a member in good standing in 1956. By February 1959, Boatin and Stellato had reached an understanding. In his campaign leaflets, Boatin aligned himself with Reuther, Bannon, and Stellato, and Stellato listed Boatin as part of his own election slate.[17]

These incumbent-slate officers rested almost exclusively on incumbency and ran campaigns without bothering to offer an identifiable, substantive program. These incumbents were, in time, challenged by the emergence of a new dissident caucus.[18] The first sign of regeneration came on February 5, 1959, in the form of 8,500 copies of an "Open Letter" distributed by a group calling itself the "Committee for Good Unionism." The leaflet, which referred to Stellato as "The Undertaker" of Local 600, noted that Stellato was "eager to skip ... He tried to escape to Washington via the 16th District." Then, in reference to the support given to Stellato by his incumbent allies, the leaflet described how "the CHAIRMEN said, 'yes, Carl' ... but the voters said, 'no, Carl." Even this minor factional blow caught the eye, not only of Stellato, but of Ken Bannon, Reuther's top staffer in the Ford Department.[19]

The dissident group came forward with a second "Open Letter" that articulated a positive program and identified leaders of the Committee for Good Unionism. The Committee demanded, "Our union must fight for humane work standards."[20] There was no mention of the shorter workweek, and, like the first "Open Letter," it contained more factional venom than substantive program. The weak program, however, was drafted by a weak slate. The group put forward Pat Rice, perhaps the most inept factional opportunist within the Rouge, to run against Stellato.[21] Rice's problem had always been that he constantly exposed himself as an opportunist, apparently unaware that even cynical opportunists needed to campaign publicly with a substantive program. Back in the 1953 Local 600 race, for example, when Rice had first broken with Stellato to run for the presidency, he had made almost no effort to propose a substantive program. In that three-way race, Stellato had won almost 19,000 votes, compared with almost 8,000 for the Reutherite candidate, whereas Rice won only 2,393 votes. Rice ignored the politically contentious issue of the shorter workweek demand.

Nevertheless, Rice was the beneficiary of a major anti-Stellato vote. Like Joe Hogan's surprise showing in 1951, Rice's 7,934 votes were not enough to win against Stellato's 13,964 votes, but the results turned many heads among those who underestimated the independence of the rank and file.[22] That a candidate like Rice—with no real program—could poll almost 8,000 votes, winning the support of more than one-third of the voting membership of Local 600, meant that there was a far greater opportunity for dissident challengers than had been previously thought. In its first "Open Letter" the Committee for Good Unionism had foolishly explained that Stellato had been "eager to split" the scene not because he feared the wrath of the rank and file in the wake of his 30-40 betrayal, but because he saw "the Local's fighting spirit . . . going down fast."[23] Stellato knew why he needed to split, but it took other observers a little longer to learn. Stellato himself took little comfort in his 1959 local union victory at Local 600. In 1960, he once again tried to find safer ground as a legislator in Washington, with even more assistance from Solidarity House, including the endorsement of Emil Mazey. Once again, however, Stellato lost in the primary.[24]

At the UAW convention in October of 1959, the shorter workweek demand once again was pushed aside. A shorter workweek resolution was submitted by the Reuther administration, much of the wording having been lifted directly from the 1957 bargaining resolution. However, one key adjustment was made. The shorter workweek was no longer introduced as "the next major goal" of collective bargaining, but as "a major collective bargaining goal" to be requested "at the earliest practicable opportunity."[25]

A group of delegates met together at the convention to discuss the formation of new dissident movement. Their chief grievance: Reuther's efforts to sidetrack the shorter workweek.[26] After forming a steering committee and holding a few preliminary meetings in Detroit from October through January, the group—calling itself the National Committee for Democratic Action (NCFDA) in the UAW—held a founding conference on February 21, 1960.[27] At the meeting, the sixty founding members, representing nineteen UAW Locals, met at the headquarters of Flint Local 599, and agreed that the central feature of its economic program was the 30-40 demand.[28] The group also urged a change in the UAW constitution that would allow the same kind of direct rank-and-file vote used in contract ratification to be used in union elections of International officers and regional directors.[29]

The timing of the founding convention of the dissident group coincided with a press report in Detroit suggesting that Reuther had declared his intention to once again make profit sharing, rather than the shorter workweek, the main goal of the 1961 negotiations. The NCFDA meeting used the occasion to criticize the Reuther announcement. Jack Crellin, the labor reporter at the *Detroit Times*, covered the conference and his article appeared on the front page with the headline, "Rebel Against Reuther on Share-Profits Plan." "UAW President Reuther had a revolt on his hands today for apparently putting profit-sharing above the shorter workweek," Crellin reported.[30]

With the new group and the shorter workweek in the spotlight, Stellato felt compelled to respond to the new formation. Many still wondered if he would lead the new movement. Putting such speculation to rest, he announced that he would have nothing to do with the band of shorter workweek advocates. In its public statements, the NCFDA had asserted the obvious, that Reuther did not favor the fight for the shorter workweek. Stellato immediately jumped to Reuther's defense in the pages of *Ford Facts*. He cited all of Reuther's 1957 pronouncements about the shorter workweek and more recent Reuther predictions that the shorter workweek fight would be made at some point in the future.[31]

On April 3, 1960, the NCFDA convened a second conference for the Detroit area locals and drew representatives from twenty-two locals. Shortly thereafter, the group issued its first "Bulletin," in which it specified that the chief aim of the organization was to "reopen all contracts for the establishment of a 30 hour week with 40 hours pay."[32] By Labor Day, 1960, the NCFDA had printed, copied, and distributed 300,000 pieces of literature.[33]

Initially, there was little representation from Local 600 within the NCFDA. In October 1960, however, a new opposition movement at Local 600, calling itself the "Ford 600 Rank and File Caucus," publicly affiliated itself with the NCFDA. In its first leaflet, the Local 600 movement reprinted the once-celebrated Ford Program of 1951.

> That's forgotten now—Today Brother Stellato and the Local 600 leadership and much of the unit leadership have forgotten about the above program. They have become part and parcel of Reuther's PETRIFIED PROGRAM, which is cutting the guts out of the auto workers and our Union ... In 1941 there were 85,000 members in Local 600; in 1950, down to 65,000; today, less than 28,000 ... The 1951 Program is Still Good ... even though Stellato has jumped on the tailgate of Reuther's bandwagon. Local 600's 1951 program is basically incorporated in the 1960 program of the National Committee for Democratic Action in the UAW ... We call upon the [NCFDA] ... to unite with us to carry it out.[34]

In January 1961, a statewide convention of the NCFDA met in Detroit. The meeting resolved to call on locals to pass resolutions demanding that 30-40 be placed at the top of UAW bargaining demands. The group also pledged to work toward the election of union officers and local committeemen willing to campaign in support of the 30-40 contract demand.[35]

In 1961, *Business Week* suggested, "Reuther managed to dump [the shorter workweek] as a central demand in 1958, [but] he can't ignore the almost universal support for it this year among the rank-and-filers.[36] It had never been quite that simple; popularity could not be equated with power. So long as the union bureaucracy remained united, Reuther, in fact, could ignore the shorter hours demand, even if it had the universal support of the rank and file.

The central threat to bureaucratic unity remained the contest for control of Local 600. On February 3, 1961, Jack Conway, Reuther's trusted aide and the administrator of Local 600 back in 1952, sent a memo to Walter Reuther that delivered some bad news. "The attached leaflet was circulated in the Rouge plant. It is the opening gun in a campaign to dump Stellato. We will have to watch this development very closely."[37] Indeed, not only did Solidarity House "watch" the campaign very closely, but when they saw that Stellato was in trouble, the Reutherites actually provided administrative support for his campaign.[38]

The political fallout in the aftermath of Stellato's retreat from the shorter workweek spread into several different areas of Local 600 politics. Stellato's willingness to champion the 30-40 movement had allowed him to accomodate and, to some extent, reconcile the collective bargaining demands of many different groups at the Rouge. He had led an impressive coalition. Stellato depended on the shorter workweek in order to hold his winning coalition together. At Local 600, the large population of African-American men and women, and the smaller group of white women who remained at work in the Rouge after World War II, did not allow Stellato to fall back on the habitual exclusivist strategies embraced by so many other labor leaders. The labor movement had always dealt with unemployment by accepting layoffs of the least senior employees. Until the 1958 press for plant-wide seniority, however, African-American workers had effectively blocked the most privileged white workers from implementing this divisive strategy. The 30-40 demand allowed Stellato to respond to the threat of layoffs with a unifying demand. Rather than taking sides among different groups of workers fighting over a limited number of jobs, Stellato had used the shorter workweek demand to propose that all workers sell less labor.

Nothing in Stellato's past had predisposed him to be the darling of the Detroit Urban League, the NAACP, or a close political ally of black community leaders like Reverend Charles Hill. Yet, he was all of these things during the height of the 30-40 movement. Throughout the 1950s, Stellato never ran for union office without a major African-American leader on his ticket and at his side. Why? Was Stellato a great, moral crusader committed to helping the "victimized" African-American workers? Not a chance. In all of his union politics, Stellato was an opportunist. So long as Local 600 remained divided by factional politics, it had been impossible for any white leader to retain local-wide office without a significant show of support from the militant African-American members who constituted a quarter of the local union membership.[39]

When Stellato abandoned the shorter workweek demand, however, he threw away his most effective method for responding to the demands of competing groups at the Rouge. Insofar as peace with Reuther demanded silence on shorter hours, Stellato could offer nothing but divisive seniority rules within Local 600 and white supremacy in his congressional races. When Stellato dumped the 30-40 demand, his grand coalition immediately disintegrated.

The first rebellion came in April 1959, from within the small group of women struggling to hang on to employment within the shrinking Rouge workforce. During the recession of 1957 and 1958, the number of women working at the Rouge had fallen from 943 to only 583. A group of approximately 300 women, led by Edna Austin, stormed the Local 600 headquarters and assailed Carl Stellato for ignoring their situation.[40] Stellato responded by saying that the women wanted him to bump men out of jobs. "We don't want to fight with anybody," she told a reporter. But neither would the women retreat. "We just want our old jobs back."[41]

Stellato's retreat from racial justice also provoked mobilization from African-American men at the Rouge. Two Rouge-based African-American leaders, Horace Sheffield, previously aligned with Reuther, and Buddy Battle, previously aligned with Stellato, helped form an African-American political alliance, the Trade Union Leadership Council (TULC), to pressure for racial justice within the UAW.[42] At Local 600, the TULC became the core of the new dissident movement, especially after the 1959 local union election.[43]

In 1959, Bill Johnson, the African-American incumbent recording secretary aligned himself with Stellato's slate. Johnson's candidacy was challenged, however, by James O'Rourke, a white worker. O'Rourke attacked Johnson, but Stellato had nothing but kind words for O'Rourke. O'Rourke beat Johnson and was then welcomed into office as a member of the Stellato team.[44]

For the first time since anyone could remember, all four of the top officers at Local 600 were white men. Even Stellato considered this situation unsustainable. On December 17, 1960, Stellato announced to the readers of Ford Facts that the four officers had agreed "that there should be Negro representation at the highest level of this Local . . . and have unanimously reached the conclusion that one of the four will not seek re-election in May of 1961."[45]

Initially, a rumor spread that Stellato himself would step aside to make room on the slate for an African-American officer.[46] On March 23, however, Stellato announced that he would run for re-election at the Rouge and, in a stunning reversal, announced that he would run an all-white slate of candidates for local-wide office.[47] Stellato did replace one of the incumbent officers on his slate, but the replacement was another white candidate.[48] The TULC was outraged. Did Stellato really plan to introduce another all-white slate of candidates? At the Rouge?

During this period, Dave Moore, a leader of the 1952 shorter hours protest at Solidarity House and one of the African-American leaders barred from office in 1953, had been reinstated as a member in good standing.[49] When he learned of Stellato's announcement, he called for the TULC and the remainder of the "Progressive Caucus" to join in a struggle against Stellato, linking the struggle against racism and the struggle for the shorter workweek. "Since 1959," Moore wrote in a leaflet, "a serious misunderstanding developed between the Negro and white leaders of our local ... an all-white slate was put forth ... We ask you, the Rank and File to join us and help prevent any of our union leaders from traveling this road of division which is so dangerous to our union ... Inseparable from the above is our need to thoroughly talk over our needs for a shorter workweek."[50]

The day after Stellato made his announcement, the leading African-American unionists at the Rouge publicly repudiated Stellato and declared that, although a rival candidate had not yet been chosen, "there definitely will be someone running against Stellato."[51] Stellato had destroyed his coalition and betrayed his winning platform. In the absence of a progressive program, Stellato crafted what one observer called "a white supremacy campaign."[52]

In an election leaflet, Stellato presented his "explanation" for the emergence of significant racial hostilities within the Local.

> The TULC bosses [told me] that if I didn't accept Buddy Battle for vice-president on our slate of candidates for Local office and a Negro to knock off O'Rourke as Recording Secretary—both to be selected by TULC—they would then see to it that I would get no Negro worker support ... Naturally, I couldn't permit anyone to threaten the Office of President of Local 600 ... we told the personally ambitious Negro leadership of TULC, which was bent on rule or ruin, to go to hell.[53]

The rival selected to run against Stellato was Harry Philo, an unknown white activist formerly aligned with the CP.[54] Following Moore's suggestion, the opposition created a joint slate representing the TULC and the "Progressive Caucus" in the formation of a "Job Security Slate."

Stellato red-baited Philo mercilessly, but his campaign remained primarily focused on race and the TULC. Stellato printed a leaflet with photographs of his entire slate on one side of the page and photos of the opposition on the other, he put his picture at the top of his own slate, but put a large picture of Horace Sheffield—rather than Harry Philo—in the comparable place on the other side of the page. The caption running across the page from Stellato to Sheffield read, "You may continue This - or - Change to This." It made no difference, apparently, that the major African-American candidate who ran on the Philo Slate was Al Wilson, not Horace Sheffield.[55]

The Philo ticket campaigned on a "Job Security" platform in which the first and most prominent demand was for a "30 hour week for 40 hours pay."[56] In one frequently repeated campaign theme, the Philo slate recalled, "In '50, '55 and '58 they said, 'This is not the time.' . . . We say 1961 must be the time."[57] Picking up Stellato's old slogan, "Within the unity of workers lies the salvation of American labor," the Job Security slate amended it to read, "Within the unity of *all* workers, *regardless of race, creed or religion*, lies the salvation of American labor."[58] In contrast, Stellato campaigned against the "TULC gang of strike-happy office seekers hell bent on taking control of the membership of Local 600."[59] Indeed, when the "Job Security Slate" pledged "a clean campaign without red-baiting, race-baiting or mud-slinging," Stellato responded, as if shocked and disappointed, "No Red-Baiting or Race-Baiting? Whenever I hear this sort of campaign plea I begin to look into the records and backgrounds."[60] He charged that the TULC had, until recently, "banned whites from membership" and—although Sheffield had been instrumental in persuading black workers at Ford to join the UAW in

1941—Stellato tried to suggest that the TULC was helping Ford break the union. "1941 Against Union—1961 Break the Union."[61]

Stellato won re-election in 1961.[62] The attempt to rebuild a shorter hours movement at Local 600 had failed. The election breakdown did, nevertheless, reveal support for the Job Security slate's 30-40 program and a significant dissident movement in opposition to Stellato's race-baiting. Stellato had, in fact, won an extremely narrow victory, even with the full support of the International administration. In the presidential race, Stellato beat Harry Philo, 12,466 to 10,528 votes. Philo, however, beat Stellato in a majority of the units at the Rouge. Stellato's base of support depended on the skilled trades units. The 1961 election demonstrated the degree to which the 30-40 demand had become a movement of production workers. Stellato carried the traditional skilled trades units, but Philo beat Stellato in the production units.[63]

In February 1961, a document signed by "The Ford Rouge Specter" had reported an additional factor that helped Stellato retain office. According to the "Specter," Stellato had arranged for the merger of a separate Ford local into the Rouge bargaining unit. The leaflet asked, "What's behind all this so-called merger talk?"[64]

The election results made clear the importance, for Stellato, of the mysterious merger. Led by Stellato loyalists, the unit delivered Stellato his margin of victory. In one of the most lob-sided victories at Local 600, the new unit went to Stellato, 647 to 101 votes. With the addition of the votes from the merged unit, Stellato's margin climbed to 51.69 percent, enough to declare victory.[65]

Employment at the Rouge had declined dramatically: from 85,000 workers in 1941 to 28,000 in 1961. Ford's decentralization program and its automation investments had taken an extraordinary toll on the employment scene at the Rouge. One little-noticed consequence of all of this was the degree to which it had also transformed the contours of the Local 600 membership. With no new hiring at the Rouge, the proportion of active workers fell in relation to retired workers. In 1961, the Philo slate learned that there were 46,000 eligible voters: 28,000 actively employed, 14,000 retired members.[66]

The size of the retiree vote posed a significant challenge to the anti-incumbent opposition because there were unique elements of the retiree's situation that differentiated it from the life of the active worker. First, in terms of communication channels, the retirees were cut off from everyday workplace chatter about union politics. For retirees, the primary channels of communication were highly structured and vertical: *Ford Facts* articles and mailings. Without a daily dose of shop-floor discourse, retirees depended on name recognition. For those retirees who left the Rouge during the years when Stellato had presented himself as a militant fighter, his name on an election slate evoked the fighting spirit of Local 600.

A more serious challenge for the shorter hours movement was the different imperatives of retired life. Active production workers demanded less work, whereas retirees had already won their freedom from labor. This did not turn them against the idea of a 30-hour workweek, but the hours of work became less urgent than pension benefits, especially after the 1958 contract settlement in which the UAW forfeited its right to bargain for retirees. The retired workers were being sold out and had their own battles to fight, especially the struggle to win cost-of-living adjustments as a part of the pension system. Nevertheless, the impact of the retired workers' vote proved to be the decisive factor in the 1963 and 1965 election fights at Local 600.

On February 15, 1965, after a bruising contract battle at Local 600 in 1964, Stellato announced that he would not run for re-election in 1965, but instead would await retirement on the payroll of the International.[67] Almost immediately, Gene Prato and Walter Dorosh organized a "retain Stellato as President" meeting to try to convince Stellato to run again, or at the very least, to identify themselves closely with his presidency. When Stellato affirmed his decision to step aside, his right-wing caucus had to choose a new presidential candidate. Walter Dorosh, a former CP activist, was Stellato's hand-picked successor.[68]

The Rank and File Caucus—which had campaigned for a "no" vote against the 1964 contract—ran a slate against Dorosh, campaigning on the demand for shorter hours. They lost to Dorosh in the primary "For the third consecutive local election," the Rank and File Caucus declared, "the in-plant dues paying membership" voted in support of the opposition, "but these votes were canceled out by the retiree votes".[69]

Some time after the election, one final leaflet appeared. The leaflet offered "a look at elections Local 600 style, now and into the future."[70] "It seems that the astute politicians in the local administration have found the formula that will enable them to dominate the elected jobs." The formula, according to the leaflet, included several steps. "Remember the international can do no wrong (keep repeating this to yourself it will help you remember)." Also, use staff members to seek out and bring retired members to vote and when dropping them off at the polls, "don't forget to continually mention the name of the Internationally supported candidate." "Buy off opposition supports with local staff jobs whenever possible." And, finally, if you must choose a successor to the top candidate, "retain the Stellato image for the all important block of retiree votes."[71] Weren't some of these men "who now praise the international union . . . open critics" in years past?

> Ah, but this was before the retired brother became a significant political power in local 600 . . . We must give credit where credit is due . . . Now the question rises why should we have elections every two years? Are they not just a farce? It seems that it is just an unnecessary expense . . . We might as well forget about local autonomy, abolish elections, and grant the International the right to appoint unit and local officers. It is apparent that the results would be the same.[72]

CONCLUSION

The decline of Local 600 as a venue for dissent within the UAW had significance far beyond the walls of the Rouge. Long after Reuther was able to use the power of his bureaucratic machine to overwhelm the political culture within smaller locals, Local 600 had been able to maintain its independence. The establishment of political stability within the UAW was incomplete until Reuther was able to win control of Local 600, if only because the local was large enough to function like an entirely independent union.

For years, headquarters of Local 600 functioned at the precarious intersection of an unruly and polarized local political culture and a more insulated, unresponsive UAW administration. If Local 600 served the interests of the UAW membership, however, it did so only because of its own thriving internal political culture. After the eclipse of factionalism at the Rouge, the bureaucracy at Local 600 became as insulated from the rank and file as Reuther's own bureaucracy. Only then was it possible for Stellato and his administration to consider peace with Reuther. Once in the hands of a united Reuther-Stellato administration, the weight of the Local

600 bureaucracy became a burden, rather than a blessing, for local dissidents.

Factional polarization provided the union membership with the leverage necessary to force incumbent leaders to be accountable to rank-and-file demands. Division between Stellato and Reuther provided the most prominent example of this phenomenon during the 1950s, but even this division was largely the consequence of divisions within Local 600, rather than any kind of personal rivalry between Stellato and Reuther. Carl Stellato was, in fact, a reluctant rival; no better and no worse than Reuther, he abandoned his erstwhile allies in the Reuther caucus as a consequence of the pressure of political forces within Local 600.

Factionalism made it possible for the rank and file to exert pressure on incumbents, but the issues that divided the factions at the Rouge were rarely, if ever, generated by basic, "bread and butter" questions of labor union policy, or even the more general battle between corporatism and syndicalism. Instead, the internal political culture of the UAW turned on a very different axis, revolving almost entirely around Cold War politics of Communism and Anti-Communism.

The Cold War and the question of Communism contributed mightily to the rise and fall of factionalism within Local 600. And yet, these issues were often only obscurely related to labor issues of immediate concern to rank-and-file workers at the Rouge. In effect, the factions were often interested in the workers for different reasons than the workers were interested in the factions.

Workers seem to have been primarily concerned with the ability of competing factions to "deliver the goods" in relation to membership demands. The rival factions, on the other hand, were animated by very different concerns. The Communist Party leadership, for example, sought control of Local 600 in order to use the Local as an institutional base for other activities related to a host of issues including, but not limited to, support for a pro-Soviet political "line." The ACTists, on the other hand, were equally motivated, if not more so, by a broad *anti*-Communism and a desire to prevent the CP from building an institutional base within the labor movement. All factions were Cold War factions in that they defined themselves and their *raison d'être*, not in relation to the "Labor" question but in relation to the "Communist" question.

Each of the competing factions did, at one time or another, find it necessary to champion the demand for a shorter workweek. None, however, were particularly inclined toward the old syndicalist labor ideologies that first gave rise to the shorter hours movement. All factions, as a matter of principle, were opposed to the workings of markets and market leverage and favored, instead, various forms of cooperative, collaborative, or planned production. This was as true of the Catholics as it was of the Communists and various groups of Socialists. And yet, insofar as they were forced to compete with one another for the support of rank-and-file workers, these same factions were forced to set aside their own corporatist inclinations and learn to embrace the language of syndicalism. It was only in this context that the various factions embraced, at one time or another, the 30-40 demand and the syndicalist ideology of the shorter workweek. The factions aimed, in essence, to accumulate political capital among union members by championing the shorter workweek, only to then spend that capital on various Cold War battles.

If ideological factions played an important role in the history of the UAW, it was probably not a role that CP-led factions intended or would have embraced. They did not aim to be factionalists; they aimed to win. They may have intended to function as vanguard parties that delivered truth to the masses, but the great contribution of each ideological group was its role in perpetuating factionalism, rather than building Communism, Socialism, anti-Communist Catholicism.

In some respects, of course, the advent of Cold War polarization witnessed a dramatic narrowing of the competitive spirit among

UAW factions, especially insofar as otherwise warring sectarian groups found common cause in anti-Communism. For example, the Association of Catholic Trade Unionists and the Shachtmanite Workers Party represented very different political traditions. During World War II, the two groups competed directly with each other for the support of the UAW rank and file. After the war, however, as the Communists began to champion the demands of dissidents within the UAW, both groups abandoned the rank and file to the Communists and joined an awkward alliance within Walter Reuther's UAW bureaucracy, commonly perceived to be the best venue for beating back the Communists.

Perhaps, then, it might be commonly argued that both the UAW, in general, and the 30-40 demand, in particular, were hurt rather than helped by the Cold War climate of the 1940s and 1950s. To be sure, Walter Reuther eagerly embraced HUAC investigations in his war against his erstwhile Communist allies and used red-scare tactics in his battle to crush legitimate shorter hours dissent within the UAW. Reuther's anti-Communist crusades aimed to enhance his own bureaucratic authority by criminalizing the shorter workweek demands of his most powerful critics.

And yet, in some respects, the political culture of the UAW managed to thrive alongside the bitterness and viciousness of Reuther's anti-Communist bureaucratic coalition. Reuther's battle against the CP, in fact, was remarkably unsuccessful, especially in light of the frightening context of domestic Cold War repression. At several points in the history of factionalism at Local 600, it was the anti-Communist fervor of the ACTists and the HUAC investigators, rather than the political commitments of the CP, that kept the factional fires burning. Stellato's drive against Local 600 Communists in 1951 and the HUAC drive against Local 600 in 1952 forced Local 600 CP activists to abandon power-sharing strategies promoted by CP leaders and to discover creative and popular factional demands for retaining the support of union members in a hostile climate. The rank and file was not particularly committed to either the Soviet Union or the civil liberties of Communists, at least in the abstract. But neither was the membership moved by Cold War anti-Communist campaigns in the UAW. Instead, the rank and file offered provisional loyalty to any faction that embraced a militant, syndicalist union program.

The autoworkers supported those factions willing to speak out and defend militant rank-and-file demands. And they remained largely diffident toward those who seemed to stand in the way of the realization of those demands. Beyond that, there were few identifiable patterns of ideological loyalty. When the Communists embraced "everything for victory" during World War II, the autoworkers followed the lead of anti-Communist factions that articulated a militant labor program. When those same anti-Communist factions abandoned this labor program, the autoworkers followed the Communists and militant socialists who picked up the fallen banner of shorter hours. So long as the CP was willing to champion the movement for a 30-hour week at 40 hours' pay, Reuther's most audacious repressive campaigns for control of Local 600 proved utterly futile. The real danger to the 30-40 movement emerged, not from the political chill of the Cold War, but from the cozy collusion of the Cold War thaw. Only after the CP made its peace with Reuther and abandoned its posture as the leading faction of the opposition did the political culture of Local 600 and the UAW finally collapse.

The Communists saved Reuther from having to follow through on his promises to pursue the demand for a shorter workweek. As the 30-40 pressure was beginning to yield serious, public concessions from Reuther, the Communists retreated from the factional fight. In exchange for a nod toward the Soviets and a place in his bureaucratic machine, the Party agreed to back away from demands that made life difficult for Reuther. There is absolutely no evidence that the Communists reached out to Reuther because they were losing the support of the rank and file in their factional demand for a shorter workweek. The Communists abandoned the rank and file, not the other way around. Indeed, the Party went out of its way to help Reuther suffocate the movement it had helped promote within Local 600.

Unity between the Communists and Reuther was established in the mid-1950s on a widespread basis throughout the UAW and the CIO. Some referred to the new CP line as "Browderism without Browder."[1] What drove the Party into the mainstream? In all likelihood, the CP was motivated by a combination of related factors. As indicated in the Party's discussion of 30-40 and factionalism in the UAW, the CP had at least one eye on U.S. foreign policy toward the Soviets. And, eventually the Party did manage to extract from Reuther some public muttering about the importance of peace initiatives with the Soviets, especially after the death of Stalin in March 1953. But the CP seemed willing to criticize its own local activists for emphasizing 30-40 several months before it ever received its minimal Cold War concessions from Reuther and long before Reuther was willing or able to make peace with Local 600.

The retreat from factionalism also coincided with a generalized Communist retreat. The Communists became preoccupied with the isolation of the Party and the status of its formal leadership. In the heyday of postwar anti-Communism, the hunt for Communists had become a national obsession, causing considerable trauma for those caught up in the government witch-hunt. The Party had been hounded by the law and many of its top leaders had been prosecuted as enemies of the state. Almost all of the leading figures of the CP were either in prison, living as fugitives, or living "voluntarily" underground.[2] The Communists had successfully maintained the support of the rank and file at Local 600, but the Party leadership was seeking legitimacy in the "higher circles" of American labor; the Communists wanted to come in from the cold.

The retreat of the Communists, and the partial rollback of the most severe elements of McCarthyism after 1954, enabled Reuther,

Stellato, and the CP to embrace each other in a power-sharing arrangement that ushered in an era of peace and stability within the political culture of the UAW. Only the rank and file remained out in the cold.

The Reuther machine emerged from the factionalism of the 1950s more secure than ever before, only to collapse at the bargaining table. The 1958 round of UAW collective bargaining negotiations was a major defeat, not only for the 30-40 demand, but for any positive labor program within the UAW. Faced with widespread unemployment and worker insecurity, Reuther dumped the 30-40 demand and the UAW moved into full retreat.

The ultimate demise of the UAW, and of the industrial union movement more generally, was delayed during the inflationary years of the Vietnam War and its aftermath. Nevertheless, the 1958 bargaining round in auto set the stage for the future of American labor. The shorter workweek movement had been decisively defeated within the industrial union movement and organized labor had demonstrated its complete helplessness in the face of recession and unemployment.

The twentieth century ended with organized labor in the United States flat on its back. Shorn of any serious strategy for battling the threat of unemployment in a post-Keynesian economy, organized labor suffered mightily during the recessions of the early 1980s and 1990s.

Today, almost fifty years after the merger of the AFL and the CIO, organized labor in the United States is so unresponsive to its own rank and file and so removed from its own history of struggle that labor leaders are no longer even compelled to venture a position on the hours question. There is no hours question. The discourse of shorter hours—the vision of less work and more pay—has vanished from the horizon of possibility.

Labor's silence has not been without consequences for the structure of the labor market and labor's capitulation has not escaped the notice of leading economic policymakers. In the summer of 1996, Federal Reserve Chairman Alan Greenspan described "a puzzling phenomenon" confronting the American economy. "I refer to the pervasiveness of job insecurity in the context of an economic recovery that has been running for more than five years . . ." Greenspan was not concerned, in his remarks, with the actual scarcity of jobs so much as popular perceptions of job scarcity, especially in relation to "the question of how people perceive . . . technological change." "This sense of job insecurity," Greenspan suggested, "is so deep that many workers are truly scared . . . Some fear their ability to make ends meet in the future. Many appear truly concerned about a prospective decline in their standard of living."

Even as late as mid-February 1999, as unemployment dropped to thirty-year lows, Greenspan continued to find evidence of this puzzling phenomenon. In remarks prepared for the American Council on Education, Greenspan suggested that the pace of technological change "has clearly raised the level of anxiety and insecurity in the workforce. As recently as 1981, in the depths of a recession, International Survey Research [a private research firm] found 12% of workers fearful of losing their jobs. In today's tightest labor market in two generations, the same organization has recently found 37% concerned about job loss."[3]

Greenspan neither challenged nor confirmed the accuracy of the growing culture of job panic within the labor market. He did emphasize, however, the very real ways that job panic might prove to be profitable for business. As a result of the perception of job insecurity, Greenspan concluded, "[workers] have increasingly forgone wage hikes for job security . . . [and] the past few years have been a period of extraordinary labor peace. In fact, 1995 had the lowest strike record for a half-century. Moreover, labor contracts . . . are now sometimes going out five and six years, as people try to lock in job security, often willing to forgo significant wage increases in the process."[4] In 1999, the Fed Chairman reaffirmed his claim that job panic had significant consequences. "Workers' underlying fear ... appeared to have suppressed labor cost pressures despite a reduced unemployment rate."[5]

As Fed Chairman, Greenspan had no intention of combating a pervasive discourse of fear and anxiety about the threat of a jobless future. His only interest was in the discourse itself and in the consequences of that discourse. For Greenspan, the discourse of technological change—the alleged threat of automation—had managed to enfold anxiety about the future back onto the practices of the present.

What Greenspan recognized was that the pretensions of labor do not simply correspond to the present level of unemployment. Labor's militancy also corresponds to the rise and fall of movements capable of projecting a future of freedom and abundance. In the last instance, the defeat and demise of the movement for a shorter workweek helped set the stage for the collapse of organized labor, the advent of job panic, and the establishment of Greenspan's "extraordinary labor peace."

NOTES

INTRODUCTION

1. "Johnson State of the Union Provides Budget of $97.9 Billion, War on Poverty, Atomic Cutback," *New York Times*, January 9, 1964, p. 1; "State of the Union: Johnson Urges a 'War on Poverty,' but Only New Plan Is Overtime Pay Study; Spurns a 35-Hour Work Week," *Wall Street Journal*, January 9, 1964, p. 3.
2. "Text of President Kennedy's Message to Congress on the State of the Union," *New York Times*, January 15, 1963, p. 4.
3. Quadagno (1994, 61–62).
4. Quadagno (1994, 76). Prior to the merger of the AFL and the CIO, Meany had served as president of the craft-unionist AFL and Reuther as president of the industrial-unionist CIO. For an excellent review of the conflict between the AFL and the CIO, see Morris (1958).
5. Edsforth (1995).
6. The *Wall Street Journal* closely monitored Meany's campaign for a shorter workweek. See, for example, "AFL-CIO to Seek Law for 35-Hour Work Week," *Wall Street Journal*, February 24, 1959, p. 3; "Kennedy Opposes Work Week Cut To Trim Jobless," *Wall Street Journal*, March 16, 1961, p. 3; "AFL-CIO Urges Unions To Seek Higher Wages, Shorter Hours," *Wall Street Journal*, December 13, 1961, p. 7; "AFL-CIO Drive for Law to Cut Work Week Likely to Be Slated by Leaders Next Week," *Wall Street Journal*, August 7, 1962, p. 5; "AFL-CIO Opens Drive for 35-Hour Week, Calls Level of Unemployment 'Intolerable,'" *Wall Street Journal*, August 14, 1962, p. 4.
7. For Kennedy administration responses to Meany's shorter hours agitation, see "Kennedy Opposes Work Week Cut To Trim Jobless," *Wall Street Journal*, March 16, 1961, p. 3; "AFL-CIO Urges Unions To Seek Higher Wages, Shorter Hours," *Wall Street Journal*, December 13, 1961, p. 7; "35-Hour Slogan," *Wall Street Journal*, March 13, 1963, p. 18; "AFL-CIO President Describes Automation as 'Curse to Society,'" *Wall Street Journal*, November 15, 1963, p. 14.
8. The most prominent instance of civil rights pressure *within* organized labor was A. Philip Randolph's Negro American Labor Council. Randolph began

mobilizing African-American trade union officials in the summer of 1959 in order to build pressure on Meany to respond to the crisis of African-American poverty and unemployment. Randolph himself was responding to a larger context of civil rights mobilization outside the labor movement. See Meier (1963) and Pfeffer (1990, 206–39).

Walter Reuther and Randolph had been Socialist Party comrades in the 1930s and were life-long allies. Reuther was, for the most part, spared the kind of high-profile pressure tactics Randolph used to force Meany's hand. Reuther did, however, face challenges within his own union from an emboldened civil rights consciousness, especially at Ford Local 600. Reuther's battles to contain these challenges constitute one of the major concerns of this book.

9. Kornhauser (1952, 444–446).

10. "Restless Reuther: He May Try to Replace Meany This Year, Make AFL-CIO More Militant," *Wall Street Journal*, June 21, 1961, p. 1.

11. For well-publicized rumors of a Reuther challenge to Meany, see "AFL-CIO to Seek Law for 35-Hour Work Week," *Wall Street Journal*, February 24, 1959, p. 3; "Restless Reuther: He May Try to Replace Meany This Year, Make AFL-CIO More Militant," *Wall Street Journal*, June 21, 1961, p. 1.; "Reuther May Bring into the Open His Feud with AFL-CIO Chiefs over Internal Splits," *Wall Street Journal*, November 15, 1961, p. 2; "Reuther, Meany Prepare to Clash," *Wall Street Journal*, December 6, 1961, p. 18; "Merged Labor's Ailments: AFL-CIO Convenes, Strained by Internal Battles, Declining Membership and Assaults on Racial Policies," *Wall Street Journal*, December 7, 1961, p. 30; "Meany, Reuther Clash over Appointment; Old AFL-CIO Enmity Likely to Erupt Again," *Wall Street Journal*, August 16, 1962, p. 2.

12. Piore and Sabel (1984, 116).

13. In her account of exclusionary gender politics and the UAW, Ruth Milkman has emphasized the urgency of "strategies that can win broad support (from men as well as women) . . . especially in the present period of economic contraction and restructuring" (1987, 159). For gender politics and the hours question in unions, see Gabin (1991) and James (1976). For an excellent account of battles between nationalism and dissident demands for a shorter workweek within the UAW, see Frank (1999).

14. Cutler and Aronowitz (1998).

15. Dubois (1935, 354–355); Ignatiev (1993, 248–249).

16. Kornhauser (1993, 22).

17. Kornhauser (1993, 1).

18. "Kennedy Opposes Work-Week Cut Below 40 Hours," *Wall Street Journal*, January 25, 1962, p. 3.

19. Quoted in Lichtenstein (1995, 530 fn43).

20. Andrew (1979); Lichtenstein (1995, 314–319).

21. Roediger (1980, 5). See also Roediger and Foner (1989).

22. Roediger (1990, 13); Lipsitz (1998).

23. Commons (1906, 471).

24. Harrington (1962). For the influence of Harrington's book, and Dwight Macdonald's prominent 1963 review of the book in the *New Yorker*, see Bernstein (1996, 91–92).
25. Harrington (1962, 167).
26. Harrington (1962, 167); Rawick (1969).
27. Harrington (1962, 135).
28. Lipsitz (1998, 218).
29. Rawick (1969, 102).
30. Harrington (1962, 156).
31. Lipsitz (1998, 22).
32. Commons (1906, 474).
33. "Mean Mr. Meany," *Wall Street Journal*, August 13, 1962, p. 8.
34. Roediger (1991, 180).
35. Rawick (1972, 132).
36. Harrington (1962, 72).
37. Harrington (1962, 126, 131).
38. Sugrue (1996, 100–101).
39. Stein (1998, 195).
40. Stein (1998, 387 fn12).
41. Lichtenstein (1995, 290, 364); Stieber (1962, 45–53, 143–53); Preis (1964, 441); Andrew (1979); Edsforth (1995); Sugrue (1996, 159).
42. Commons (1906, 471).
43. McNeill (1887, 470).
44. For a recent discussion of syndicalism, see Kimeldorf (1999).
45. For a well-known discussion of "corporate ideology" among American labor leaders, see Radosh (1966).
46. Hardman (1928, 8). An almost identical passage can be found in Mills (1948, 117). The connection is not arbitrary: Mills dedicated the 1948 book to Hardman, his mentor.
47. Commons (1906, 471).
48. Commons (1906, 472).
49. Commons (1906, 470, 472).
50. Golden and Ruttenberg (1942, 5).
51. Golden and Ruttenberg (1942, 230).
52. The "prophetic vision" quoted is that of Louis Brandeis. See Fraser (1991, 150).
53. Mills (1948, 253).
54. Mills (1948, 252).
55. Nelson Lichtenstein correctly argues that Reuther's corporatism "put him at odds" with those in organized labor who "retained much of their pre-New Deal worldview, which saw competition for a limited set of jobs as a fundamental constraint faced by the labor movement . . . Like Kennedy, Reuther argued that 'there is enough work to do in America to keep us busy,' if only the economy were geared to full production . . . Reuther therefore rejected a reduction in statutory hours." (1995, 364).

56. Panitch (1980).
57. Golden and Ruttenberg (1942, 212).
58. Collier and Collier (1979).
59. As Mark Leff has noted, Nelson Lichtenstein's biography of Reuther reads, "as if Lichtenstein's narrative were immersed in Reuther's own consciousness ... [The] considerations shaping Reuther's initiatives, alliances, ideological rationales, and compromises get top billing" (1996, 348).
60. Brody (1975, 121).
61. "Auto Workers and 32-Hour Week," *Workers Age*, November 12, 1938, p. 6. *Workers Age* was the newspaper of Reuther's factional opponents, followers of Jay Lovestone, a one-time CP leader in the United States who became a leading anti-Communist figure of the Cold War. During the late 1930s, the so-called "Lovestoneites" were aligned with UAW president Homer Martin and were careful students of Reuther's dissident faction. They took note of Reuther's leadership of the shorter hours movement and reckoned with the potential threat the movement posed to the incumbent administration of Homer Martin. See Morgan (1999) and Alexander (1981).
62. "32-Hour Week Idea May Become Troublesome Issue," *Wall Street Journal*, October 11, 1938, p. 1.
63. "32-Hour Week Idea May Become Troublesome Issue," *Wall Street Journal*, October 11, 1938, p. 1.
64. "The 32-Hour Week and Labor's Demands," *Ward's Automotive Reports*, December 17, 1938.
65. Babson (1991).
66. McPherson (1940, 33).
67. Proceedings of the Special Convention of the International Union, United Automobile Workers of America, Cleveland, OH, 1939, p. 505.
68. Proceedings of the Special Convention of the International Union, United Automobile Workers of America, Cleveland, OH, 1939, p. 506.
69. "Labor and General Motors," *Ward's Automotive Reports*, January 27, 1940.
70. "Labor Situation Unchanged," *Ward's Automotive Reports*, February 18, 1939.
71. For the use of the exclusive representation principle in the case of GM and the UAW, see Boyle (1986).

    Although scholars of American labor have taken little notice of the corporatist dimension of the principle of exclusive representation, the notion is commonplace within the field of political science and the comparative analysis of corporatism. Collier and Collier, for example, argue that legal provision of a "monopoly of representation" to labor organizations can accelerate "the tendency for labor leadership to become an oligarchy less responsive to the needs of the workers" (1979).

    For labor and labor-law scholarship suggesting that rivalry might enhance the vitality and responsiveness of organized labor, see Brooks (1960) and Schwab (1992).

72. "The Labor Situation," *Ward's Automotive Reports*, August 12, 1939.

73. "CIO Wins Most General Motors Plants," *Ward's Automotive Reports*, April 20, 1940.

74. "Negotiations Between GM and UAW to Start Soon," *Automotive Industries*, May 1, 1940.

75. "Inter-Union Truce? AFL and CIO Chiefs Meet Today, Seek End to Membership Raids," *Wall Street Journal*, June 2, 1953, p. 1. For a positive "labor" interpretation of the merger written by one of its chief architects, see Goldberg (1956).

76. "NLRB Bans Union Representation Elections During 5-Year Contracts," *Wall Street Journal*, February 9, 1953, p. 2.

77. "General Motors Corporation Detroit Transmission Division," in *Decisions and Orders of the National Labor Relations Board* (1953), 1143.

78. Tomlins (1985, 233).

79. "Speech by Walter P. Reuther at GM Conference, February 9, 1941," in Box 18, Folder 17, Walter P. Reuther Collection, Wayne State University Labor Archives, Detroit, MI. See also Lichtenstein (1977).

80. Hirschman (1970). For a discussion of the bases for and meanings of factionalism and union democracy, see Lipset et al. (1956); McConnell (1958); Martin (1968); and Stepan-Norris (1997).

81. Studies of American Communism and the labor movement include Foster (1947); Kampelman (1957); Sapppos (1959); Prickett (1969); Cochran (1977); and Levenstein (1981).

   Studies of American Communism and the UAW include Andrew (1979); Keeran (1979a); Keeran (1979b); Keeran (1980); Pintzuk (1992); and Stepan-Norris and Zeitlin (1996).

82. See Levenstein (1981); Seaton (1981); and Rosswurm (1992).

83. Barnes (1976); Wald (1987); Fields (1988); and Breitman et al. (1996).

84. Wald (1987); Buhle (1988); Drucker (1994); and Worcester (1996).

85. Wald (1987).

86. Mintz and Schwartz (1985, xviii) discuss the accuracy of evidence that runs "against the grain of the bias" of business sources. The same discussion holds equally well for the bias of political sources.

C H A P T E R 1

1. Stepan-Norris and Zeitlin (1996, 16–18); Paul Weber memorandum to Philip Murray, December 3, 1939, "Ford Local 600, 1946–50" file, box 24, Association of Catholic Trade Unionists Collection, Wayne State University Labor Archives, Detroit, MI.

2. Memorandum from Paul Weber to Philip Murray, "Local Union 600, 1939–45" file, box 24, Association of Catholic Trade Unionists Collection, Wayne State University Labor Archives, Detroit, MI.

3. Keeran (1979).

4. Foster (1947, 296).

5. "Local 600—clippings and bulletins" file, box 25, Association of Catholic Trade Unionists Collection, Wayne State University Labor Archives, Detroit, MI. On Fitzpatrick's involvement with ACTU, see Stepan-Norris and Zeitlin (1996, 218).

6. Glaberman (1980, 76).

7. Glaberman (1980, 114).

8. Glaberman (1980, 115).

9. Quoted in an article published in *Ford Facts*, November 6, 1954, that recalls Reuther's various positions on the shorter workweek. *Ford Facts* was the weekly newspaper of UAW Local 600. For a complete collection of *Ford Facts* for the period under consideration, see the UAW Newspaper Collection, Wayne State University Labor Archives, Detroit, MI.

10. "Economic Security—Plans and Ballyhoo," *American Socialist*, February 1954, p. 16.

11. Johanningsmeier (1994, 295–296, 302); Klehr and Haynes (1992, 97); and Jaffe (1975).

12. Johanningsmeier (1994, 302) and Klehr and Haynes (1992, 97).

13. Johanningsmeier (1994, 304–313); Klehr and Haynes (1992, 102–109); and Pintzuk (1992).

14. James Weinstein suggests that "Foster had a gut commitment to the class struggle as he understood it and an instinctive revulsion of Browder's vision of domestic class harmony" (1975, 99).

15. Johanningsmeier (1994, 296). An article by George Morris, labor writer for the *Daily Worker*, described the dissolution and reconstitution of the clubs. See copy of undated article, "Local 600–clippings and bulletins" file, box 25, Association of Catholic Trade Unionists Collection, Wayne State University Labor Archives, Detroit, MI.

16. *Wage Earner*, October 12, 1945; *Wage Earner*, December 7, 1945, "Local 600–clippings and bulletins" file, box 25, Association of Catholic Trade Unionists Collection, Wayne State University Labor Archives, Detroit, MI.

17. *Wage Earner*, December 21, 1945, "Local 600–clippings and bulletins" file, box 25, Association of Catholic Trade Unionists Collection, Wayne State University Labor Archives, Detroit, MI.

18. Halpern (1988,103).

19. Ben Hall, "UAW Convention Issues Blurred," *Labor Action*, March 11, 1946, p. 4.

20. Drucker (1994, 46).

21. Max Shachtman, "Two Policies in UAW" *Labor Action*, December 8, 1947, p. 1.

22. Howe and Widick (1949). Widick had published within the WP press under the pseudonym Jack Wilson.

23. Drucker (1994, 242).

24. Worcester (1996, 88).

25. Barnes (1976, 147).

26. Shachtman was quick to expose SWP squirming. "The SWP ... has more than one position and it does not seem to have found the time to try to bring them into harmony with one another. If it has one policy ... it is the policy of localized, unthought-out, unanalyzed, haphazard opportunism, from which a heavy dose of adventurism is not absent. In some unions, it opposes the Stalinist group and supports conservative and even chauvinistic groups. In other unions, it supports the Stalinist groups against the anti-Stalinists" (Max Shachtman, "Two Policies in UAW," *Labor Action*, December 8, 1947, p. 1).

27. The Socialist Union published a monthly periodical called *American Socialist* that included coverage of factional fights within the UAW, especially at Local 600. For profiles of Cochran and Braverman, see Wald (1987, 298–300). See also Glaberman (1980, 142n4).

28. Cochran (1977). See also, Preis (1964).

    Shortly after the war, a hesitant merger occurred between the Johnsonites and the SWP. Paul Buhle (1988, 88) called it a "marriage of convenience." The SWP could not hold the Johnsonite group for long and the marriage ended in mid-August, 1951 when the Johnsonites split from the SWP. See "Johnsonites Split from SWP—at 8:30 Sharp," *Labor Action*, August 27, 1951.

    In the late 1940s and early 1950s, these Johnsonite and SWP groups continued to compete for the support of the rank and file, alongside and in the shadow of the CP. The SWP proximity to the CP would lead Shachtman to quip, "It seems there are some 'Trotskyists' who are not sure whether they are writing for the *Militant* or for the *Daily Worker*" (Max Shachtman, "Two Policies in UAW," *Labor Action*, December 8, 1947, p. 1).

29. Reuther won 4,438 votes; Thomas won 4,320 votes. The basis for and political meaning of Reuther's victory have been the subject of considerable scholarly debate. See Halpern (1988) and Goode (1994).

30. "Longer Work Week Is Urged By Industry to Raise Wages," *New York Times*, December 6, 1947, p. 1.

31. Proceedings of the Eleventh Convention, UAW-CIO, Atlantic City, NJ, November 9–14, 1947, p. 16.

32. "What Reuther Victory Means," *Business Week*, November 15, 1947, p. 92–93.

33. *Ford Facts*, January 17, 1948.

34. "Reuther Says Industry Cuts Back Production Vital to U.S. and ERP," *New York Times*, February 6, 1948, p. 1.

35. "Reuther Asks Bigger ERP," *Detroit News*, February 5, 1948, p. 50; "Reuther Says Industry Cuts Back Production Vital to U.S. and ERP," *New York Times*, February 6, 1948, p. 1; "New U.A.W. Strategy Awaited," *Business Week*, November 22, 1947, p. 101.

36. "Reuther Echoes NAM On Longer Hours," *The Militant*, February 16, 1948, p. 1; article by Nat Ganley in "Michigan struggle for trade union unity, 1943–51," file 24, box 1, Ganley-Wellman Collection, Wayne State University Labor Archives, Detroit, MI.

37. For the new "concentration" see Andrew (1979, 231). See also the testimony of an ex-Communist, Lee Romano in United States House of Representatives, Committee on Un-American Activities, *Communism in the Detroit Area.* Washington, DC: U.S. Government Printing Office, 1952, pp. 3060–3061.

38. "Reuther's 44-Hours OK Stirs Debate in UAW," *Daily Worker,* February 10, 1948, p. 5. In February 1948, the CP-sponsored *Michigan Herald* merged with the CP's national weekly, the *Worker.* After the merger, the *Worker* published a Michigan Edition that featured locally generated and edited material about Michigan. All subsequent references to the *Worker* are drawn from the Michigan Edition, unless otherwise noted.

39. "Labor Sacrifices Is the New 'Reuther Plan,'" *Worker,* February 15, 1948, p. 2-A.

40. The Communists took aim, not only at Reuther, but also at the corporatist ideology of Catholic labor activists, including the well-known Bishop Francis Haas who used the occasion of a CIO convention invocation to advocate, "Let each of us be ready to do a little more, rather than a little less," in what he called "a fair day's work." "Autotown Alley," *Worker,* July 4, 1948, p. 14.

41. "Ford: More Cars, Less Men," *Worker,* January 9, 1949, p. 13.

42. "Thousands Suffer As Auto Layoffs Mount," *Worker,* January 23, 1949, p. 1.

43. "Autotown Alley," *Worker,* February 20, 1949, p. 14.

44. "Ford Workers Say: 'You Must Live NOW to Enjoy Pensions Later,'" *Worker,* February 6, 1949, p. 2-A.

45. "Laid-Off Workers Ask: What's Percentage in Marshall Plan 'Boom,'" *Worker,* February 6, 1949, p. 2-A.

46. Although a popular demand among older workers nearing retirement, the pension plan—linked to 25 years of service with a single employer—provoked questions from delegates concerning the portability of the benefit. One conference delegate asked Reuther how this would affect workers "who move around from company to company, and from one plant of a company to another plant of a company … [the current plan] will not probably tie into a man's life in the industry, and might leave him short of what we are seeking." Secretary-Treasurer Mazey agreed, noting that a company pension was no substitute for solving the problem "on a federal basis so we can tie this thing together for all the people, not only in our industry, but people who migrate between industries" ("National Conference on Economic Objectives," file 1, box 56, Walter P. Reuther Collection, Wayne State University Labor Archives, Detroit, MI).

47. "National Conference on Economic Objectives," file 1, box 56, Walter P. Reuther Collection, Wayne State University Labor Archives, Detroit, MI.

48. "National Conference on Economic Objectives," file 1, box 56, Walter P. Reuther Collection, Wayne State University Labor Archives, Detroit, MI.

49. For a careful analysis of the 1949 speedup strike, see Asher (1995).

50. "Strike Betrayal" Pamphlet, file 16, box 88, Walter P. Reuther Collection, Wayne State University Labor Archives, Detroit, MI. A manuscript version of this pamphlet can also be found in "Ford Strike vs. Speed Up: Ganley notes and articles, 1949," file 4, box 5, Nat Ganley Collection, Wayne State University Labor Archives, Detroit, MI.

   The inclusion of "women" in this passage was a new addition. Although never particularly focused on the demands of women auto workers, the CP did attempt to give some voice to their concerns. The "Strike Betrayal" pamphlet included a call for "better job opportunities for Negro and women workers, and for youth." The CP also noted the active participation of approximately 5,000 women among the 62,000 workers involved in the speedup strike. "Ford Women Want Right to Rest," *Worker*, May 22, 1949, p. 1-A.

51. For Ganley's advocacy, see "Internal Democracy Crucial Question at UAW Convention," *Worker*, June 19, 1949, p. 2-A. For the convention issue, see "Follow the UAW Convention in the *Worker*," *Worker*, June 26, 1949, p. 1.

52. "After the Ford Pact—3-Day Week," *Worker*, November 20, 1949, p. 1.

53. See undated *Wage Earner* article in "Local 600 1950–52, Clippings" file, box 25, Association of Catholic Trade Unionists Collection, Wayne State University Labor Archives, Detroit, MI.

54. "Autotown Alley," *Worker*, January 15, 1950, p. 10.

55. The "Old-Timer"—anonymous author of "Autotown Alley"—accused Hood of "playing a double game" by trying to appear "friendly" to the left-wing while backing Thompson. Hood was reported by the "Old-Timer" to have taken the floor in support of a red-baiting resolution introduced by Lee Romano at a December 1948 mass meeting on the speed-up ("Autotown Alley," *Worker*, December 19, 1948, p. 14).

56. "Ford Layoff Delay Will Be Short-Lived," *Worker*, November 13, 1949, p. 2-A. The Michigan Edition of the *Worker* incorrectly lists the publication date on page 2-A as October 30, 1949.

57. The *Worker* was almost certainly putting words in Thompson's mouth. "'Jobs in 1950', said Thompson, 'will be a key issue for auto workers.' The union should seriously think of doing something on a program of the 30-hour week with 40-hour pay as one of the ways to ease developing unemployment." Neither of the two sentences included a quote from Thompson and the second sentence was not even formally attributed to Thompson, although the implication was that Thompson had said something along those lines. "Thompson on T-H," *Worker*, January 15, 1950, p. 2-A.

58. For biographical information on Stellato, see Andrew (1979); Stieber (1962, 144); Election Leaflet, file 18, box 249, Walter P. Reuther Collection, Wayne State University Labor Archives, Detroit, MI; Election Leaflet, Art Fox Collection (Unprocessed), Michigan State University Library, Special Collections Division, Detroit, MI.

59. "Autotown Alley," *Worker*, March 5, 1950, p. 10.

60. Election Leaflet, file 18, box 249, Walter P. Reuther Collection, Wayne State University Labor Archives, Detroit, MI.

61. *Wage Earner* article, undated clipping, in "Local 600 1950–52, Clippings" file, box 25, Association of Catholic Trade Unionists Collection, Wayne State University Labor Archives, Detroit, MI.

62. "Crack Caucus Lines To Back Art McPhaul," *Worker*, April 9, 1950, p. 1-A. The leaflet was issued during the run-off campaign, not the primary, but it was indicative of Stellato's attempt to align himself with the progressives.

63. "Llewellyn Runs for West Side UAW Director," *Worker*, June 26, 1949, p. 1-A. John Orr, rather than Llewellyn, was the progressive regional director candidate at the 1949 convention (Proceedings of the Twelfth Convention, UAW-CIO, Milwaukee, Wisconsin, July 10–15, 1949, pp. 476–477).

64. Phil Schatz clipping, "Ford Material, 1947–52," file 9, box 3, Ganley-Wellman Collection, Wayne State University Labor Archives, Detroit, MI.

65. The *Worker* reproduced an election leaflet that asked, "Want Real Unity? Select the Best from Each Slate." See "Here's How Rank-File Broke Through at Ford," *Worker*, April 9, 1950, p. 1-A.

66. These militants were "independent" of the CP, which claimed that they were "Trotskyites." This may have been so, but the SWP's *Militant* took no notice of the election, even as it published reports about Trotsky-aligned electoral campaigns in much smaller UAW Locals. There was no mention of the Local 600 election in the *Militant* until May 29, 1950, when a "Letter to the Editor" provided an analysis of the election results. That "letter" noted the importance of the election, although made no claims regarding any role played by Trotskyists in the campaign.
    The CP referred to followers of Leon Trotsky as Trotskyites, rather than Trotskyists. Trotskyists usually referred to CP members as Stalinists.

67. "Ford, 1948–50," file 32, box 4, Nat Ganley Collection, Wayne State University Labor Archives, Detroit, MI.

68. "Ford Locals Gave Mandate for Unity, Not Factionalism," *Worker*, April 9, 1950, p. 10.

69. See Primary Election Results, file 22, box 249, Walter P. Reuther Collection, Wayne State University Labor Archives, Detroit, MI; "Biggest UAW Local Rebuffs Reuther," *Worker*, April 2, 1950, p. 1; "Letters From Our Readers: Analysis of Ford Local 600 Election," *Militant*, May 29, 1950.

70. Primary Election Results, file 22, box 249, Walter P. Reuther Collection, Wayne State University Labor Archives, Detroit, MI; "Biggest UAW Local Rebuffs Reuther," *Worker*, April 2, 1950, p. 1; "Letters From Our Readers: Analysis of Ford Local 600 Election," *Militant*, May 29, 1950.

71. See Progressive Slate Election Leaflet, file 18, box 249, Walter P. Reuther Collection, Wayne State University Labor Archives.

72. Election Leaflet, file 1, box 1, Percy Llewellyn Collection, Wayne State University Labor Archives.

73. "Some Lessons of the United-Front Victory in the Ford Elections," *Political Affairs*, July 1950, pp. 79–86.

74. Phil Schatz clipping in "Ford Material, 1947–52," file 9, box 3, Ganley-Wellman Collection, Wayne State University Labor Archives, Detroit, MI.

75. Run-off Election Results, "Ford Local 600, 1946–50" file, box 24, Association of Catholic Trade Unionists Collection, Wayne State University Labor Archives, Detroit, MI.

76. Undated *Wage Earner* article in "Local 600 1950–52, Clippings" file, box 25, Association of Catholic Trade Unionists Collection, Wayne State University Labor Archives, Detroit, MI.

77. Phil Schatz clipping in "Ford Material, 1947–52," file 9, box 3, Ganley-Wellman Collection, Wayne State University Labor Archives, Detroit, MI.

78. "Some Lessons of the United-Front Victory in the Ford Elections," *Political Affairs*, July 1950, pp. 79–86.

79. "Some Lessons of the United-Front Victory in the Ford Elections," *Political Affairs*, July 1950, pp. 79–86.

80. "Some Lessons of the United-Front Victory in the Ford Elections," *Political Affairs*, July 1950, pp. 79–86.

81. Klehr & Haynes (1992, 127). In retrospect, John Williamson, who called for the CP to embrace the 30-40 program in January of 1949 did not even consider the program significant enough in the history of the CP to deserve mention in his memoir, published twenty years later, long after the demand had been jettisoned from the CP agenda. See Williamson (1969).

82. Andrew (1979, 240). "Ford Local Head Promises End of Speedup; Gag Law Voided," *Labor Action*, May 29, 1950; "Pledge Local 600 To Fight Speedup," *Worker*, May 21, 1950, p. 1-A.

83. "Autotown Alley," *Worker*, April 23, 1950, p. 10.

84. "We Accuse" (a single-issue newspaper/leaflet produced by the Ford Communists) in "Labor—UAW Ford" file, Saul Wellman Collection (Unprocessed), Michigan State University Library, Special Collections Division, Detroit, MI. See also, Andrew (1979, 240–241).

85. "We Accuse," in "Labor—UAW Ford" file, Saul Wellman Collection (Unprocessed), Michigan State University Library, Special Collections Division; Andrew (1979, 241).

86. "Labor News: Big Ford Local Union Raises Threat Of Strike to Win Wage Increase," *Wall Street Journal*, August 14, 1950, p. 2.

87. "Labor News: Ford, UAW Scrap Old Contract, Sign New 5-Year Pact Granting Pay Increase of 8 Cents an Hour Now," *Wall Street Journal*, September 5, 1950, p. 2; "CIO Auto Local Accepts Ford Pact," *Los Angeles Times*, September 14, 1950, p. 20; "Ford Pact Irks Commies, Say Reuther Made Under-the-Table Deal With Co.," *Wage Earner*, September 1950, p. 1; "Reuther Tries to Steal Credit for Wage Raises," *Militant*, September 25, 1950.

88. Article from *Detroit Free Press*, January 7, 1951 in "Local 600, clippings and bulletins" file, box 25, Association of Catholic Trade Unionists Collection, Wayne State University Labor Archives; *Proceedings of the Fourteenth Convention, UAW-CIO, March 22–27, 1953, Atlantic City, NJ*, pp. 207–209.

89. "Rank and File Stupidity," *Wage Earner*, November 1950, p. 1.

90. Andrew (1979, 242); "Local 600—clippings, 1950–52" file, box 25, Association of Catholic Trade Unionists Collection, Wayne State

University Labor Archives; Proceedings of the Fourteenth Convention, UAW-CIO, Atlantic City, NJ, March 22–27, 1953, pp. 207–209.

91. "Thompson Set To Oppose Stellato at 600," *Wage Earner*, December 1950.

92. Article from *Detroit Free Press*, January 7, 1951 in "Local 600, clippings and bulletins" file, box 25, Association of Catholic Trade Unionists Collection, Wayne State University Labor Archives, Detroit, MI.

93. "Ford UAW Local President Tries to Suppress Election Opponents," *Militant*, February 5, 1951.

94. Article from *Detroit Free Press*, January 22, 1951, in "Local 600, clippings and bulletins" file, box 25, Association of Catholic Trade Unionists Collection, Wayne State University Labor Archives, Detroit, MI.

95. Election Leaflets in "Labor—UAW Local 600 Elections, 1951" file, Saul Wellman Collection (Unprocessed), Michigan State University Library, Special Collections Division; "Ford Election Nears As 30,000 Face Layoffs," *Worker*, February 18, 1951, p. 1.

96. "Labor—UAW Local 600 Elections, 1951" file, Saul Wellman Collection (Unprocessed), Michigan State University Library, Special Collections Division.

97. *Ford Facts*, February 24, 1951.

98. "Labor—UAW Local 600 Elections, 1951" file, Saul Wellman Collection (Unprocessed), Michigan State University Library, Special Collections Division.

99. Hogan Anti-Dues Increase Leaflet, "Labor—UAW Local 600 Elections, 1951" file, Saul Wellman Collection (Unprocessed), Michigan State University Library, Special Collections Division.

100. *Ford Facts*, February 3, 1951; Hogan Anti-Dues Increase Leaflet, "Labor—UAW Local 600 Elections, 1951" file, Saul Wellman Collection (Unprocessed), Michigan State University Library, Special Collections Division.

101. "Redbaited Candidates Win in Ford Election," *Worker*, March 4, 1951, p. 7.

102. "UAW Elections—Reutherites Sweep Vote," *Labor Action*, March 5, 1951.

103. "Reuther Suffers Setback In UAW Local Elections," *Militant*, March 12, 1951; "Redbaited Candidates Win in Ford Election," *Worker*, March 4, 1951, p. 7.

104. In his election coverage, Allan argued that "Stellato, watching the issues and the type of campaign of Hogan in the last days of the primary election, was forced to drop his well-known red-baiting towards the end of the campaign." This was a bit of wishful thinking. The run-off campaign saw an *increase*, not a decrease in red-baiting. The CP had narrowed its "conditions" for coalition partnership to the single issue of red-baiting, without serious regard for trade union issues. See "Redbaited Candidates Win in Ford Election," *Worker*, March 4, 1951, p. 7.

105. "Redbaited Candidates Win in Ford Election," *Worker*, March 4, 1951, p. 7.

106. Hogan Run-off Election Leaflet, "Labor —UAW Local 600 Elections, 1951" file, Saul Wellman Collection (Unprocessed), Michigan State University Library, Special Collections Division.

107. "Reuther Suffers Setback In UAW Local Elections," *Militant*, March 12, 1951.
108. "Cut Speedup, Say Hogan, 4 Prexies," *Worker*, March 11, 1951, p. 8; Hogan Run-off Election Leaflet, "Labor—UAW Local 600 Elections, 1951" file, Saul Wellman Collection (Unprocessed), Michigan State University Library, Special Collections Division.
109. *Ford Facts*, March 10, 1951.
110. *Ford Facts*, March 4, 1951.
    The "Old-Timer" reported that the Stellato administration was now working to "get the House Un-American Committee to come into the Ford situation" ("Autotown Alley," *Worker*, March 18, 1951, p. 8).
111. Shachtman's *Labor Action* could not quite make sense of Local 600's left-wing, calling it "a mish-mash . . . not dominated by Stalinists" ("Detroit: Post-Convention Reactions," *Labor Action*, April 23, 1951).
112. The *Worker* reported the election results to be 17,111 votes for Stellato, 16,682 for Hogan, with a difference of 429 votes. The *Wage Earner* reported that Stellato beat Hogan 16,664 to 16,188, for a difference of 476 votes. "Vote for Hogan Shows Mettle of Ford Workers," *Worker*, March 25, 1951, p. 1; Undated *Wage Earner* article in "Local 600—clippings, 1950–52" file, box 25, Association of Catholic Trade Unionists Collection, Wayne State University Labor Archives, Detroit, MI. Andrew (1979, 243) uses the 429-vote difference to describe the run-off outcome.
    B. J. Widick reported that Hogan made "an amazing showing . . . in spite of a fantastic 'Moscow plot' story cooked up against him" ("Ranks Balk at Reuther Stress on Dues Hike, 2-Yr. Convention," *Labor Action*, April 2, 1951, p. 1).
113. Andrew (1979, 244) reports that "between the time of the referendum and the start of the convention, Stellato had actually pledged to Reuther that he would support a dues increase." The only event between the referendum and the convention which could have changed Stellato's thinking was the run-off election.
114. *Ford Facts* declared, "For the first time since he was elected to the presidency of Local 600 in May 1950, Stellato now has a majority of the members of the Local Executive Board in his corner" (March 24, 1951).
    The CP was similarly confident in its calculation, noting, "The 26-man Executive Board of the 65,000 member local now lines up as follows: Stellato, 10, the progressives, 11, and five members who are rated as independents" ("It Was a Vote for Peace And Jobs at Local 600," *Worker*, April 8, 1951, p. 8).
    Labor Action reported that the majority of the executive board members were "against Reuther" ("Detroit: Post-Convention Reactions," *Labor Action*, April 23, 1951). In any event, Stellato was in for a rough ride.
115. *Ford Facts*, March 24, 1951.
116. *Ford Facts*, March 31, 1951.

117. "Ranks Balk at Reuther Stress on Dues Hike, 2-Yr. Convention," *Labor Action*, April 2, 1951, p. 1.

118. "UAW Convention Meets," *Labor Action*, April 9, 1951, p. 1.

119. Widick reported that the attack on Stellato came as "quite a shock" to some who had thought that Widick's own April 2, 1951 article had been too critical of Reuther's moves to increase bureaucratic power and stifle union democracy. Widick reported that the "language of the Reuther leaders was different than in other years. Stellato was an 'enemy of the union,' and anyone agreeing with him was 'sabotaging the union.'" "Automobile Workers—CIO," *Labor Action*, April 16, 1951, p. 7.

120. Proceedings of the Thirteenth Convention, UAW-CIO, Cleveland, OH, April 1–7, 1951, p. 96.

121. *Ford Facts*, April 23, 1951.

122. The CP recognized that Stellato was emerging as a powerful opposition figure. The *Worker* reported, "Stellato, seriously concerned about his narrow victory in the recent elections, is making overtures in all directions seeking new realignments." The CP was simultaneously dismayed that Stellato's *Ford Facts* editor, Dave Averill, was still "red-baiting in the old way." The CP identified Averill as a Trotskyite. "Autotown Alley," *Worker*, May 13, 1951, p. 8.

123. See James F. Ryan Letter, file 19, box 249, Walter P. Reuther Collection, Wayne State University Labor Archives, Detroit, MI.

124. Lewis had temporarily become the darling of militant unionists within the UAW who perceived his 1950 fighting spirit and contract victories to be a model of old-style labor struggle preferable to Reuther's statesmanly vision of "social unionism." Lewis himself added fuel to the fire, offering up scathing attacks on Reuther's leadership of the UAW. The Lewis-Reuther feud and the 10th Anniversary Celebration at Local 600 are discussed in Zieger (1990).

125. "Stellato-Reuther Conflict Heats Up in Auto Union," *Labor Action*, June 11, 1951, p. 2; Zieger (1990, 54).

126. "Lewis Hurls Reuther Blast," *Detroit News*, June 24, 1951, p. 1.

127. Zieger (1990, 53); "UAW Chiefs Snub Lewis," *Detroit News*, June 22, 1951, p. 1; and "They Cheered John L. Lewis—To Rebuke Walter P. Reuther," *Labor Action*, July 2, 1951, p. 1.

128. "They Cheered John L. Lewis—To Rebuke Walter P. Reuther," *Labor Action*, July 2, 1951, p. 1.

129. "They Cheered John L. Lewis—To Rebuke Walter P. Reuther," *Labor Action*, July 2, 1951, p. 1; "Rally Celebrates Tenth Year of Ford Local 600," *Militant*, July 2, 1951, p. 1; and "50,000 at Local 600 Birthday Cheer Calls for Unity," *Worker*, July 1, 1951, p. 1.

130. "Ford Hit By New Bid for UAW Power," *Business Week*, June 9, 1951, p. 32. By September 1951, *Business Week* had discovered in Stellato a "shrill president of Ford Local 600 . . . calling for action almost daily" ("UAW: War of Words," *Business Week*, September 8, 1951).

131. The quote is from the *Flint Weekly Review*, as reproduced in the *Worker*. "Blame Speedup in Buick Foundry Layoffs; Ask 30 Hours at Full Pay," August 26, 1951, p. 1.
132. "Ford Local Head Asks UAW Act on Mass Layoffs," *Daily Worker*, July 13, 1951, p. 2.
133. For the Chrysler stewards, see "Demand Parley on Chrysler Speedup," *Worker*, July 22, 1951, p. 1. For the Chevrolet assembly workers, see "11 Chevrolet Locals Set for Parley to Alter Pact," *Daily Worker*, August 28, 1951, p. 2. For the leadership of Ford Local 600, see "Restless UAW Ranks Seek Action; Leaders Hope to Ride out Storm," *Labor Action*, September 24, 1951.
134. "Local to Ask 25% Speedup Cut, 30-Hour Week, in Parley with Ford," *Worker*, September 16, 1951, p. 1.
135. Preis (1964, 440); "Convene GM, Ford, Chrysler Meets on Layoffs," *Worker*, September 20, 1951, p. 1.

    The term "GM conference" or "Chrysler conference" signified a conference of UAW delegates representing workers from these auto companies. The companies were not represented at the union conferences.
136. "Ford Local's Pamphlet Urges Moves for Peace," *Daily Worker*, August 28, 1951, p. 1. For a copy of the booklet, see "UAW, Local 600, 1950–1960" file, Art Fox Collection (Unprocessed), Michigan State University Library, Special Collections Division.
137. "UAW, Local 600, 1950–1960" file, Art Fox Collection (Unprocessed), Michigan State University Library, Special Collections Division.

    It is difficult to reconcile the history of the Ford Program with Boyle's (1995, 77) discussion of the same period, in which he suggests that "Stellato could have offered a radical, even syndicalist alternative to Reuther's social democratic agenda ... But Stellato did not create a radical movement. Rather, he channeled the rank and file's anger in an essentially conservative direction." Boyle claims that Stellato's demand for "a thirty-hour work week for forty hours' pay ... simply demanded that the UAW leadership seek a bigger share of wartime spoils." It is difficult to imagine what Boyle means when he suggests that the program "channeled" this anger into "an essentially conservative direction." The "Fighting Program" was articulated as an explicit alternative to Reuther's dependence upon military spending as the basis for job creation.

    Boyle notes that, Stellato's 1950, pro-Reuther program included support for all efforts to increase defense spending in Detroit. It also included a commitment to a wartime "equality of sacrifice" program. Boyle (1995, 77) mentions that "Stellato switched his allegiance shortly thereafter," but does not recognize that Stellato's new allegiance included a new program. Instead, Boyle mistakenly blames Stellato for pushing Reuther to the right. "By adopting a portion of Stellato's program as his own, similarly, the UAW president deepened the union's subordination to the military industrial complex that [some] had complained of in early 1951" (Boyle 1995, 80).

Boyle (1995, 284n43) notes, "Much of Stellato's attack on the International was nothing more than gamesmanship." No doubt. Stellato was an opportunist, not an ideological radical. Stellato's gamesmanship, however, was a calculated response to pressure from a militant membership. Thus, it is all the more surprising to find Boyle (1995, 77) arguing that "Stellato's actions also reinforced a growing perception at UAW headquarters that the rank and file had itself swung to the right." If anything, Stellato's actions demonstrated that the membership was to the left of the UAW headquarters.

138. Reuther built his UAW career as leader of Local 174, an amalgamated local in Detroit. For Reuther's early years at Local 174, see Lichtenstein (1995).

139. "Progressives Give Program to UAW-GM Parley," *Daily Worker*, October 2, 1951, p. 2; "The Ford Local's Fighting Program," *Daily Worker*, October 5, 1951, p. 1.; "The Fight of UAW Ford Local 600 Is Much Bigger Than That of Faction," *Daily Worker*, October 10, 1951, p. 2; "Stellato Raps Moves to Disrupt Opposition," *Militant*, November 5, 1951.

140. "Urge GM Conferees to Scrap 5-Yr. Contract," *Worker*, October 7, 1951, p. 1. The leaflet also proposed a 10 percent wage increase, abrogation of the five-year contract, and a continued fight against speedup.

141. The "metal shortage" would continue to be Reuther's primary concern for some time. Reuther's argument was essentially that employers were incompetent, especially when contrasted with his own planning expertise. George Morris ridiculed Reuther's discussion of the issue. especially the implicit assumption that "labor will solve its problems if it first helps the boss solve his . . . the only thing left for us to do . . . is to organize the membership into junk-collection squads" ("Reuther—Mighty Hunter of Metals," *Daily Worker*, October 8, 1951). See also Reuther's remarks in "Official Proceedings, National Emergency Conference on Problems of Unemployment" in file 3, box 250, Walter P. Reuther Collection, Wayne State University Labor Archives, Detroit, MI.

142. Preis (1964, 441); "Jobless Problem Ducked at Flint UAW Conference," *Militant*, October 15, 1951; "They Wanted Action on Layoffs, Get 4 Hours of Reuther's Oratory," *Worker*, October 7, 1951, p. 4.

143. "Dare Reuther to Make GM Pay for Layoffs," *Worker*, October 14, 1951, p. 1.

144. "30-Hour Week 'Out of Order,'" *Detroit News*, October 12, 1951.

145. B. J. Widick reacted sharply to this language: "Very frankly, we are quite suspicious of this latest move because we have seen far too many examples where Reuther leaders identify themselves as the union" ("Reuther in Bureaucratic Move against Stellato Opposition," *Labor Action*, October 22, 1951).

146. Western Union Telegram (October 12, 1951), file 19, box 249, Walter P. Reuther Collection, Wayne State University Labor Archives.

147. The "Reuther in Bureaucratic Move Against Stellato Opposition," *Labor Action*, October 22, 1951. The *Militant* suggested, "From accused, Stellato became the accuser" ("Ford Local 600 Fights Gag Attempt by Reuther," *Militant*, October 29, 1951).

148. "Board Guns for Stellato," *Detroit News*, October 13, 1951, p. 1; "UAW Ford Local 600's Council Demands 10c Hike, 30-Hour Wk.," *Daily Worker*, October 17, 1951, p. 3; "Reuther in Bureaucratic Move Against Stellato Opposition," *Labor Action*, October 22, 1951; "Ford Local 600 Fights Gag Attempt by Reuther," *Militant*, October 29, 1951.

149. The *Daily Worker* reported only six opposition votes. "UAW Ford Local 600's Council Demands 10c Hike, 30-Hour Wk.," *Daily Worker*, October 17, 1951, p. 3; "Ford Local 600 Fights Gag Attempt by Reuther," *Militant*, October 29, 1951.

150. "Ford Local Asks End to Pact To Break Through Pay Freeze," *Daily Worker*, November 13, 1951, p. 3; *Militant*, November 19, 1951. For mention of Ford's "revolutionary" plans, see "Ford Plans New Layoff," *Worker*, November 4, 1951, p. 1.

151. Western Union Telegram (November 7, 1951), file 23, box 249, Walter P. Reuther Collection, Wayne State University Labor Archives.

152. Western Union Telegram (November 7, 1951), file 23, box 249, Walter P. Reuther Collection, Wayne State University Labor Archives.

153. Proceedings of the Thirteenth Convention, Congress of Industrial Organizations, New York, NY, November 5–9, 1951, pp. 554–556 (Resolutions, Indexed by Subject), pp. 288–292 (Reuther on Metals).

   It was not until this time, after the CIO convention, that the William Allan, *Worker* correspondent at the Rouge, began to list the 30 for 40 demand as its top demand. See "Spark United Action against War Layoffs," *Worker*, November 18, 1951, p. 1.

154. "Commies Use Stellato to Disrupt Local 600," *Wage Earner*, November 1951, p. 3.

155. "Commies Use Stellato to Disrupt Local 600," *Wage Earner*, November 1951, p. 3.

156. "UAW Palace Repels Visit," *Detroit News*, November 19, 1951, p. 1; "40,000 Ask Reuther Back 30-40," *Worker*, November 25, 1951; "Paradox in Detroit," *Fortune*, January 1952, p. 40–42.

CHAPTER 2

1. "Commies Use Stellato to Disrupt Local 600," *Wage Earner*, November 1951, p. 3.
2. "Official Proceedings, National Emergency Conference on Problems of Unemployment" in file 3, box 250, Walter P. Reuther Collection, Wayne State University Labor Archives, Detroit, MI.
3. "Official Proceedings, National Emergency Conference on Problems of Unemployment" in file 3, box 250, Walter P. Reuther Collection, Wayne State University Labor Archives, Detroit, MI, p. 21.
4. The eight-point program demanded: (1) enact a federal unemployment compensation bill; (2) continue essential civilian production until defense jobs are available; (3) dovetail defense and civilian work in existing plants;

(4) place defense and civilian work in existing plants; (5) break the machine-tool bottleneck; (6) establish a technical task force on critical materials; (7) initiate nationwide scrap campaign (i.e., collect metals, etc.); and (8) free the American economy from the stranglehold of monopoly and scarcity. "Official Proceedings, National Emergency Conference on Problems of Unemployment" in file 3, box 250, Walter P. Reuther Collection, Wayne State University Labor Archives, Detroit, MI.

5. "Official Proceedings, National Emergency Conference on Problems of Unemployment" in file 3, box 250, Walter P. Reuther Collection, Wayne State University Labor Archives, Detroit, MI, p. 28.

6. Ibid, p. 29.

7. Ibid, p. 29.

8. Ibid, pp. 12–13.

9. Ibid, p. 18.

10. Ibid, p. 33.

11. The magazine to which Reuther referred was the *March of Labor*.

12. "Official Proceedings, National Emergency Conference on Problems of Unemployment" in file 3, box 250, Walter P. Reuther Collection, Wayne State University Labor Archives, Detroit, MI, pp. 33–34.

13. Ibid, p. 38.

14. Ibid, pp. 31–32.

15. The "board" to which Stellato referred was a poster that listed the Reuther administration's eight-point program.

16. "Official Proceedings, National Emergency Conference on Problems of Unemployment" in file 3, box 250, Walter P. Reuther Collection, Wayne State University Labor Archives, Detroit, MI, p. 32.

    Stellato glossed over the fact that he had shifted his stance since 1950. If one were to attempt to characterize Stellato's opposition movement based exclusively on his comments at this conference, rather than his campaign at Local 600, before and after the Washington conference, one might conclude, with Boyle (1995, 77), that Stellato's position was one that simply pushed Reuther closer to the defense establishment. The clearest evidence that Stellato had been pushing a very different program came not from Stellato, however; it came from Reuther. Reuther identified the real terms of the debate when he lashed out against the "Fighting Program" and its bold advocacy of 30 for 40 as an alternative to his own military Keynesianism.

17. "Official Proceedings, National Emergency Conference on Problems of Unemployment" in file 3, box 250, Walter P. Reuther Collection, Wayne State University Labor Archives, Detroit, MI, p. 32.

18. Andrew (1979, 251); "Un-Americans Move on Local 600," *Daily Worker*, November 22, 1951.

19. "UAW Palace Repels Visit," *Detroit News*, November 19, 1951, p. 1.

20. Stellato was subsequently compelled to reclaim his more militant posture at Local 600. In so doing, he produced a revised account of his heroic fight for

shorter hours while characterizing Reuther as promoting a corporatist "'let's help the bosses' program" (*Ford Facts*, March 8, 1952).

21. "Un-Americans to 'Probe' UAW," *Labor Action*, February 4, 1952, p. 1.

22. Excellent coverage of the hearings appeared in *Labor Action* beginning in March 1952. "For any social historian anxious to get the 'feel' of dark epochs like the Salem witch hunt or the Stalin purges in Russia, there is fertile soil in this tense febrile city since the opening of the hearings by the congressional Committee on Un-American Activities last week" ("Detroit Becomes Salem: Probe Looses Hysteria," *Labor Action*, March 10, 1952, p. 1). Details of the reaction in Detroit can also be found in Andrew (1979, 251–252).

23. "Detroit Becomes Salem: Probe Looses Hysteria," *Labor Action*, March 10, 1952, p. 1.

24. "A New 'Ally' for Reuther," *Business Week*, March 22, 1952, p. 162. See also Cochran (1977, 328).

25. United States House of Representatives, Committee on Un-American Activities, *Communism in the Detroit Area*. Washington, DC: U.S. Government Printing Office, 1952, p. 3052.

26. United States House of Representatives, Committee on Un-American Activities, *Communism in the Detroit Area*. Washington, DC: U.S. Government Printing Office, 1952, p. 3053.

27. Andrew (1979).

28. "Reuther Joins in Witch Hunt Attack on Ford Local," *Militant*, March 17, 1952, p. 1; "A New 'Ally' for Reuther," *Business Week*, March 22, 1952, p. 162.

29. "Reuther Imposes Dictatorship on Ford Local 600," *Militant*, March 24, 1952, p. 1.

30. "UAW Exec Takes Over Ford Local," *Labor Action*, March 24, 1952, p. 1. Several reports, filed by Fred Collins for the editors of *Time* and *Life*, contain interesting details about the events of mid-March, especially the hearing at Solidarity House. See "Reuther 1952—FE/CP," file "K," box 7, Daniel Bell Collection, Tamiment Institute Library, New York University.

31. "A New 'Ally' for Reuther," *Business Week*, March 22, 1952, p. 162; Stieber (1962, 146).

Many ex-Trotskyists and those aligned with the Shachtmanites inside the Reuther caucus defended Reuther's actions. Horace Sheffield, one of the few Shachtmanite-aligned African American activists in the Reuther camp at Local 600 recalled, "I had no problems with [Reuther's administratorship of Local 600], because I had come out of the local, and I know some of the things that happened in the local" (Stepan-Norris & Zeitlin 1996, 221). William Johnson estimated, "Ninety-nine percent of all blacks were in the anti-Reuther caucus." Paul Boatin similarly recalled, "The only right-winger out of the blacks was [Horace] Sheffield. Every other black was either middle-of-the-roader or a progressive." Stepan-Norris & Zeitlin (1996, 171, 172). For an excellent description of Sheffield's role as a youth leader within the NAACP during the recognition battle at Local 600, see Meier and Rudwick (1979).

Some Shachtmanites, however, were uncomfortable with Reuther's alliance with HUAC and with his undemocratic grab for power. *Labor Action*'s B. J. Widick posed the question rhetorically: "Why has the Reuther faction been unable, with 90 per cent of the UAW in its control, to build a cadre of union leaders and unite them on a sound progressive program that would smash the influence of Stalinism in the way that counts most, by defeating them in elections, by winning the rank and file away from their influence? . . . There seems little question but that Reuther has disavowed his one-time method of defeating Stalinism by a superior program and leadership" ("UAW Exec Takes Over Ford Local," *Labor Action*, March 24, 1952, p. 1).

32. Nelson Lichtenstein notes that Reuther was well aware of the power of an opposition newspaper because he had once used his own local's *West Side Conveyor* as a weapon in his factional battles against the incumbent administration of Homer Martin. "Stellato and company made *Ford Facts* a union-wide organ of Reuther's opposition" (Lichtenstein 1995, 314). For Reuther's efforts to control the union press throughout the UAW, see Stieber (1962, 140–143). For details of the hearing and the justification for the administratorship, see Stieber (1962, 146).

　　Political Affairs, a CP journal, also noted that "the Ford Local did distribute its local paper to other plants" ("Reuther's Seizure of the Ford Local," *Political Affairs*, July 1952, p. 12).

33. *Ford Facts*, March 29, 1952.

34. "Reuther 1952—FE/CP," file "K," box 7, Daniel Bell Collection, Tamiment Institute Library, New York University.

35. "Reuther 1952—FE/CP," file "K," box 7, Daniel Bell Collection, Tamiment Institute Library, New York University.

36. "Reuther 1952—FE/CP," file "K," box 7, Daniel Bell Collection, Tamiment Institute Library, New York University.

37. "UAW Exec Takes Over Ford Local," *Labor Action*, March 24, 1952, p. 1.

38. *Business Week* reported that "industry in Detroit is betting Reuther can't do it." Nevertheless, *Business Week* argued that "Reuther took the initiative in the fight. He could have kept ducking it . . . Now in the ring, he's playing for keeps." "A New 'Ally' for Reuther," *Business Week*, March 22, 1952, p. 162.

39. "Reuther Imposes Dictatorship on Ford Local 600," *Militant*, March 24, 1952, p. 1.

40. Levenstein (1981, 317).

41. "Auto Workers' Demands Paramount in May-June Local Union Elections," *Michigan Party Forum*, March 1952, p. 2. See also, "On the Crisis in Local 600," *Michigan Party Forum*, April 1952, p. 1.

42. "Ford Material, 1947–52," file 9, box 3, Ganley-Wellman Collection, Wayne State University Labor Archives, Detroit, MI.

43. "Reds Slowed Down—But Not Stopped," *Wage Earner*, April 1952, p. 1. See also, "Ford Local Heads Urge Fight on Dictatorship," *Militant*, March 31, 1952; "Reuther Rejects Ford Election; Stellato Group Issues New Paper," *Militant*, April 21, 1952.

44. "A New 'Ally' for Reuther," *Business Week*, March 22, 1952, p. 162; "Reuther Purge Board Removes Six More Ford Local Officers, *Militant*, April 7, 1952.
45. "Local 600 Starving For Pirated Leaders," *Wage Earner*, March 1952, p. 1; Lichtenstein (1995, 318).
46. "Local 600 Apr–May 1952 IEB Administratorship," file 5, Box 250, Walter P. Reuther Collection, Wayne State University Labor Archives, Detroit, MI.
47. "Call for Meeting" Leaflet, file 1, Box 249, Walter P. Reuther Collection, Wayne State University Labor Archives, Detroit, MI.
48. The *Wage Earner* tried to calm the anger of "loyal right-wingers" who were "antagonistic to the administrators place over them by the International to erase Communist influence." The responsibly pro-Reuther newspaper advised its diminished ranks that they could "still switch the balance of power" to the right if they could somehow move beyond their "hereditary dislike of 'ordered thinking' from above." "Local 600 Right Wingers Kept Hopping Guarding Autonomy While Ousting Reds," *Wage Earner*, July, 1952, p. 3.
49. Walter Dorosh, at one time a CP-aligned leader, recalled, "[W]e started raising hell, and we took about a thousand guys, I guess, out to Solidarity House. I guess that scared [Reuther]. We had a big riot out in front of the building there." Stepan-Norris and Zeitlin (1996, 218).

    Although there is no reason to doubt that workers were angered by Reuther's decision to deny calls for elections, there is little evidence, other than that provided by Dorosh's memory, of any so-called "big riot" about elections. The only such "riot" confirmed by other sources was the 30-40 action at Solidarity House in November of 1951.
50. "The Defeat of Reuther in the Elections of #600" in "Reuther #4" file, Saul Wellman Collection (Unprocessed), Michigan State University Library, Special Collections Division.
51. Election Leaflet, "Local 600 Apr–May 1952 IEB Administratorship," file 5, Box 250, Walter P. Reuther Collection, Wayne State University Labor Archives, Detroit, MI.
52. "Right Wing Maps Strategy To Win Local 600 Election," *Wage Earner*, May 1952, p. 1.
53. "Right Wing Maps Strategy To Win Local 600 Election," *Wage Earner*, May 1952, p. 1.
54. Campaign Leaflet, file 18, box 249, Walter P. Reuther Collection, Wayne State University Labor Archives, Detroit, MI.
55. "Local 600 Right Wingers Kept Hopping Guarding Autonomy While Ousting Reds," *Wage Earner*, July, 1952, p. 3.
56. Campaign Leaflet, file 18, box 249, Walter P. Reuther Collection, Wayne State University Labor Archives, Detroit, MI.
57. "Many Upsets in UAW Elections," *Militant*, August 11, 1952.
58. Campaign Leaflet, file 18, box 249, Walter P. Reuther Collection, Wayne State University Labor Archives, Detroit, MI.

59. See the many Campaign Leaflets, file 18, box 249, Walter P. Reuther Collection, Wayne State University Labor Archives, Detroit, MI.
60. "UAW Woos Ford Workers with Highbrow Tabloid," *Wage Earner*, July 1952, p. 3.
61. "UAW Woos Ford Workers with Highbrow Tabloid," *Wage Earner*, July 1952, p. 3.
62. Campaign Leaflets, file 18, box 249, Walter P. Reuther Collection, Wayne State University Labor Archives, Detroit, MI.
63. The name John Swift was a pseudonym for Gil Green. See Levenstein (1981, 327fn5).
64. "Some Problems of Work in Right-Led Unions," *Political Affairs*, April 1952, p. 31
65. "Some Problems of Work in Right-Led Unions, II," *Political Affairs*, May 1952, p. 31.
66. "Reuther's Seizure of the Ford Local," *Political Affairs*, July 1952, p. 13.
67. "Reuther's Seizure of the Ford Local," *Political Affairs*, July 1952, pp. 13–15.
68. "Reuther's Seizure of the Ford Local," *Political Affairs*, July 1952, pp. 18–19.
69. "Some Problems of Work in Right-Led Unions, II," *Political Affairs*, May 1952, p. 32.
70. "Auto Workers Urge Govt Accept Malenkov Peace Bid," *Worker*, March 29, 1953, p. 1; "Reuther Talks Peace," *Worker*, May 3, 1953. Malenkov was the General-Secretary of the Soviet Union in the immediate aftermath of Stalin's death.
71. "Auto Workers Urge Govt Accept Malenkov Peace Bid," *Worker*, March 29, 1953, p. 1.
72. *Worker*, May 3, 1953.
73. "The Ford Local Union Election," *Political Affairs*, November 1952, p. 31.
74. "Reuther Talks Peace," *Worker*, May 3, 1953.
75. See, for example, the article about Reuther and Ford Motor Company, "Reuther Plan for Peace Economy," *Worker*, April 19, 1953.
76. *Worker*, January 18, 1953.
77. *Worker* (National Edition), January 25, 1953.
78. "Michigan Communist Party, 1950s," file 31, box 31, Nat Ganley Collection, Wayne State University Labor Archives, Detroit, MI.
79. "Michigan Communist Party, 1950s," file 31, box 31, Nat Ganley Collection, Wayne State University Labor Archives, Detroit, MI.

Nelson Lichtenstein suggests that CP activists like Walter Dorosh "reached a mutual accommodation" in 1955 when Reuther needed the help of old-time Communists to defuse a revolt of skilled trades workers. This revolt is particularly ironic because it demonstrates the degree to which Reuther's "new" social unionism was based, in part, on the strategy of supplementing the insufficient labor market leverage of production workers by linking them with the old craft leverage of the remaining skilled workers in the big auto companies. As skilled workers recognized that Reuther was relying on them to subsidize the wages of production workers without embracing any strategy for building autonomous market leverage for production workers (e.g., shorter workweek), these skilled workers increasingly refused to "go down" with the production worker ship.

Some CP activists, notably John Orr, president of the Rouge tool and die workers, had championed that crusade. See *Worker*, beginning May 6, 1951. Lichtenstein correctly notes that Reuther wanted to get the Communists to abandon various rank-and-file struggles, but he does not mention the reason for the Communist accommodation to Reuther. Although undoubtedly a minor oversight, the point is important, lest it seem as though the CP had reached an accommodation with Reuther because he had transformed his labor movement program in some substantive way that satisfied these "militants." See Lichtenstein (1995, 323).
80. Pintzuk (1997, 158–59).

CHAPTER 3

1. "Admitting Poor Early Strategy Ford Right Wingers Race Time to Hammer Out Slate, Program," *Wage Earner*, August 1952, p. 1.
2. "Anti-Reutherites Win Ford Local Election," *Militant*, September 22, 1952.
3. See "Local 600 1947–52 Political Pamphlets, Literature," folder 18, box 249, Walter P. Reuther Collection, Wayne State University Labor Archives, Detroit, MI.
4. See "Local 600 1947–52 Political Pamphlets, Literature," folder 18, box 249, Walter P. Reuther Collection, Wayne State University Labor Archives, Detroit, MI. See "Admitting Poor Early Strategy Ford Right Wingers Race Time to Hammer out Slate, Program," *Wage Earner*, August 1952, p. 1; "Many Upsets in UAW Elections," *Militant*, August 11, 1952.
5. "The Defeat of Reuther in the Elections of #600" in "Reuther #4" file, Saul Wellman Collection (Unprocessed), Michigan State University Library, Special Collections Division.
   Johnson also served as defense attorney for the five accused Communists. In an interview with Stepan-Norris and Zeitlin, Johnson's recollection of this period contains a comment that is unintelligible without an understanding of the CP's new pro-Reuther "peace" agenda. "So," Johnson recalled, "when they held the election, we defeated every one of them. The membership returned all the guys to office ... We had a certified public accountant who supervised the election and we swept the election and defeated all of the Reuther team. So, after that time we sat down, and we felt, 'Well, maybe the fight has gone on long enough. Maybe, we ought to seek an accommodation on each side'—and that's what happened."
   Johnson was asked, "When did that happen?" "In 1952–53," he responded, "and from then on, there was very little infighting between the local and the international union."
   Stepan-Norris and Zeitlin asked, "Was that a policy of Carl Stellato?" Johnson was reluctant to attach Stellato's name to the peace deal. "It was a

policy that we all more or less agreed to. I myself felt that it was becoming destructive, and it was not really doing the local union, or the international union, for that matter, any good." See Stepan-Norris and Zeitlin (1996, 216).

6. "Election Results from Local 600," *Worker*, August 31, 1952, p. 11.

7. "Labor Notes," *Fortune*, September 1952, p. 74.

8. "Labor Notes," *Fortune*, September 1952, p. 74.

9. "Admitting Poor Early Strategy Ford Right Wingers Race Time to Hammer Out Slate, Program," *Wage Earner*, August 1952, p. 1.

10. "Admitting Poor Early Strategy Ford Right Wingers Race Time to Hammer Out Slate, Program," *Wage Earner*, August 1952, p. 1.

11. "Admitting Poor Early Strategy Ford Right Wingers Race Time to Hammer Out Slate, Program," *Wage Earner*, August 1952, p. 1.

12. "Admitting Poor Early Strategy Ford Right Wingers Race Time to Hammer Out Slate, Program," *Wage Earner*, August 1952, p. 1.

13. "Right Wing Charges 'Whitewash' as UAW Administrators Concede Local 600 to Stellato Machine," *Wage Earner*, September 1952, p. 1; "End of UAW-Reuther Era Seen in Events at 600," *Wage Earner*, September 1952, p. 1.

14. "Right Wing Charges 'Whitewash' as UAW Administrators Concede Local 600 to Stellato Machine," *Wage Earner*, September 1952, p. 1.

15. Andrew (1979, 254).

16. "Right Wing Settles Down to Era of Watch and Wait," *Wage Earner*, October 1952, p. 3; "The Defeat of Reuther in the Elections of #600" in "Reuther #4" file, Saul Wellman Collection (Unprocessed), Michigan State University Library, Special Collections Division; Cochran (1977, 328).

One excellent historian, Harvey Levenstein, makes the mistake of prematurely "writing off" Local 600. Levenstein (1981, 317) suggests, "Many months of continuing rule by the Reuther emissaries and the purges finally paid off with the victory in the next elections of a pro-Reuther slate of committeemen to accompany Stellato, who ran unopposed, into office. The last outpost of Communist strength in the UAW had been beaten down mainly through bureaucratic power."

Lichtenstein (1995, 318–19) suggests that the administratorship "turned into an enormous embarrassment" and that "Reuther's humiliation at the Rouge proved but one index of his declining capacity to mobilize a politically coherent movement." According to Lichtenstein (1995, 318–19) Stellato remained "a thorn in Reuther's side for the balance of the decade" but suggests that "Reuther's real problem was that his faction had lost the capacity to reproduce itself when it was not in control of the union apparatus." During the administratorship, however, Reuther was in control of the union apparatus.

17. "Backstage Agreement at Ford," *Business Week*, September 6, 1952, p. 165.

18. "How Administrators Kept 'Hands Off' Ford Facts Policy," *Wage Earner*, September 1952.

19. "In the Middle," *Business Week*, September 20, 1952, p. 145.

20. "UAW Showdown," *Business Week*, May 2, 1953, p. 155.

21. "Labor," *Fortune*, October 1952, p. 94.

22. "In the Middle," *Business Week*, September 20, 1952, p. 145; "End of UAW-Reuther Era Seen in Events at 600," *Wage Earner*, September 1952, p. 1; "Before Convention Starts: Local 600's Threats of Fireworks Fizzle," *Wage Earner*, March 1953, p. 1.

23. "Right Wing Charges 'Whitewash' as UAW Administrators Concede Local 600 to Stellato Machine," *Wage Earner*, September 1952, p. 1; "UAW Replies to Charge," *New York Times*, December 31, 1952, p. 2; "UAW Showdown," *Business Week*, May 2, 1953, p. 155.

24. *Ford Facts*, February 28, 1953.

25. Proceedings of the Eleventh Convention, UAW-CIO, Atlantic City, NJ, November 9–14, 1947, p. 15.

26. Proceedings of the Eleventh Convention, UAW-CIO, Atlantic City, NJ, November 9–14, 1947.

27. The 1955 *Labor Fact Book* noted, "The word 'automation' has come into use during the past two years to describe the automatic production of goods with a minimum of human assistance—also called push-button methods of production ... The Ford Motor Co. has taken the lead in applying automation to manufacture. At Ford's engine plant in Cleveland, Ohio, installed in March, 1952, electronic 'brains' operating from several big panels control the huge assembly lines ... In one section it now takes only three machines and nine men to do the same job that was formerly done by 29 machines and 39 men" (Labor Research Associates (1955, 34).

28. Proceedings of the Fourteenth Convention, UAW-CIO, Atlantic City, NJ, March 22–27, 1953, p. 144.

29. In his discussion of "Collective Bargaining" and the UAW, Jack Stieber notes that this "Thirty-Hour Week" resolution constituted the "first major debate on a collective bargaining issue" to be brought before delegates. He also asserts that the resolution "was an obvious attempt by the Reuther administration to rout the forces supporting the shorter workweek rather than the guaranteed annual wage as the major demand for the 1955 negotiations, and at the same time to puncture a growing opposition led by Carl Stellato, president of Ford Local 600." Stieber (1962, 45).

30. Proceedings of the Fourteenth Convention, UAW-CIO, Atlantic City, NJ, March 22–27, 1953, p. 150.

31. Proceedings of the Fourteenth Convention, UAW-CIO, Atlantic City, NJ, March 22–27, 1953, p. 150.

32. Proceedings of the Fourteenth Convention, UAW-CIO, Atlantic City, NJ, March 22–27, 1953, p. 150.

The resolution included the practical demand that an education campaign be initiated, not to inform the membership of the importance of the shorter workweek, but "to inform the membership of the political sources of the demand for a 30-hour week" (Proceedings of the Fourteenth Convention, UAW-CIO, Atlantic City, NJ, March 22–27, 1953, p. 152).

33. Proceedings of the Fourteenth Convention, UAW-CIO, Atlantic City, NJ, March 22–27, 1953, p. 151.

34. Ibid, p. 150.

35. Ibid, p. 151.

36. Ibid, pp. 151–52.

Reflecting upon the argument that "with less work there is less produced," Jack Stieber notes, "In its zeal to discredit supporters of the shorter workweek, the Resolutions Committee even espoused a theory . . . generally put forth by management groups and disavowed by unions" (Stieber 1962, 46).

37. Proceedings of the Fourteenth Convention, UAW-CIO, Atlantic City, NJ, March 22–27, 1953, pp. 151–52.

38. Emphasis in original. Proceedings of the Fourteenth Convention, UAW-CIO, Atlantic City, NJ, March 22–27, 1953, p. 152.

39. Proceedings of the Fourteenth Convention, UAW-CIO, Atlantic City, NJ, March 22–27, 1953, p. 151.

40. Ibid, p. 155.

41. Ibid, pp. 158–59.

42. Ibid, p. 159.

43. Ibid, p. 159.

44. Ibid, pp. 156–57.

45. Ibid, p. 152.

46. Ibid, p. 159.

Local 600 submitted a total of twenty-eight different resolutions to the convention. As the convention began, the resolution that received the most attention was one "which specifies flatly that all future contracts should have one year's life." See "Auto Wages: The Five-Year Contract Faces General Assault at UAW Convention," *Wall Street Journal*, March 21, 1953, p. 1.

Local 600 allegedly sent copies of its resolutions to 900 local unions of the UAW. This certainly explains some of Reuther's defensiveness. See "Local 600 Resolutions for UAW Convention," *Worker* (National Edition), January 25, 1953.

47. Proceedings of the Fourteenth Convention, UAW-CIO, Atlantic City, NJ, March 22–27, 1953, p. 153.

48. Ibid, p. 153.

49. Ibid, p. 155.

50. Ibid, p. 154.

Reuther responded to the charge that the UAW had become undemocratic. Reuther asked, "How do you keep a union free and democratic with rank-and-file control and yet prevent a small group of people who will hide behind all the democratic slogans, who will exploit all the democratic privileges from tearing the guts out of the organization? It is not easy. That is how unions get bureaucratic . . . so you can chop down anybody who raises a voice. We don't want that kind of a union . . . but . . . we are going to protect [the union] against the small minority." (Proceedings of the Fourteenth Convention, UAW-CIO, Atlantic City, NJ, March 22–27, 1953, p. 163).

51. Proceedings of the Fourteenth Convention, UAW-CIO, Atlantic City, NJ, March 22–27, 1953, p. 153.
52. Ibid, p. 156.
53. Ibid, p. 153.
54. Ibid, pp. 155–156.
55. Ibid, p. 157.
56. Mike Donnelly, a unit leader at Local 600, challenged Reuther to test the resolution's support with a roll-call vote. Reuther responded that, according to the UAW Constitution, Donnelly was within his rights to call for such a vote, so long as 775 delegates supported his demand. Reuther then asked for a show of hands in favor of a roll-call vote, ruled that "there are less than 125 hands up," and put the issue to rest without leaving behind a record of delegate voting behavior. Proceedings of the Fourteenth Convention, UAW-CIO, Atlantic City, NJ, March 22–27, 1953, p. 162.
57. Proceedings of the Fourteenth Convention, UAW-CIO, Atlantic City, NJ, March 22–27, 1953, p. 182.
58. Proceedings of the Fourteenth Convention, UAW-CIO, Atlantic City, NJ, March 22–27, 1953, pp. 119–128; Stieber (1962, 147–148); "Guaranteed Wages: UAW Parley to Vote on Proposal Aimed at 'Full-Time' Employment," *Wall Street Journal*, March 24, 1952, p. 2.
59. Proceedings of the Fourteenth Convention, UAW-CIO, Atlantic City, NJ, March 22–27, 1953, pp. 191–198.
60. As noted above, Reuther would soon receive similarly "kind treatment" from the Communist Press in appreciation for his willingness to talk "peace" in relation to the Soviets. "Reuther Plan for Peace Economy," *Worker*, April 19, 1953.
61. Proceedings of the Fourteenth Convention, UAW-CIO, Atlantic City, NJ, March 22–27, 1953, p. 201.
   Moore's reference to Reuther's alleged "pro-Soviet" past was centered upon a famous postcard sent from the Soviet Union and signed by "Walt and Vic" Reuther. The note on the card concluded, "Yes . . . we must Sovietize Ford and Detroit, and I will go even further . . . we must Sovietize America."
   Reuther denied that he wrote the letter. He told the delegates, "The Communist Party has been peddling that letter for years along with every fascist group in America . . . I will sit before any Congressional Committee any day of the week and I will swear under oath and take all the risk involved that I never wrote such a letter at any time . . . Now, my brother, Victor . . . also denies that he wrote the letter." Proceedings of the Fourteenth Convention, UAW-CIO, Atlantic City, NJ, March 22–27, 1953, pp. 206–207.
62. Proceedings of the Fourteenth Convention, UAW-CIO, Atlantic City, NJ, March 22–27, 1953, p. 210.

63. Proceedings of the Fourteenth Convention, UAW-CIO, Atlantic City, NJ, March 22–27, 1953, p. 211.

64. Stellato was quite harsh in recalling the fact that UAW staffers testified against Local 600 members before the HUAC. Referring to Romano, Stellato suggested, "I am just trying to point out to you in order to be a hero and deserve a Congressional Medal, and maybe even stay on the International pay roll in the cases of some guys, maybe you have to go down to the Un-American Activities Committee." The comment about testifying in order to stay on the payroll was undoubtedly a reference to Tappes, who, unlike Romano, was a reluctant and relatively uncooperative witness. Proceedings of the Fourteenth Convention, UAW-CIO, Atlantic City, NJ, March 22–27, 1953, p. 212.

65. The convention transcript actually recorded the date of the Detroit *Times* article as "October 11, 1950," but the article described appeared on October 11, 1951.

66. Proceedings of the Fourteenth Convention, UAW-CIO, Atlantic City, NJ, March 22–27, 1953, pp. 212–14.

67. Ibid, p. 213.

68. Ibid, pp. 222–223.

69. Ibid.

70. Ibid.

71. Proceedings of the Fourteenth Convention, UAW-CIO, Atlantic City, NJ, March 22–27, 1953, p. 214.
    For details about the famous May 26, 1937 "Battle" at the overpass near Gate 4 of the Rouge complex, see Lichtenstein (1995, 83–87).

72. Proceedings of the Fourteenth Convention, UAW-CIO, Atlantic City, NJ, March 22–27, 1953, p. 224.

73. Proceedings of the Fourteenth Convention, UAW-CIO, Atlantic City, NJ, March 22–27, 1953, pp. 224–229.

CHAPTER 4

1. "Election Results," *Business Week*, May 16, 1953, p. 168.

2. Reuther's hostility toward the NNLC is briefly discussed in Korstad and Lichtenstein (1988) and in Harris (1982, 264).

3. "UAW Showdown," *Business Week*, May 2, 1953, p. 155.

4. "Left Wingers Win Top Posts at Local 600," *Wage Earner*, June 1953.

5. "Ford Local Vote Victory for Autonomy," *Worker*, May, 17, 1953. *Business Week* reported a "2-to-1 margin" of victory for Stellato ("Election Results," *Business Week*, May 16, 1953, p. 168).

6. "Election Results," *Business Week*, May 16, 1953, p. 168.

7. "Reuther Foe Wins Election," *Wall Street Journal*, May 9, 1953, p. 2.

8. "Stellato Slate Wins Ford 600 Elections," *Militant*, May 18, 1953; "Ford Local Vote Victory for Autonomy," *Worker*, May, 17, 1953.

9. "Left Wingers Win Top Posts at Local 600," *Wage Earner*, June 1953.

10. "Stellato Slate Wins Ford 600 Elections," *Militant*, May 18, 1953; "Ford Local Vote Victory for Autonomy," *Worker*, May, 17, 1953.
11. "Election Results," *Business Week*, May 16, 1953, p. 168.
12. "Election Results," *Business Week*, May 16, 1953, p. 168.
13. "Election Results," *Business Week*, May 16, 1953, p. 168.
14. "Jitters in Detroit," *Fortune*, October 1953, p. 120.
15. For Murphy's electoral platform, see "Mass Caravan Will Demand More Jobless Aid in Michigan," *Militant*, March 1, 1954.
16. "Signs of Slump Point Up Demand to Slash Hours," *Militant*, August 3, 1953, p. 1.
17. "Jitters in Detroit," *Fortune*, October 1953, p. 120. In a telegram, Mazey and Ed Cote, director of the Kaiser division, formally stated, "We demand you rescind this cancellation of the Kaiser Motors Corp. aircraft contracts … and give the UAW, as representatives of the workers whose livelihood you have endangered, an opportunity to be heard" ("UAW Hits Cancellation," *Wall Street Journal*, June 25, 1953, p. 2).
18. "Jitters in Detroit," *Fortune*, October 1953, p. 120; *Militant*, August 3, 1953.
19. "California CIO Backs 30-Hour Week Program," *Militant*, November 23, 1953.
20. "Letter from Stellato to Reuther—November 12, 1953," folder 12, box 250, Walter P. Reuther Collection, Wayne State University Labor Archives, Detroit, MI.
21. *Ford Facts*, November 21, 1953.
22. "Reuther 'Not Disturbed,'" *New York Times*, April 27, 1953, p. 19.
23. *Ford Facts*, November 21, 1953.
24. *Ford Facts*, November 21, 1953. Emphasis in original.
25. *Ford Facts*, November 21, 1953.
26. *Ford Facts*, November 21, 1953.
27. See "Letter from Stellato to Reuther," in file 3, box 250, Walter P. Reuther Collection, Wayne State University Labor Archives, Detroit, MI.
28. "Muddle-Headed Logic Characterizes Demand for 30-Hour Week," *Wage Earner*, December 1953, p. 1; "Ford 600 Offers Fighting Program on Unemployment," *Militant*, November 30, 1953, p. 1.
29. For Weinberg's document, see "Final Draft" (November 11, 1953) in "Shorter Workweek, 1956–61" file, box 59, UAW Research Department Collection, Wayne State University Labor Archives, Detroit, MI.
30. "Final Draft (November 11, 1953)" in "Shorter Workweek, 1956-61" file, box 59, UAW Research Department Collection, Wayne State University Labor Archives, Detroit, MI.
31. "Final Draft" (November 11, 1953) in "Shorter Workweek, 1956–61" file, box 59, UAW Research Department Collection, Wayne State University Labor Archives, Detroit, MI.
32. "Final Draft" (November 11, 1953) in "Shorter Workweek, 1956–61" file, box 59, UAW Research Department Collection, Wayne State University Labor Archives, Detroit, MI.

33. *Ford Facts*, December 12, 1953.

34. "Economic Security—Plans and Ballyhoo," *American Socialist*, February 1954, p. 16.

35. *Ford Facts*, December 12, 1953.

36. "Autotown Alley," *Worker*, January 24, 1954, p. 15.

37. "Mass Caravan Will Demand More Jobless Aid in Michigan," *Militant*, March 1, 1954.

38. "GM Lie of 'Healthy Economy' Exploded by Chevrolet Union," *Militant*, February 15, 1954.

39. "UAW Board Takes Over Flint Local," *Wall Street Journal*, May 10, 1954, p. 2; *Labor Action*, May 17, 1954; *Labor Action*, June 14, 1954. See also, Stieber (1962, 142–143).

40. "Proceedings of the International Economic Conference, UAW-CIO, November 12–13, 1954, Detroit, Michigan" in box 75, UAW Region 6 Collection, Wayne State University Labor Archives, Detroit, MI, p. 150.

41. "Proceedings of the International Economic Conference, UAW-CIO, November 12–13, 1954, Detroit, Michigan" in box 75, UAW Region 6 Collection, Wayne State University Labor Archives, Detroit, MI, p. 167.

42. "Proceedings of the International Economic Conference, UAW-CIO, November 12–13, 1954, Detroit, Michigan" in box 75, UAW Region 6 Collection, Wayne State University Labor Archives, Detroit, MI, pp. 154, 168.

43. "Reuther Warns UAW Would Strike to Win Demands; Union Set to Authorize Walkout at Chrysler Plants," *Wall Street Journal*, November 15, 1954, p. 2. See also, "Behind UAW's Goals for 1955," *Business Week*, November 20, 1954, p. 166.

44. *Ford Facts*, November 20, 1954.

45. In 1959, for example, nine of every ten delegates to the UAW convention were union officers. Twenty-five percent were local presidents. Nevertheless, "fully 45 percent were attending their first convention as delegates" (Stieber 1962, 17).

46. Stieber (1962, 101).

47. See Stieber (1962, 100–101).

48. For this assessment, see "Michigan Family Spat: "U.A.W. Local Head Shakes Up Democrats by Challenging Incumbent in House Race," *Wall Street Journal*, July 17, 1958, p. 10.

49. Proceedings of the Fourteenth Convention, UAW-CIO, Cleveland, OH, March 27–April 1, 1955.

50. "Fifteenth Convention of the Auto Union," *American Socialist*, May 1955, p. 10.

51. "Fifteenth Convention of the Auto Union," *American Socialist*, May 1955, p. 10.

52. "Fifteenth Convention of the Auto Union," *American Socialist*, May 1955, p. 10. See also, "Reuther Slate Wins Top U.A.W. Posts Despite Surprise Challenge," *Wall Street Journal*, March 31, 1955, p. 2.

53. Proceedings of the Fourteenth Convention, UAW-CIO, Cleveland, OH, March 27–April 1, 1955, pp. 194–195.

54. "Auto Union Convention Shows Organized Left-Wing Needed," *Militant*, April 11, 1955, p. 1.

55. Proceedings of the Fourteenth Convention, UAW-CIO, Cleveland, OH, March 27–April 1, 1955, pp. 194–195.

56. Ibid.

57. Ibid.

58. Ibid.

59. Ernest Mazey, a dissident UAW activist—and brother of the UAW Secretary Treasurer, Emil Mazey—reported that "the so-called 'pork-choppers,' the paid international representatives, worked all night [the night before the roll call vote] and half the next morning, trying to get the situation under control." See "What's Ahead for Labor? A Symposium," *American Socialist*, December 1955, p. 12.

60. Proceedings of the Fourteenth Convention, UAW-CIO, Cleveland, OH, March 27–April 1, 1955, pp. 376–575. Stieber (1962, 62) noted that this was "the last and most serious" challenge to the vice-presidential candidates faced by the Reuther administration.

61. "Ford Local 600 Election Results," *Militant*, June 6, 1955; *Ford Facts*, May 14, 1955.

62. *Ford Facts*, May 14, 1955. See also, "Ford, 1955" file in box 4, Nat Ganley Collection, Wayne State University Labor Archives, Detroit, MI.

63. "Ford Settles for Semi-Annual Jobless Benefits Supplement," *Militant*, June 13, 1955, p. 1.

64. "Labor News," *Wall Street Journal*, June 8, 1955, p. 2; "Settlement in Auto," *American Socialist*, July 1955, p. 8; "Ford Settles for Semi-Annual Jobless Benefits Supplement," *Militant*, June 13, 1955, p. 1.

65. "Stumbling Blocks to G.A.W.," *Fortune*, August 1955, p. 55.

66. Glaberman (1984).

67. "Stumbling Blocks to G.A.W.," *Fortune*, August 1955, p. 55.

68. Cited in "Settlement in Auto," *American Socialist*, July 1955, p. 8.

69. "Settlement in Auto," *American Socialist*, July 1955, p. 9.

70. "Stumbling Blocks to G.A.W.," *Fortune*, August 1955, p. 55; "Settlement in Auto," *American Socialist*, July 1955, p. 8; "Ford Settles for Semi-Annual Jobless Benefits Supplement," *Militant*, June 13, 1955, p. 1.

71. "Settlement in Auto," *American Socialist*, July 1955, p. 9.

72. Quoted in "Why the Ford Workers Dislike Contract," *Militant*, June 20, 1955, p. 3.

73. "Settlement in Auto," *American Socialist*, July 1955, p. 8.

74. "Don't Put All Your Eggs in One Basket," *Worker*, May 9, 1954, p. 3.

75. "Ford Settles for Semi-Annual Jobless Benefits Supplement," *Militant*, June 13, 1955, p. 1; "Estimate of the 1955 Contract Struggle in Auto" in the "Labor—UAW Auto 1954" file, Saul Wellman Collection (Unprocessed), Michigan State University Library, Special Collections Division.

76. "Ford Settles for Semi-Annual Jobless Benefits Supplement," *Militant*, June 13, 1955, p. 1; "Settlement in Auto," *American Socialist*, July 1955, p. 9.
77. "Stumbling Blocks to G.A.W.," *Fortune*, August 1955, p. 55; "Demands of Auto Workers Shown During Strikes," *Militant*, June 27, 1955, p. 1.
78. "Stumbling Blocks to G.A.W.," *Fortune*, August 1955, p. 55.

CHAPTER 5

1. Proceedings of the Sixteenth Convention, UAW-AFL-CIO, Atlantic City, NJ, April 7–12, 1957, p. 19.
2. Proceedings of the Sixteenth Convention, UAW-AFL-CIO, Atlantic City, NJ, April 7–12, 1957, p. 19.
3. Quoted—from the 1957 convention proceedings—in "After the Auto Settlement," *American Socialist*, December 1958, p. 5.
4. Proceedings of the Sixteenth Convention, UAW-AFL-CIO, Atlantic City, NJ, April 7–12, 1957, p. 159.
5. Proceedings of the Sixteenth Convention, UAW-AFL-CIO, Atlantic City, NJ, April 7–12, 1957, pp. 163–168. Dallesandro's comment was also published in "Next Big Labor Issue: Shorter Work Week," *Business Week*, April 20, 1957, p. 42.
6. Proceedings of the Sixteenth Convention, UAW-AFL-CIO, Atlantic City, NJ, April 7–12, 1957, p. 243.
7. "UAW's Goal Is Cold Cash," *Business Week*, April 13, 1957, p. 155.
8. "Two Caucus Meetings," *Militant*, April 15, 1957, p. 2.
9. *Ford Facts*, May 11, 1957; "Stellato Wins," *Business Week*, May 18, 1957, p. 157.
10. "UAW Opens . . . ," *Business Week*, May 11, 1957, p. 154; "Reuther Requests Auto Men to Join in Study of Shorter Work Week," *Wall Street Journal*, May 3, 1957, p. 13; "UAW Press Release, Thursday May 2, 1957," in box 6, Ken Bannon Collection, Wayne State University Labor Archives, Detroit, MI.
11. "GM Spurns Invitation By UAW for a Study of Shorter Work Week," *Wall Street Journal*, May 8, 1957, p. 4; "Ford Rejects UAW Proposal to Study Short Work Week," May 14, 1957, p. 4; "UAW Opens," *Business Week*, May 11, 1957, p. 154.
12. For a transcript of the address, see "UAW Union Democracy" file, box 17, Daniel Bell Collection, Tamiment Institute Library, New York University. Back in 1953, Daniel Bell, writing in *Fortune*, had suggested a relationship between labor militancy and technological innovation. "[L]abor demands have helped give U.S. capitalism [a] dynamic quality . . . By becoming costly, labor has spurred industry to more efficient planning and to mechanization" ("The Next American Labor Movement," *Fortune*, April 1953, p. 123).
13. "Radio Reports, Inc. Memo to UAW" in file 4, box 59, UAW Research Department Collection, Wayne State University Labor Archives, Detroit, MI.
14. "Big Three Auto Makers Expected to Reject Reuther's Proposal for $100 a Car Reduction in 1958 Prices," *Wall Street Journal*, August 19, 1957, p. 2; "Opening Gun," *Business Week*, August 24, 1957, p. 34; "Reuther Offers

Auto 'Big 3' Wages Deal for Cut in Prices," *Militant*, August 26, 1957, p. 1; "Reuther's Wage-Price Proposal Puts Auto Industry on the Spot," *Labor Action*, August 26, 1957, p. 1.

15. "Curtice Snubs Reuther Plan to Cut '58 Car Prices $100, But Has Own Proposal: Extend Wage Pacts 2 Years," *Wall Street Journal*, August 23, 1957, p. 2; "Ford, Chrysler Reject Reuther Bid for Price Cuts, Ask Lower Wages," August 26, 1957, p. 5; "Auto Heads Decide to Parry Blow with Blow," *Business Week*, August 31, 1957, p. 104; "Auto 'Big 3' Reject Reuther's Price-Wage Deal," *Militant*, September 2, 1957.

16. "Companies View Reuther Proposal As Clever Move in '58 Negotiations," *Labor Action*, September 9, 1957, p. 3.

17. "UAW Leads Cause of Whole People in Fight Against Profit Inflation," *Labor Action*, September 9, 1957, p. 1.

18. "Reuther Asks President to Support Plea for $100 Cut on 1958 Autos," *Wall Street Journal*, August 20, 1957, p. 22; "UAW Leads Cause of Whole People In Fight Against Profit Inflation," *Labor Action*, September 9, 1957, p. 1.

19. "UAW Leads Cause of Whole People in Fight Against Profit Inflation," *Labor Action*, September 9, 1957, p. 1.

20. "Auto Heads Decide to Parry Blow with Blow," *Business Week*, August 31, 1957, p. 104; "UAW Concentrates on Wages," October 26, 1957, p. 155; "Ford Says Labor Costs Caused Price Hikes on Both 1957, 1958 Cars," *Wall Street Journal*, November 5, 1957, p. 20.

21. "UAW Concentrates on Wages, October 26, 1957, p. 155.

22. "Stalemate in Detroit," *Fortune*, October 1957, p. 239.

23. "UAW Leads Cause of Whole People in Fight Against Profit Inflation," *Labor Action*, September 9, 1957, p. 4.

24. *Ford Facts*, August 24, 1957. Emphasis in original.

25. *Ford Facts*, October 26, 1957.

26. *Ford Facts*, November 16, 1957.

27. *Ford Facts*, November 2, 1957.

28. *Ford Facts*, November 16, 1957.

29. Stieber (1962, 48); "Auto Executives Assail UAW Profit-Split Plan," *Detroit Free Press*, January 14, 1958, p. 1.

30. Quoted in "Walter Reuther Presents A New Program for the UAW," *Labor Action*, January 27, 1958, p. 2.

31. "Walter Reuther Presents A New Program for the UAW," *Labor Action*, January 27, 1958, p. 2; "Auto Executives Assail UAW Profit-Split Plan," *Detroit Free Press*, January 14, 1958, p. 1.

32. "Poor Carl! Up Against Reuther, the Russians," *Detroit Times*, January 19, 1958; "Walter Reuther Presents a New Program for the UAW," *Labor Action*, January 27, 1958, p. 2.

33. "UAW to Ask Auto Makers to Share Pre-Tax Profit Over 10% of Net Capital; Drops 4-Day Week Demand," *Wall Street Journal*, January 14, 1958, p. 3; "Walter Reuther Presents a New Program for the UAW," *Labor Action*, January 27, 1958, p. 2.

34. "Big 3 Tells UAW: NO," *Detroit Times*, January 14, 1958, p. 1; "Big 3 to Fight UAW Profit Plan," *Detroit News*, January 14, 1958, p. 1; "Auto Executives Assail UAW Profit-Split Plan," *Detroit Free Press*, January 14, 1958, p. 1.
35. "The Reuther Plan—Advance or Retreat," *American Socialist*, March 1958, p. 8.
36. "Big 3 Tells UAW: NO," *Detroit Times*, January 14, 1958, p. 1; "Big 3 to Fight UAW Profit Plan," *Detroit News*, January 14, 1958, p. 1; "Auto Executives Assail UAW Profit-Split Plan," *Detroit Free Press*, January 14, 1958, p. 1.
37. "Auto Executives Assail UAW Profit-Split Plan," *Detroit Free Press*, January 14, 1958, p. 1.
38. "Stellato to Battle Reuther," *Detroit Free Press*, January 14, 1958, p. 1.
39. "Stellato to Battle Reuther," *Detroit Free Press*, January 14, 1958, p. 1.
40. "Stellato Press Release, January 14, 1958" in box 6, Ken Bannon Collection, Wayne State University Labor Archives, Detroit, MI.
41. "UAW Revolt Grows on 4-Day Week Ban," *Detroit Times*, January 16, 1958.
42. "Short Week Vies with Profit Plan," *Detroit Free Press*, January 16, 1958; "UAW Revolt Grows on 4-Day Week Ban," *Detroit Times*, January 16, 1958.
43. The "dissident" status of this group is unclear, but some clues about the political culture of the locals can be drawn from the roll-call vote from the 1955 convention, during which Stellato was a candidate for vice president of the UAW. For example, in 1955 the Local 7 delegation—which included a young delegate (and future Congressman) named John Conyers—was entirely loyal to the Reuther administration. See the roll-call vote in proceedings of the Fourteenth Convention, UAW-CIO, Cleveland, OH, March 27–April 1, 1955, pp. 378–379, 416–417.
44. "UAW Bloc to Press Short-Week Demand: Would Ask for Profit Split, Too: 20 Union Officials in 'Rebel' Group," *Detroit Free Press*, January 17, 1958.
45. *Ford Facts*, January 18, 1958.
46. *Ford Facts*, January 18, 1958.
47. *Ford Facts*, January 18, 1958.
48. Proceedings of the Special Constitutional Convention, UAW-AFL-CIO, Detroit, MI, January 22–24, 1958, p. 59.
49. Ibid.
50. Ibid.
51. Ibid.
52. Proceedings of the Special Constitutional Convention, UAW-AFL-CIO, Detroit, MI, January 22–24, 1958, p. 70.
53. Ibid.
54. Ibid.
55. Ibid.
56. See "The Reuther Plan—Advance or Retreat," *American Socialist*, March 1958, p. 9.
57. Proceedings of the Special Constitutional Convention, UAW-AFL-CIO, Detroit, MI, January 22–24, 1958, pp. 91–92.
58. Ibid, p. 92.

59. Ibid, p. 67.
60. Ibid, p. 63.
61. Ibid, p. 64.
62. Ibid, p. 95.
    The *American Socialist* reported that Reuther probably overestimated his margin of victory. "A number of observers were of the opinion that a 25 percent delegate opposition was a closer figure, and with the heavier representation for delegates in the Michigan area, this would account for roughly a third of the convention. In the corridors, many delegates expressed reluctance to repudiate the leadership on the eve of negotiations" ("The Reuther Plan—Advance or Retreat," *American Socialist*, March 1958, p. 9).
63. Proceedings of the Special Constitutional Convention, UAW-AFL-CIO, Detroit, MI, January 22–24, 1958, p. 94.
64. Proceedings of the Special Constitutional Convention, UAW-AFL-CIO, Detroit, MI, January 22–24, 1958, p. 95.
65. The official transcription seems to have misquoted this candid delegate. In the record of the proceedings, the phrase is reported as, "If you want a place in the sun you have got to expect some whispers." However, a reporter for the *Militant* confirmed the more likely term, "blister." See Proceedings of the Special Constitutional Convention, UAW-AFL-CIO, Detroit, Michigan, January 22–24, 1958, p. 79; "At Auto Union Convention Big Locals Hit Reuther Gimmick," *Militant*, February 3, 1958, p. 1.
66. "At Auto Union Convention Big Locals Hit Reuther Gimmick," *Militant*, February 3, 1958, p. 1.
67. Proceedings of the Special Constitutional Convention, UAW-AFL-CIO, Detroit, MI, January 22–24, 1958, p. 95.
68. Proceedings of the Special Constitutional Convention, UAW-AFL-CIO, Detroit, MI, January 22–24, 1958, p. 96.
69. Proceedings of the Special Constitutional Convention, UAW-AFL-CIO, Detroit, MI, January 22–24, 1958, p. 95.
70. Ibid.
71. Ibid.
72. Ibid.
73. *Ford Facts*, March 15, 1958.
74. Ibid; "From 600 to 16?" *Wage Earner*, April 1958.
75. "Michigan Family Spat: U.A.W. Local Head Shakes Up Democrats by Challenging Incumbent in House Race," *Wall Street Journal*, July 17, 1958, p. 10; "From 600 to 16?" *Wage Earner*, April 1958; "Election Time," *Wage Earner*, July 1958; "Stellato Runs for Congress Against Fair Deal Democrat," *Labor Action*, August 11, 1958, p. 2.
76. "Stellato Runs for Congress Against Fair Deal Democrat," *Labor Action*, August 11, 1958, p. 2.
77. *Ford Facts*, March 29, 1958; "Stellato Runs for Congress Against Fair Deal Democrat," *Labor Action*, August 11, 1958, p. 2.

78. *"Challenger,* July 1958" in box 250, Walter P. Reuther Collection, Wayne State University Labor Archives, Detroit, MI.
79. "Stellato Runs for Congress Against Fair Deal Democrat," *Labor Action,* August 11, 1958, p. 2.
80. "From 600 to 16?" *Wage Earner,* April 1958.
81. "Stellato and Brown Defeated in Michigan Primaries," *Militant,* August 18, 1958.
82. "Michigan Family Spat: U.A.W. Local Head Shakes Up Democrats by Challenging Incumbent in House Race," *Wall Street Journal,* July 17, 1958, p. 10.
83. "Stellato and Brown Defeated in Michigan Primaries," *Militant,* August 18, 1958; "Michigan Communist Party, 1958," file 35, box 31, Nat Ganley Collection, Wayne State University Labor Archives, Detroit, MI.

CHAPTER 6

1. "UAW Won't Ask Short Work Week in Ford Talks, Union Official Says," *Wall Street Journal,* March 6, 1958, p. 2.
2. "UAW Won't Ask Short Work Week in Ford Talks, Union Official Says," *Wall Street Journal,* March 6, 1958, p. 2.
3. "UAW Won't Ask Short Work Week in Ford Talks, Union Official Says," *Wall Street Journal,* March 6, 1958, p. 2.
4. *Ford Facts,* May 24, 1958.
5. Lichtenstein is correct when he asserts, "For the next half-decade Reuther would hold but the weakest cards. The 1957–1958 recession proved a dress rehearsal for the disasters that would befall American unionism at the end of the Vietnam War boom." The only problem is that, by neglecting the historic struggle over the 30-40 demand, Lichtenstein does not indicate the degree to which Reuther's "hand"—and ours—is dealt by the house dealer, according to house rules, within the house of labor itself. To suppose, as Lichtenstein does, that labor is necessarily a dependent variable, inevitably at the mercy of "the economy"—that is, at the mercy of capital—is to abandon the very idea of an autonomous labor movement and move swiftly toward capitulation to the demands of capital. See Lichtenstein (1995, 349).
6. Boyle (1995, 135).
7. "Auto Workers Face Arrogant Corporations," *Militant,* May 26, 1958.
8. "Reuther Plans to Enter Contract Talks with General Motors Today," *Wall Street Journal,* September 5, 1958, p. 20; "Auto Workers Choose Ford as Target for Strike, Set September 17 Deadline; Move Is Termed a Surprise," *Wall Street Journal,* September 11, 1958, p. 2.
9. "Ford, UAW Sign 3-Year Contract Boosting Pensions, Jobless Pay, Skilled Workers' Wage, Other Benefits," *Wall Street Journal,* September 18, 1958, p. 3.
10. "Ford, UAW Sign 3-Year Contract Boosting Pensions, Jobless Pay, Skilled Workers' Wage, Other Benefits," *Wall Street Journal,* September 18, 1958, p. 2.
11. "Indicated Cost of Auto Labor Pacts to Big 3 is Below '55, Short of Reuther's Initial Goal," *Wall Street Journal,* October 6, 1958, p. 3.

12. "Indicated Cost of Auto Labor Pacts to Big 3 is Below '55, Short of Reuther's Initial Goal," *Wall Street Journal*, October 6, 1958, p. 3.
13. Stieber (1962, 51).
14. "Walkout at Ford Mill Cut Stell Output Last Week," *Wall Street Journal*, September 23, 1958, p. 5.
15. "Indicated Cost of Auto Labor Pacts to Big 3 is Below '55, Short of Reuther's Initial Goal," *Wall Street Journal*, October 6, 1958, p. 3; "After the Auto Settlement," *American Socialist*, December 1958, p. 5.
16. "Local 600 Leaflets, 1959–60" in box 10, UAW Ford Department Collection, Wayne State University Labor Archives, Detroit, MI.
17. "Memo from Boatin to Mazey" in file 20, box 250, Walter P. Reuther Collection, Wayne State University Labor Archives, Detroit, MI; "Local 600 Leaflets, 1959–60" in box 10, UAW Ford Department Collection, Wayne State University Labor Archives, Detroit, MI.
18. For the absence of any program in the campaign leaflets of the Stellato slate, see "Local 600 Leaflets, 1959–60" in box 10, UAW Ford Department Collection, Wayne State University Labor Archives, Detroit, MI.
19. "Local 600 Leaflets, 1959–60" in box 10, UAW Ford Department Collection, Wayne State University Labor Archives, Detroit, MI.
20. Ibid.
21. Ibid.
22. Ibid.
23. Ibid.
24. For Stellato's second Congressional run and Mazey's endorsement, see *Ford Facts*, April 30, 1960; June 18, 1960 and August 13, 1960.
25. Proceedings of the Seventeenth Convention, UAW-AFL-CIO, Atlantic City, NJ, October 9–16, 1959, p. 571.
    Stieber (1962, 51) noted, "UAW leaders, having once had to reverse their field on this issue were being careful not to be caught again in the same predicament."
26. See "UAW—Committee for Democratic Action in UAW" in the Art Fox Collection (Unprocessed), Michigan State University Library, Special Collections Division; "Labor," *Business Week*, March 12, 1960, p. 43.
27. "New Group Wins Attention in UAW," *Militant*, November 20, 1960; "UAW—Committee for Democratic Action in UAW" in the Art Fox Collection (Unprocessed), Michigan State University Library, Special Collections Division.
28. "New Group Wins Attention in UAW," *Militant*, November 20, 1960; "UAW—Committee for Democratic Action in UAW" in the Art Fox Collection (Unprocessed), Michigan State University Library, Special Collections Division.
29. "New Group Wins Attention in UAW," *Militant*, November 20, 1960.
30. Article from *Detroit Times*, February 22, 1960 in the Art Fox Collection (Unprocessed), Michigan State University Library, Special Collections Division. See also, Stieber (1962, 149–153).

31. *Ford Facts*, March 5, 1960. *Business Week* also quoted Reuther's prediction that "by 1975 we will have a four-day week as a general proposition, and in the auto industry and most other industries will get it far in advance of that." Emphasis added. "A Shorter Week, but Not in '59," *Business Week*, April 4, 1959, p. 61.

32. "UAW—Committee for Democratic Action in UAW" in the Art Fox Collection (Unprocessed), Michigan State University Library, Special Collections Division.

33. "New Group Wins Attention in UAW," *Militant*, November 20, 1960.

34. The reference to Reuther's "petrified program" was appropriated by the Rank and File Caucus from Stellato's own 1951 speeches. In an interesting slip, the leaflet also made reference to the NCFDA as a movement within the "UAW-CIO," rather than the UAW-AFL-CIO. See "Local 600, Leaflets, 1959–60" in box 10, UAW Ford Department Collection, Wayne State University Labor Archives, Detroit, MI.

35. "UAW Group Adopts Fighting Program," *Militant*, February 6, 1961.

36. "How Tough Can UAW Get?" *Business Week*, February 11, 1961, p. 55.

37. "Conway Memo, February 3, 1961" in box 250, Walter P. Reuther Collection, Wayne State University Labor Archives, Detroit, MI.

38. See Stieber (1962, 178n35).

39. This analysis of the racial politics and union factionalism draws its inspiration from Kornhauser (1952).

40. "Grandmothers Joining Fight over Ford Jobs," *Detroit News*, April 17, 1959. The *Detroit News* did not mention the racial composition of the women who stormed the Local 600 headquarters.

41. "Grandmothers Joining Fight over Ford Jobs," *Detroit News*, April 17, 1959.

42. Lichtenstein (1995).

43. See "UAW Local 600, 1960–" in the Art Fox Collection (Unprocessed), Michigan State University Library, Special Collections Division.

44. See "Local 600, Leaflets, 1959–60" in box 9, UAW Ford Department Collection, Wayne State University Labor Archives, Detroit, MI.

45. *Ford Facts*, December 17, 1960.

46. Article from *Detroit Free Press*, March 24, 1961, in "Local 600 Leaflets, 1959–60" in box 10, UAW Ford Department Collection, Wayne State University Labor Archives, Detroit, MI.

47. Article from *Detroit Free Press*, March 24, 1961, in "Local 600 Leaflets, 1959–60" in box 10, UAW Ford Department Collection, Wayne State University Labor Archives, Detroit, MI.

48. "If It's Time for a Change, You Ought to Know . . ." Leaflet, in box 9, UAW Ford Department Collection, Wayne State University Labor Archives, Detroit, MI.

49. Stieber (1962, 148).

50. See "UAW Local 600, 1960–" in the Art Fox Collection (Unprocessed), Michigan State University Library, Special Collections Division.

51. Article from *Detroit Free Press*, March 25, 1961, in "Local 600 Leaflets, 1959–60" in box 10, UAW Ford Department Collection, Wayne State University Labor Archives, Detroit, MI.

52. The charge was made in a letter from James Theriet of Local 600 to Walter P. Reuther, dated July 18, 1961. See "Theriet letter" in box 250, Walter P. Reuther Collection, Wayne State University Labor Archives, Detroit, MI.

53. None of the historical records reviewed presented a TULC account of any alleged meeting with Stellato. For Stellato's version, see "If It's Time for a Change, You Ought to Know . . ." Leaflet, in box 9, UAW Ford Department Collection, Wayne State University Labor Archives, Detroit, MI.

54. Article from *Detroit News*, April 16, 1961, in "Local 600 Leaflets, 1959–60" in box 10, UAW Ford Department Collection, Wayne State University Labor Archives, Detroit, MI. For the characterization of Philo as having run without name recognition, see article from *Detroit Free Press*, February 17, 1965, in "Clippings," box 16, UAW Ford Department Collection, Wayne State University Labor Archives, Detroit, MI.

55. For the Stellato layout, see "If It's Time for a Change, You Ought to Know . . ." Leaflet, in box 9, UAW Ford Department Collection, Wayne State University Labor Archives, Detroit, MI. For the Philo slate, see "Time for a Change" Leaflet, in box 9, UAW Ford Department Collection, Wayne State University Labor Archives, Detroit, MI.

56. "Job Security Slate" Election Leaflet, in box 9, UAW Ford Department Collection, Wayne State University Labor Archives, Detroit, MI.

57. "Job Security Slate" Election Leaflet, in box 9, UAW Ford Department Collection, Wayne State University Labor Archives, Detroit, MI.

58. Emphasis in original. See "Job Security Slate" Election Leaflet, in box 9, UAW Ford Department Collection, Wayne State University Labor Archives, Detroit, MI.

59. "If It's Time for a Change, You Ought to Know . . ." Leaflet, in box 9, UAW Ford Department Collection, Wayne State University Labor Archives, Detroit, MI.

60. "Job Security Slate" Election Leaflet, in box 9, UAW Ford Department Collection, Wayne State University Labor Archives; "If It's Time for a Change, You Ought to Know . . ." Leaflet, in box 9, UAW Ford Department Collection, Wayne State University Labor Archives, Detroit, MI.

61. "If It's Time for a Change, You Ought to Know . . ." Leaflet, in box 9, UAW Ford Department Collection, Wayne State University Labor Archives, Detroit, MI. For Sheffield's brilliant role in 1941, see Meier and Rudwick (1979).

62. Election Results, in box 9, UAW Ford Department Collection, Wayne State University Labor Archives, Detroit, MI.

63. Election Results, in box 9, UAW Ford Department Collection, Wayne State University Labor Archives, Detroit, MI.

64. "Conway Memo Attachment, February 3, 1961" in box 250, Walter P. Reuther Collection, Wayne State University Labor Archives, Detroit, MI.

65. Election Results, in box 9, UAW Ford Department Collection, Wayne State University Labor Archives, Detroit, MI.

66. Article from *Detroit News*, March 25, 1961, in "Local 600 Leaflets, 1959–60" in box 10, UAW Ford Department Collection, Wayne State University Labor Archives, Detroit, MI.

67. Article from *Detroit Free Press*, March 5, 1965 in "Clippings," box 16, UAW Ford Department Collection, Wayne State University Labor Archives, Detroit, MI. See also a "Kravens-Tate-Zuzak-Fodera" Leaflet, in "UAW Local 600, 1960–" file, Art Fox Collection (Unprocessed), Michigan State University Library, Special Collections Division.

68. Article from *Detroit Free Press*, March 6, 1965 in "Clippings," box 16, UAW Ford Department Collection, Wayne State University Labor Archives, Detroit, MI; Dorosh Leaflet, Art Fox Collection (Unprocessed), Michigan State University Library, Special Collections Division. For biographical information on Dorosh, see Stepan-Norris and Zeitlin (1996).

69. "Thank You" Leaflet, Art Fox Collection (Unprocessed), Michigan State University Library, Special Collections Division.

70. "A Look at Elections" Leaflet, Art Fox Collection (Unprocessed), Michigan State University Library, Special Collections Division.

71. "A Look at Elections" Leaflet, Art Fox Collection (Unprocessed), Michigan State University Library, Special Collections Division.

72. "A Look at Elections" Leaflet, Art Fox Collection (Unprocessed), Michigan State University Library, Special Collections Division.

CONCLUSION

1. See Shannon (1959); Aronowitz (1973; 2003); Cochran (1977); and Levenstein (1981).

2. Pintzuk (1997).

3. "Greenspan—Worker Insecurity Up Despite Tight Labor Markets," *Market News International*, Feburary 16, 1999.

4. "Remarks by Alan Greenspan at the 40th Economic Conference of the Federal Reserve Bank of Boston," *FDCH Regulatory Intelligence Database*, June 6, 1996.

5. "Greenspan—Worker Insecurity Up Despite Tight Labor Markets," *Market News International*, Feburary 16, 1999.

BIBLIOGRAPHY

Alexander, Robert J. (1981). *The Right Opposition: The Lovestoneites and the International Communist Opposition of the 1930s*. Westport, CT: Greenwood Press.

Andrew, William D. (1979). "Factionalism and Anti-Communism: Ford Local 600." *Labor History* 20:227–255.

Aronowitz, Stanley (1973). *False Promises: The Shaping of American Working Class Consciousness*. New York: McGraw-Hill Books Company.

Aronowitz, Stanley (2003). *How Class Works: Power and Social Movement*. New Haven, CT: Yale University Press.

Asher, Robert (1995). "The 1949 Ford Speedup Strike and the Post War Social Compact, 1946–1961." In *Autowork*, edited by Robert Asher and Ronald Edsforth. Albany: State University of New York Press.

Babson, Steve (1991). *Building the Union: Skilled Workers and Anglo-Gaelic Immigrants in the Rise of the UAW*. New Brunswick, NJ: Rutgers University Press.

Barnes, Jack (1976). *James P. Cannon as We Knew Him*. New York: Pathfinder Press.

Bernstein, Irving (1996). *Guns or Butter: The Presidency of Lyndon Johnson*. New York: Oxford University Press.

Boyle, Kevin (1986). "Rite of Passage: The 1939 General Motors Tool and Die Strike." *Labor History* 27:188–203.

Boyle, Kevin (1995). *The UAW and the Heyday of American Liberalism*. Ithaca, NY: Cornell University Press.

Breitman, George, Paul Le Blanc, and Alan Wald (1996). *Trotskyism in the United States: Historical Essays and Reconsiderations*. Atlantic Highlands, NJ: Humanities Press.

Brody, David (1975). "Radical Labor History and Rank-and-File Militancy." *Labor History* 16:117–127.

Brooks, George (1960). *The Sources of Vitality in the American Labor Movement*.

Ithaca: New York State School of Industrial and Labor Relations, Cornell University.

Buhle, Paul (1988). *C.L.R. James: The Artist as Revolutionary.* New York: Verso.

Cochran, Bert (1977). *Labor and Communism: The Conflict That Shaped American Unions.* Princeton, NJ: Princeton University Press.

Collier, Ruth Berins, and David Collier (1979). "Inducements versus Constraints: Disaggregating 'Corporatism'." *American Political Science Review* 73:967–986.

Commons, John R. (1906). "Restrictions by Trade Unions." *Outlook* 84:470–476.

Cutler, Jonathan and Stanley Aronowitz (1997). "Quitting Time: An Introduction," In *Post-Work: The Wages of Cybernation*, edited by Stanley Aronowitz and Jonathan Cutler. New York: Routledge.

Drucker, Peter (1994). *Max Shachtman and His Left: A Socialist's Odyssey through the "American Century."* Atlantic Highlands, NJ: Humanities Press.

Dubois, W.E.B. (1935). *Black Reconstruction in America.* New York: Atheneum.

Edsforth, Ronald (1995). "Why Automation Didn't Shorten the Work Week: The Politics of Work Time in the Automobile Industry." In *Autowork*, edited by R. Asher and R. Edsforth. Albany: State University of New York Press.

Fields, A. Belden (1988). *Trotskyism and Maoism: Theory and Practice in France and the United States.* Brooklyn, NY: Autonomedia.

Foster, William Z. (1947). *American Trade Unionism: Principles and Organization Strategy and Tactics.* New York: International Publishers.

Frank, Dana (1999). *Buy American: The Untold Story of Economic Nationalism.* Boston, MA: Beacon Press.

Fraser, Steven (1991). *Labor Will Rule: Sidney Hillman and the Rise of American Labor.* Ithaca, NY: Cornell University Press.

Gabin, Nancy (1991). "Time out of Mind: The UAW's Response to Female Labor Laws and Mandatory Overtime in the 1960s." In *Work Engendered: Toward a New History of American Labor*, edited by Ava Baron. Ithaca, NY: Cornell University Press.

Glaberman, Martin (1980). *Wartime Strikes: The Struggle against the No-Strike Pledge in the UAW.* Detroit, MI: Bewick Editions.

Glaberman, Martin (1984). "Vanguard to Rearguard." *Political Power and Social Theory* 4:37–61.

Goldberg, Arthur J. (1956). *AFL-CIO: Labor United.* New York: McGraw-Hill Book Company.

Golden, Clinton S, and Harold J. Ruttenberg (1942). *The Dynamics of Industrial Democracy.* New York: Harper & Brothers Publishers.

Goode, Bill. (1994). *Infighting in the UAW: The 1946 Election and the Ascendancy of Walter Reuther.* Westport, CT: Greenwood Press.

Halpern, Martin (1988). *UAW Politics in the Cold War Era*. Albany, NY: State University of New York Press.

Hardman, J.B.S. (1928). "Postscripts to Ten Years of Labor Movement." In *American Labor Dynamics: In the Light of Post-War Developments*, edited by J.B.S. Hardman. New York: Harcourt Brace and Company.

Harrington, Michael (1962). *The Other America: Poverty in the United States*. New York: Macmillan Company.

Harris, William H. (1982). *The Harder We Run: Black Workers Since the Civil War*. New York: Oxford University Press.

Hirschman, Albert O. (1970). *Exit, Voice, and Loyalty: Responses to Decline in Firms, Organizations, and States*. Cambridge, MA: Harvard University Press.

Howe, Irving, and B. J. Widick (1949). *The UAW and Walter Reuther*. New York: Random House.

Ignatiev, Noel (1993). "'The American Blindspot': Reconstruction According to Eric Foner and W.E.B. Du Bois." *Labour/Le Travail* 31:243–251.

Jaffe, Philip J. (1975). *The Rise and Fall of American Communism*. New York: Horizon Press.

James, Selma (1976). *Women, the Unions, and Work: Or, What Is Not to Be Done*. Bristol, CT: Falling Wall Press.

Johanningsmeier, Edward P. (1994). *Forging American Communism: The Life of William Z. Foster*. Princeton, NJ: Princeton University Press.

Kampelman, Max M. (1957). *The Communist Party vs. the CIO: A Study in Power Politics*. New York: F. A. Praeger.

Keeran, Roger (1979a). "Communist Influence in the Automobile Industry, 1920–1933: Paving the Way for an Industrial Union." *Labor History* 20:189–225.

Keeran, Roger (1979b). "'Everything for Victory': Communist Influence in the Auto Industry during World War II." *Science and Society* 43:1–28.

Keeran, Roger (1980). *The Communist Party and the Auto Workers' Unions*. New York: International Publishers.

Kimeldorf, Howard (1999). *Battling for American Labor: Wobblies, Craft Workers, and the Making of the Union Movement*. Berkeley: University of California Press.

Klehr, Harvey, and John Earl Haynes (1992). *The American Communist Movement: Storming Heaven Itself*. New York: Twayne Publishers.

Kornhauser, Anne M. (1993). "Craft Unionism and Racial Equality: The Failed Promise of Local 3 of the International Brotherhood of Electrical Workers in the Civil Rights Era." M.A. Essay, Department of History, Columbia University, New York.

Kornhauser, William (1952). "The Negro Union Official: A Study of Sponsorship and Control." *American Journal of Sociology* 57:443–452.

Korstad, Robert, and Nelson Lichtenstein (1988). "Opportunities Found and Lost: Labor, Radicals, and the Early Civil Rights Movement." *Journal of American History* 75:786–811.

Labor Research Associates (1955). *Labor Fact Book*, volume 12. New York: International Publishers.

Leff, Mark (1996). "The House That Reuther Built: Assessing 'Labor Liberalism.'" *Labor History* 37:347–352.

Levenstein, Harvey A. (1981). *Communism, Anticommunism, and the CIO.* Westport, CT: Greenwood Press.

Lichtenstein, Nelson (1977). "Ambiguous Legacy: The Union Security Problem during World War II." *Labor History* 18:214–238.

Lichtenstein, Nelson (1985). "UAW Bargaining Strategy and Shop-Floor Conflict: 1946-1970." *Industrial Relations* 24:369.

Lichtenstein, Nelson (1995). *Walter Reuther: The Most Dangerous Man in Detroit.* Urbana: University of Illinois Press.

Lipset, Seymour Martin, Martin A. Trow, and James S. Coleman (1956). *Union Democracy: The Internal Politics of the International Typographical Union.* New York: The Free Press.

Lipsitz, George (1998). *The Possessive Investment in Whiteness: How White People Profit from Identity Politics.* Philadelphia: Temple University Press.

Martin, Roderick (1968). "Union Democracy: An Explanatory Framework." *Sociology* 2:205–220.

McConnell, Grant (1958). "Factionalism and Union Democracy." *Labor Law Journal* 9:635–640.

McNeill, George (1887). "The Hours of *Labor.*" In *The Labor Movement: The Problem of Today*, edited by G. McNeill. Boston, MA: A. M. Bridgman & Co.

McPherson, William Heston (1940). *Labor Relations in the Automobile Industry.* Washington, DC: The Brookings Institution.

Meier, August (1963). "Negro Protest Movements and Organizations." *Journal of Negro Education* 32:437–450.

Milkman, Ruth (1987). *Gender at Work: The Dynamics of Job Segregation by Sex during World War II.* Urbana: University of Illinois Press.

Mills, C. Wright (1948). *The New Men of Power: America's Labor Leaders.* New York: Harcourt Brace and Company.

Mintz, Beth, and Michael Schwartz (1985). *The Power Structure of American Business.* Chicago: University of Chicago Press.

Morgan, Ted (1999). *A Covert Life: Jay Lovestone, Communist, Anti-Communist, and Spymaster.* New York: Random House.

Morris, James O. (1958). *Conflict within the AFL: A Study of Craft versus Industrial Unionism, 1901–1938.* Ithaca, NY: Cornell University Press.

Panitch, Leo (1980). "Recent Theorizations of Corporatism: Reflections on a Growth Industry." *British Journal of Sociology* 31:159–187.

Perrot, Michelle (1987). *Workers on Strike.* New Haven, CT: Yale University Press.

Pfeffer, Paula F. (1990). *A. Philip Randolph, Pioneer of the Civil Rights Movement.* Baton Rouge: Louisiana State University Press.

Pintzuk, Edward C. (1992). "Going Down Fighting: The Michigan Communist Party after World War II." Ph.D. Dissertation, Wayne State University, Detroit, MI.

Pintzuk, Edward C. (1997). *Reds, Racial Justice, and Civil Liberties: Michigan Communists during the Cold War.* Minneapolis, MN: MEP Publications.

Piore, Michael J., and Charles F. Sabel (1984). *The Second Industrial Divide: Possibilities for Prosperity.* New York: Basic Books.

Preis, Art (1964). *Labor's Giant Step: The First Twenty Years of the CIO: 1936–1955.* New York: Pathfinder.

Prickett, James R. (1969). "Some Aspects of the Communist Controversy in the CIO." *Science & Society* 33:299–321.

Quadagno, Jill (1994). *The Color of Welfare: How Racism Undermined the War on Poverty.* New York: Oxford University Press.

Radosh, Ronald (1966). "The Corporate Ideology of American Labor Leaders from Gompers to Hillman." *Studies on the Left* 6:66–88.

Rawick, George (1969). "Working Class Self-Activity." *Radical America* 3:23–31.

Rawick, George (1972). *From Sundown to Sunup: The Making of the Black Community.* Westport, CT: Greenwood Press.

Roediger, David (1980). "The Movement for a Shorter Working Day in the United States before 1866." Ph.D. Dissertation, Department of History, Northwestern University, Evanston, IL.

Roediger, David (1990). "Notes on Working Class Racism: A Tribute to George Rawick." In *Within the Shell of the Old: Essays on Workers' Self-Organization, A Salute to George Rawick,* edited by D. Fitz and D. Roediger. Chicago: Charles H. Kerr Publishing.

Roediger, David (1991). *The Wages of Whiteness: Race and the Making of the American Working Class.* London: Verso.

Roediger, David R., and Philip S. Foner (1989). *Our Own Time: A History of American Labor and the Working Day.* London: Verso.

Rosswurm, Steve (1992). "The Catholic Church and the Left-Led Unions: Labor Priests, Labor Schools, and the ACTU," pp. 119–137. In *The CIO's Left-Led Unions,* edited by S. Rosswurm. New Brunswick, NJ: Rutgers University Press.

Russell, Thaddeus (2003). *Out of the Jungle: Jimmy Hoffa and the Remaking of the American Working Class*. Philadelphia: Temple University Press.

Saposs, David J. (1959). *Communism in American Unions*. New York: McGraw-Hill Book Co.

Schwab, Stewart J. (1992). "Union Raids, Union Democracy, and the Market for Union Control." *University of Illinois Law Review* 25:367–416.

Seaton, Douglas P. (1981). *Catholics and Radicals: The Association of Catholic Trade Unionists and the American Labor Movement, from Depression to Cold War*. Lewisburg, PA: Bucknell University Press.

Shannon, David A. (1959). *The Decline of American Communism: A History of the Communist Party of the United States since 1945*. Chatham, NJ: The Chatham Bookseller.

Stein, Judith (1998). *Running Steel, Running America: Race, Economic Policy, and the Decline of Liberalism*. Chapel Hill: University of North Carolina Press.

Stepan-Norris, Judith (1997). "The Making of Union Democracy: Comparing UAW Local 600 with the International Typographical Union." *Social Forces* 76:475–510.

Stepan-Norris, Judith, and Maurice Zeitlin (1996). *Talking Union*. Urbana: University of Illinois Press.

Stieber, Jack (1962). *Governing the UAW*. New York: John Wiley & Sons, Inc.

Sugrue, Thomas J. (1996). *The Origins of the Urban Crisis: Race and Inequality in Postwar Detroit*. Princeton, NJ: Princeton University Press.

Tomlins, Christopher L. (1985). *The State and the Unions: Labor Relations, Law, and the Organized Labor Movement in America, 1880-1960*. Cambridge: Cambridge University Press.

U.S. House of Representatives, Committee on Un-American Activities (1952). *Communism in the Detroit Area*. Washington, DC: U.S. Government Printing Office.

U.S. Senate, Committee on the Judiciary (1957). *Scope of Soviet Activity in the United States*, p. 4031. Washington, DC: U.S. Government Printing Office.

Wald, Alan M. (1987). *The New York Intellectuals: The Rise and Decline of the Anti-Stalinist Left from the 1930s to the 1980s*. Chapel Hill: The University of North Carolina Press.

Weinstein, James (1975). *Ambiguous Legacy: The Left in American Politics*. New York: New Viewpoints.

Williamson, John (1969). *Dangerous Scot: The Life and Work of an American "Undesirable."* New York: International Publishers.

Worcester, Kent (1996). *C.L.R. James: A Political Biography*. Albany, NY: State University of New York Press.

Zieger, Robert (1990). "Showdown at the Rouge." *History Today* 40:49–56.

INDEX

AFL-CIO: Industrial Union Department of, 139–40, 216n.12; Meany's leadership of, 3, 5–6, 185n.4

African-American union members: class politics and, 10; Communist Party and, 39–40, 47, 193n.55; grassroots politics of, 4–6, 185n.8; Local 600 elections and, 115–16, 166–71; plant-wide seniority proposal and, 160; Reuther and, 203n.31; shorter workweek proposals and, 64–65; unemployment among, 3–6, 185n.8; as union election candidates, 128

Allan, William, 29, 35, 196n.104

American Federation of Labor (AFL), 3–4, 56–57, 185n.4. *See also* AFL-CIO

American Socialist, 23, 132, 145, 191n.27

anti-Communism: shorter workweek proposals and, 56, 69–70, 101–7; UAW and, 32–40, 176–83; in union election campaigns, 49–53, 197n.110

Association of Catholic Trade Unionists (ACTU), 22–23, 25–27, 30–31, 38–39, 84, 192n.40; Reuther and, 67–68, 80, 95–96, 98–99, 115–16; shorter workweek proposal and, 67–68; Stellato Congressional campaign and, 155; union factionalism and, 176–83

Austin, Edna, 168

automation, UAW and threat of, 100–102, 121–22, 209n.27

Automotive Industries, 20

Averill, Dave, 198n.122

Bannon, Ken, 155, 159–60, 162

Battle, Buddy, 168

Bell, Daniel, 216n.12

Benson, Herman, 141–42, 156

Boatin, Paul, 29, 33–34, 43, 47, 162, 203n.31

Boyle, Kevin 199n.137

Braverman, Harry, 23, 31

Brody, David, 15

Browder, Earl, 28–29, 180

Bugas, John S., 161

Buhle, Paul, 191n.28

Buick Local 599: shorter workweek campaign and, 58, 164; union elections and, 128

Business Week, 24, 33, 58, 74, 78, 97–98, 115–17, 141, 166, 204n.38, 222n.31

Cannon, James, 27, 31

Challenger, The, 156

Chantres, Jesus, 149

Chevrolet Local 659, 60, 118–20, 123–24

Chrysler Corporation: price-cut proposal rejected by, 140–41; UAW negotiations with, 161

Chrysler Local 7, 146–47, 218n.43

Ciccone, Louis, 108

civil rights: demise of progressive politics and, 10–11; grassroots pressure politics in, 4–5, 185n.8; racial restrictions in unions and, 5; union support for, 2–3

Clarke, George, 31

class politics: shorter workweek movement and, 7–8; wartime shifts in, 28

Cochran, Bert, 23, 31

Cold War politics, union factionalism and, 22–23, 176–83

collective bargaining, Reuther's conception of, 6

Collins, Fred, 77, 203n.30

Commons, John R., 7–8, 11–14

Communist Party (CP): American labor movement and, 22–25; Cold War

opposed by, 6–7, 16–19, 24, 33–40,
55–56, 61–65, 68–71, 104–9, 117–35,
137, 143–57, 163–66, 188n.61, 211n.56;
Stellato and, 54–60, 71–72, 96–99,
111–13, 175–83, 198n.119, 199n.137,
200n.15; support for shorter workweek,
120–26, 139–43; unemployment
program of, 68–69, 201n.4
Rice, Pat, 40, 43, 49, 51, 61–62, 77, 83,
116, 162–63
Riesel, Victor, 53, 140
River Rouge plant (Ford): African-
American workers at, 166–71;
Communist Party and elections at,
22–23, 40–55; contract negotiations of
1958 at, 159–62; employment declines
at, 171–72; postwar layoffs at, 35–36,
38; shorter hours movement and,
34–40, 59–65, 192n.40; strike of 1949,
39–40, 192n.49; union factionalism at,
25–27, 40–43, 176–83
Roediger, David, 6–9
Romano, Lee, 74–75, 192n.37, 212n.64
Roosevelt, Franklin, 28
Rouge clubs, 29, 190n.15
Ruttenberg, Harold, 13
Ryan, James, 56

Schrade, Paul, 109, 113
Score, The, 84
Searchlight, The, 119, 124
Shachtman, Max, 26–27, 29–31, 178,
191n.26, 197n.111, 203n.31
Sheffield, Horace, 117, 168, 170, 203n.31
shorter hours movement: Cold War politics
and, 20–24; Communist Party and,
34–65, 194n.81; demise of, 159–60;
evolution of, 1–2, 4–5; Ford Local 600
purge and, 78–91, 94; Guaranteed
Annual Wage proposal and, 101–4,
209n.29; HUAC investigations and,
74–76; impact of retirees on, 172–73;
Local 600 election of 1953 and, 117–35;
racial politics in, 167–71; Reuther's
campaign for, 32–33; Reuther's opposition to, 6–7, 16–19, 24, 34–40, 55–56,
61–65, 68–71, 188n.61; Stellato's campaign for, 55–65, 105–8; union corporatism and, 11–15; union factionalism
and, 176–83

Smithey, Roger, 105
Socialist Party: labor union links to, 30–31,
186n.8; shorter workweek issue and, 177
Socialist Union, 23, 31, 191n.27
Socialist Workers Party (SWP), 22–23, 27,
31, 82, 93, 156, 178, 191n.26; 191n.28
Ste. Marie, Paul, 25–26
Steffes, Herman, 149–50
Stein, Judith, 10
Stellato, Carl, 40–65, 196n.104, 197n.110;
197n.113–14; Committee for a
Democratic UAW and, 60;
Congressional campaigns of, 155–57,
163–64; contract negotiations and,
131–35; election to IEB, 127–30; Ford
Local 600 purge and, 76–78, 108–9;
HUAC investigations and, 73, 108–13,
178–79, 202n.20; Local 600 election of
1951, 49–54, 197n.110; 197n.113–14;
Local 600 election of 1957, 139; Local
600 election of 1961, 166–71; Local 600
election of 1953 and, 115–17; Murphy
alliance with, 118; NCFDA and,
164–65; racial issues and, 167–69;
retirement from Local 600 of, 172–73;
retreat from militancy by, 72–73,
202n.16; Reuther and, 54–60, 96–99,
127–35, 138–39, 142–44, 159–62,
175–83, 198n.119, 202n.15; revolt
against Reuther purge, 79–84, 94–96,
207n.5; shorter workweek proposals
and, 55–65, 67–68, 71–72, 106–13,
117–35, 146–57, 199n.137, 218n.43;
unemployment conference called by, 68
Stieber, Jack, 209n.29, 210n.36, 215n.60
"Strike Betrayal" pamphlet, 38-39, 193n.50
Sugrue, Tom, 10
Sunday Mirror, 53
Swift, John, 85–88
syndicalist theory: shorter workweek movement and, 119–20, 177–83; union corporatism and, 11–15, 59–60, 199n.137
Szluk, John, 147

Tavenner, Frank, 75
technology: Guaranteed Annual Wage
(GAW) proposal as response to,
100–102, 209n.27; labor costs and
development of, 216n.12
Thomas, R. J., 32, 191n.29

Jonathan Cutler is an assistant professor in the department of sociology at Wesleyan University and co-editor of *Post-Work*.